Writer and researcher Philip Orr lives in (
He taught English and Drama for many yea
include *Field of Bones: An Irish Division at*
Sentry Hill and the Great War (2007) and *N*
the Protestant Working Class (2008).

the communication
Of the dead is tongued with fire beyond the language
of the living

T.S. Eliot, 'Little Gidding'

THE ROAD TO THE
SOMME

MEN OF THE ULSTER DIVISION TELL THEIR STORY

PHILIP ORR

BLACKSTAFF PRESS

BELFAST

First published in 1987 by Blackstaff Press

This edition first published in 2008 by
Blackstaff Press
4C Heron Wharf, Sydenham Business Park
Belfast BT3 9LE

Typeset by CJWT Solutions, St Helens, Merseyside

Printed in England by Cromwell Press

A CIP catalogue for this book is available from the British Library

ISBN 978-0-85640-824-3

www.blackstaffpress.com

CONTENTS

In memory of my great-uncle, John Martin,
died 16 June 1918,
and my grandmother, Eleanor Taylor (née Martin),
died 3 January 1982

PREFACE TO THE 2008 EDITION

PATTERNS OF RECRUITMENT

Any invitation to re-publish an historical work that was written two decades ago compels the author to check the accuracy of his facts and judgements in light of more recent scholarship. I feel that imperative with regard to one statistic that appeared in the 1987 edition of *The Road to the Somme*. The figure for the Irish war-dead that I accepted without much query was approximately fifty thousand. It is an estimate that has been revised downwards by respected scholars to a number between thirty and thirty-five thousand. The original figure was based on the inaccurate assumption that every soldier serving in Irish regiments was an Irishman.[1] On the other hand, it is clear that many Irish-born soldiers fought with other units.[2] But do we count as Irish those men who, though not born in Ireland, had Irish or Scots-Irish names and were raised in Irish or Scots-Irish communities in places such as Toronto, Glasgow or Liverpool, and joined up along with their pals from those communities?[3] Given the difficulties of assessing what was truly 'Irish' in 1914, perhaps what really matters in 2008 is the public recognition that a truly accurate figure for the Irish war-dead is not only impossible but inapplicable.

Since 1987 there has been much painstaking research into the national, religious and regional patterns of Irish recruitment. Keith Jeffery has assessed the available official military figures – categorised by religion and by province from August 1914 to January 1918 – and notes 64,607 Catholics and 52,365 Protestants who volunteered to serve. This indicates a slight majority of Catholics among those Irish troops who were wartime volunteers between those dates; but given that Catholics formed a considerably greater proportion of the Irish population, clearly Protestants were thus more likely to 'join up'. Jeffery also notes that out of the total of 116,972 men, 62,890 were from the nine counties of Ulster, making it the most 'willing' province. Of these Ulster recruits, 45,798 were Ulster Protestants, establishing their contribution to the war effort as a very substantial one.

Jeffery also puts the overall figures for Irish involvement with the British army within an interesting statistical context – he indicates that in the 1911 census, there were just over seven hundred thousand young men between the ages of fifteen and thirty-five in Ireland. We know that by November 1918, approximately two hundred thousand Irishmen had been in the forces – including 'regular' and 'reserve' soldiers, as well as wartime volunteers. The vast majority of those men would have fallen within the 15–35 age-bracket in 1911, so Jeffery assumes that between a quarter and a third of all the available young males in the country served in the war – a strikingly high proportion.[4]

As the recruitment rate was higher among Ulster Protestants, the proportion of young men who went to war from Ulster Protestant homes was even greater: no wonder then that this war has left such an indelible impression on public and private memory within Protestant culture in the north of Ireland. Nothing comparable – by way of family disruption, temporary mass emigration, the 'militarisation' of an entire generation and the widespread loss of young male life – has happened since in the north of Ireland.

But the First World War scholar, Nicholas Perry, offers a much less impressive set of statistics regarding Irish recruiting, noting that during the first five months of the war, only ninety thousand men joined up, which amounts to 8 per cent of the male population between the ages of fifteen and forty-nine. The equivalent rate in England and Wales was twenty-four per cent, and in Scotland it was twenty-seven per cent. The recruitment rate in Ireland diminished even further as the war progressed; however, Perry does note that in Antrim, Down and Armagh in the opening period of the conflict, the figure was as high as twenty per cent, suggesting a rate of enlistment among the young Protestants – who predominated in these counties – comparable to the overall rate across the Irish Sea, and certainly better than in some agricultural areas of England.[5]

Despite this variety of statistics, which offer themselves for differing interpretations, what is clear to all those who have studied Ulster's First World War recruitment patterns in recent years is that the levels of volunteering varied greatly from place to place, and also that the Ulster Division did not necessarily find a ready supply of men from 'Carson's Army' to swiftly fill up all of its ranks in the autumn of 1914.

Timothy Bowman has suggested that the 36th Division sometimes had 'serious recruitment problems', in part because of its links with the UVF, which he believes 'prevented Catholics from joining it in large numbers, which provided serious recruiting difficulties in rural areas ...' He explains how, by October 1914, the average strength of the rural battalions was just 768 men – well short of the thousand-plus needed for full strength. The 16th Royal Irish Rifles battalion did not in fact reach its full quota until June 1915. He therefore reckons that 'overlap' between local UVF units and their respective regional British army battalions varied greatly. The 'elite' Young Citizen Volunteer unit within the UVF filled less than three quarters of its specified battalion, and 25 per cent of the ranks had to be drafted in from England, Scotland and Wales. One of the four companies of the 11th Inniskilling battalion also had to be raised in Britain.[6] And, as we know, recruitment dried up in Ulster as it did all across Ireland as this grim war progressed.

On the other hand, according to Amanda Moreno, curator of the Royal Irish Fusilier Museum in Armagh, there is plenty of evidence that this county's UVF units joined up in vast groups, filling almost all the places in the 9th Irish Fusilier battalion.[7] Presumably, this helped give it the *esprit de corps* that made it, in some observers' eyes, the best group of fighting men in the division. But even when battalions were well filled up with UVF men, as in north Armagh or parts of Belfast, Bowman suggests that the majority of the locals who had been in 'Carson's Army' still stayed at home. He explains how, on 4 September 1914, Carson himself saw 800 men of the North Belfast UVF march off to enlist – a statistic that becomes much less impressive when it is remembered that the UVF at this time had 6,000 men in the north of the city.[8]

In other words, recent scholarship seems to back up what this writer found in the 1980s. The 36th Division was not homogeneously an Ulster unionist formation, although it was dominantly so, and the job of recruiting young men to its ranks in the late summer and autumn of 1914 was often difficult in rural areas, where farmers and agricultural workers were busy with the harvest, and where there was a real fear that if the local 'Protestant boys' marched off to fight and die with the army, then that would leave local nationalists in a very advantageous position at home, where the imposition of Home Rule still loomed.

Bowman's recent work on the Ulster Volunteer Force is also of interest as it gives a more critical view of that body of men than the one I offered in 1987, influenced as I was by the historian A.T.Q. Stewart's robust and adventurous account of its nocturnal military manoeuvres, and by the nostalgic recollections of veterans whom I interviewed. I had been impressed by the complex structure, social mix and conspiratorial bravado of the UVF.

Bowman perhaps expects professional military standards from an amateur army, and is thus bound to find the UVF lacking in many ways. However, he certainly offers plenty of evidence in his recent book *Carson's Army* that the Ulster Volunteers were far from streamlined, and that they had made 'few preparations to provide food, clothing, accommodation or transport in the event of hostilities.' He reckons that the organisation functioned 'on the assumption either that British troops would never fire on UVF personnel ...', or that the Ulster Volunteers would 'in the finest traditions of the British armed forces, be able to "muddle through"'.

Bowman also suggests that 'the military efficiency of the UVF was far from uniform', with variable levels of training and instruction in evidence, as well as a high degree of absenteeism in the ranks. In particular, he points out the somewhat chaotic mix of ammunition and weapons at the UVF's disposal, even after the *Clyde Valley*'s famous gun-running. He speculates that the organisation would have made 'a poorly armed military force but a very well armed police force ...' This comment is of interest because many former UVF men, including 36th Division veterans, did in fact join the large supplementary police force – the Ulster Special Constabulary – that was raised in the new Northern Ireland state to 'support the forces of law and order' in what was a fragile and contested political entity. In fact, the UVF itself was briefly re-formed in the immediate post-war period, with many members then being steered in the direction of the new constabulary.[9]

It was therefore a mistake on my part in 1987 to conclude a history of the Ulster Division without mentioning the role that some ex-soldiers played in the highly political task of Northern Irish post-war policing. Numerous First World War veterans returned to become IRA men, and it makes sense to recognise that a number of servicemen from a pro-Union background also got sucked into the latest phase of the conflict.

I can recall one old man, whom I interviewed about his soldiering days, telling me that on returning from the trenches he had joined the police and walked up and down the Falls Road with a loaded gun in his hand, 'taking shots at the chimney pots', as he chose to express it. I did not press him any further, but wish now that I had. At the time, I was reluctant to 'muddy the waters' of my Great War narrative or to challenge my deeply naive belief that the horrors of the First World War must have turned all its survivors into ardent pacifists.

THE POST-WAR DECADES

There are other aspects of Ulster's First World War story to which I might have given rather more thought in 1987. Some of these aspects have now been carefully researched, and merit attention as Northern Ireland strives to remember the war and its legacy in an accurate manner, ninety years after the Armistice. One aspect of the aftermath of war that has come to light is how difficult it was for many Somme veterans to find work when they came home. It might be assumed that they would have been first in the queue for post-war employment. However, even in the unionist heartland of Portadown, where UVF membership had been strong and numerous young men had been 'local heroes' with the Ulster Division, the employment situation was bad for veterans.

The letter columns of post-war newspapers in Portadown contained comments by those who felt distressed at the way returning soldiers were being treated, especially if they were disabled. One man wrote on 19 July 1919 that 'the heroes of 1914–1915 ... are returning after four years of weary warfare, duty accomplished, only to find that the men who stayed at home have cuckoo-like stolen their nests ... men are refused work because they are disabled, and for this reason, the Discharged Certificate which should be a blessing is more often a curse.' The letter writer went on to attack employers who had promised an employee 'with most holy unction, that the job would be his when he returned.' The writer knew many local ex-soldiers who found that such promises were 'shelved' or that a job was being offered back at 1914 rates of pay.[10]

Another issue that has come to my attention since the first edition was published is the public and often disturbing manifestation of the unemployment, personal misery, and physical and mental disability faced by many ex-combatants after the First World War. Ninety years ago, society lacked the systems of social security, medical care, disability assistance and post-trauma counselling that now exist. As Catherine Switzer has pointed out, several autobiographies of Ulstermen and women who grew up in the 1920s and 1930s reveal vivid memories of war veterans in their vicinity who 'now had no work and often no decent clothes to wear', and 'seemed never to have left the war'.

She noted how many men were 'blind or with one eye or one arm or one leg'. There was the legless Belfast veteran who 'sat outside the GPO in Royal Avenue' begging for money. There were the ex-servicemen who 'whiled away the day in an old brickworks off the Limestone Road' playing cards or pitch and toss. And there were the 'shell-shock' victims, often seen 'holding their sticks like rifles, shouting at nobody, in a language that nobody understood' or making 'machine-gun noises' or 'stopping to look up at the sky and run for cover in the nearest doorway'.[11] As the First World War historian Joanna Bourke has pointed out, an inordinately high number of patients with psychiatric illness was presented to military hospitals in Ireland compared with elsewhere in these islands.[12] This was a trend assuredly brought about by the added stresses of returning to a country that was not only struggling with a steep economic downturn but divided by intense civil strife.

Both Catherine Switzer and Jane Leonard have looked at another aspect of the post-war years: the creation of public memorials. If the damaged and workless veterans are long since gone from Ulster's public places, the memorials definitely are not – and their solidity and air of permanence deceives the modern observer into thinking that they were all erected immediately the war ended in a communal display of solemn gratefulness.[13] Switzer notes sixty-two public memorials in the north, including twenty statues and thirteen obelisks. However, as she points out, these monuments were often seen as a misuse of money that would have been better spent on more practical projects. As one parent of a local First World War soldier expressed it: 'I feel sure that had a field been taken and converted into a public park where the wounded men might be able to go and sit instead of hanging round the corners and the Labour Exchange it would have been more appropriate.'[14] Some distinctive memorials – such as the clock-tower in

Waringstown, County Armagh – were erected as early as 1921,[15] but because of a shortage of donations, some of Northern Ireland's most notable commemorative monuments were not erected until well into the mid-1930s, including the handsome County Antrim War Memorial, which stands on the Knockagh heights, overlooking Belfast Lough.[16]

MILITARY STRENGTHS AND WEAKNESSES
OF THE ULSTER DIVISION

As for the 36th Division's military conduct throughout the war, several features have become apparent since 1987. The historian Timothy Travers has seen a likely reason why the Ulstermen were able to advance with such notable if temporary success on the morning of 1 July. He has discovered that the artillery officers attached to the 36th Division possessed high-quality 1:10,000-scale maps of the German sector that lay opposite the Ulster lines. This would have allowed them to achieve some accuracy rather than engaging in the positional guesswork that characterised too much of the British gunnery at the Somme.[17]

Gary Sheffield has written favourably about the 36th Division's performance in the Battle of Messines, on 7 June 1917. He describes how the soldiers advanced 'benefiting from a highly effective and thoroughly scientific use of artillery … using rifle grenades and bringing machine-gun fire to bear from a flank.' He applauds these 'sophisticated tactics' as evidence that the 'conduct of the war had changed dramatically' since the days of costly and simplistic tactics employed by the British Expeditionary Force (BEF) at the beginning of the Battle of the Somme, less than a year before.[18]

However, much of the research that has been done in the last few years has served to point up the fact that the 36th was a bunch of ordinary men drawn together by extraordinary circumstances and manifesting all kinds of military shortcomings, particularly during the early years when it was being turned from a crowd of civilians into a fighting unit.

It is now known that early in their training in southern County Down, some men of the Belfast Brigade headed for home, disgusted by the poor accommodation, as manifested by the fact that their tents had collapsed in the wet, windy weather. They had to be persuaded to return to the camp by senior officers who chased after them and did not dare to court-martial them for their indiscipline. Bowman also reveals evidence of a serious 'mass mutiny', when men throughout the division 'believed, wrongly, they were to be sent overseas immediately without home leave first'. He also notes the 'management' problems caused by having too many officers who were given posts merely because of UVF prominence or because they 'were prominent businessmen' or 'on the basis that they had attended a grammar school in Belfast'. This was a situation that General Nugent tried to rectify once he had assumed command of the division in 1915, weeding out 'suspect cases' and replacing them with better 'officer material'.

Bowman speculates that problems also arose in the division because there were relatively few experienced NCOs available to train the thousands of novice soldiers in the ranks, many of whom had been unskilled labourers in heavy industry. Skilled workers would have been capable of quickly becoming good NCOs, as they did in several other New Army divisions. However, in Ulster they were at a premium within local manufacturing industry in the ongoing economic war effort. It is now clear that Nugent was doubtful of his division's war-readiness as it prepared for France in the autumn of 1915, referring in correspondence to the Belfast Brigade as 'awful': 'I am very much distressed about them ... I don't think they are fit for service'. Nugent's opinions were confirmed by various acts of indiscipline during the early days in France. It is obvious why this brigade was chosen out of the three in the division to be sent to serve with another division: they were to be toughened up by serving alongside more experienced soldiers in the front line for an extended period.[19]

Presumably, it is all the more credit to the men in the ranks and the officers who led them that the 36th Division did make the transition from a mutinous and inexperienced miscellany to a disciplined and regimented unit capable of capturing the formidable Schwaben Redoubt less than two years after its formation. Certainly, Nugent's scepticism about his men was radically altered after the heroism of Thiepval, as his letters to his wife, to his superiors and to the king so clearly show.[20] However, as Stephen Walker has pointed out, Nugent's toughening regime came at a cost. In *Forgotten Soldiers*, Walker draws attention to the fact that the Shankill man whose death I noted in my 1987 edition was not the only man from the troublesome Belfast battalions to be executed. Privates McCracken and Templeton of the 15th Royal Irish Rifles were both court-martialled and shot in March 1916 for desertion from the line, bringing the total 'shot at dawn' in this brigade to three, well before the Somme battle had commenced. As the veteran Leslie Bell would later say: 'They thought that these two lads had been sacrificed to set an example to the rest of us. We never had the same respect for the officers when we found out anyone could meet the same fate.'[21]

The research of the last two decades has only helped to confirm the brutality that most Ulstermen experienced and witnessed while serving in the First World War, and the ultimate powerlessness of the individual soldier trapped in the military system without any right to protest when injustice seemed to be his lot.

PREFACE TO THE FIRST EDITION

John Martin
(great-uncle of the author),
16th Battalion,
Royal Irish Rifles
PHILIP ORR

This book owes much to my childhood fascination with the sepia portrait of my great-uncle John, in army uniform, that hung on the shadowy landing of the staircase in my grandmother's house. I knew only that he had gone missing during the latter part of the First World War, and that for several months his mother had waited in anticipation as each train pulled into the village railway station, until she finally obtained news that he had been killed a few months before the Armistice.

In 1980 I met Hugh James Adams, who had been my great-uncle's friend and with whom he had gone off to join the Ulster Division. The clarity of his memories inspired me to try to interview other veterans of the First World War who might still be alive in an attempt to piece together what it had been like for my great-uncle and his generation to be submerged in that, now distant, cataclysm.

I was privileged to meet several frail, tenacious old men who were survivors of the war – men like Tommy Ervine, who produced his mouth-organ for me during one visit and played 'It's a Long Way to Tipperary', much as he had played it in the trenches to entertain not only his colleagues but also the listening Germans across the narrow divide of no-man's-land.

The next stage took me into the archives of institutions like the splendid Royal Ulster Rifles Regimental Museum in Belfast. There I discovered – dusty but carefully preserved – diaries, letters, postcards and sketchbooks that yielded up secrets about that deeply bonded group of young men whose fate had been sealed on 1 July 1916, the disastrous opening day of the Battle of the Somme.

I was also tremendously helped by Robert H. Stewart, of Waringstown, who, in the previous few years, had interviewed numerous veterans in and around the Waringstown area. He deserves great credit for the rich store of recollections he carefully recorded and subsequently made available to me.

One thing I became aware of is that a wide range of men went from Ireland to fight in the British army during the First World War. Although it was to become politically expedient to emphasise the Ulster Protestant contribution to the war effort, and to play down the death and suffering of Irish Catholics, it must be realised that Irishmen of every kind fought on the British side. So though this book follows the story of a largely Protestant division of men formed out of the old Ulster Volunteer Force, it is also my intention to commemorate all the Irishmen who gave so much in a war that they found difficult to understand.

All I discovered in my researches, and all that I saw in the world around me during the time I was writing this book, convinced me that to question the supposed glory of dying or killing for one's country is a task we must continually undertake. *The Road to the Somme* is intended as a contribution to that questioning process that is, surely, more necessary than ever before.

Readers should note that while every effort has been made to avoid factual inaccuracies in this book, it is not always possible or even desirable to alter a veteran's recollections of a long-ago battle in the interests of strict historical fact. Any clear-cut and misleading errors have been discarded, but it should be remembered that the fascination of the oral testimony in history is its subjectivity, revealing how things were, or seemed to be, for the participant in, or witness to, historic events.

Without descending into any 'folksy' attempt to render the phonetics of the Ulster accent, I have tried to preserve the colloquialisms and grammar of the vernacular as used by several interviewees. Much of the vigour of the oral record from this period is due to the earthy, colourful and direct language of the speakers.

Philip Orr
1987

1

'HAYFOOT! STRAWFOOT!'
THE ULSTER VOLUNTEERS 1911–14

Five 'Special Service' UVF men, with bayonets mounted,
guard an Ulster Volunteer camp of instruction
SOMME MUSEUM

A EUROPEAN WAR

This book follows the fortunes of a body of Irishmen who were banded
into the 36th Division of 'Kitchener's Army' in the First World War. The
vast majority of the men recruited to this division in 1914 had been
members of a recently formed, oath-bound organisation based in the north
of Ireland and known as the Ulster Volunteer Force.

For the majority of people in Europe, and certainly for the Irish, the
outbreak of a general war in the summer in 1914 was completely unfore-
seen, although arguably it was inevitable given the imperialist ambitions of

1

the great powers. Dreams of domination, fears of decline, a feverish arms race running out of control, clumsy diplomacy, instability in the Balkans, and – finally – blind panic combined to drive Europe into the worst military conflict the world had yet seen. It was to cost the lives of at least fifteen million people.

A complex sequence of events drew the United Kingdom into the Great War. Archduke Franz Ferdinand, heir to the Austro–Hungarian imperial throne, was murdered during an official visit to Sarajevo, capital of the recently acquired province of Bosnia. Suspicion was immediately directed at neighbouring Serbia, the state to which most Bosnians wished to belong. For Vienna, this assassination was a unique, if unexpected, opportunity to smash nationalism in the Balkans, which had long threatened the internal stability of the empire. Austria's powerful ally, Germany, gave its blessing. But when Austria declared war on Serbia, the Russian Tsar, posing as protector of the Balkan people, ordered his own huge army to make ready. Russian mobilisation threatened German strategic plans to avoid a war on two fronts: the German generals had long accepted that the Tsar's ally, France, must be knocked out by an invasion through Belgium before the ponderous Russian 'steamroller' moved west. Now, as Russian soldiers pulled on their boots, there was panic in the German imperial court. There might not be enough time to knock out France if Russia was in such an advanced state of readiness – while the Germans were still approaching Paris, the Tsar's army could be taking Berlin. By the first day of August 1914 Germany had declared war not only on Russia but on France. The German war machine was the first to crank into action, and von Moltke's troops poured into Belgium. Britain was not only France's ally but was also treaty-bound to protect the freedom of the Belgians. Besides, the world's most extensive empire and greatest naval power could not stand by and see the German army smash its way through to the English Channel. By 4 August Britain was at war with Germany, and soon after, much of Europe was aflame.

As a result of the conflagration, more than sixty-five million soldiers from all across the world would be mobilised during the ensuing four years of conflict. The nature of warfare, of politics, and of many aspects of human life would be changed for ever; and amongst these changes would be lasting alterations in the development of Ireland and in the everyday lives of Irish people.

The impact of war was soon felt. In Britain, Lord Kitchener, the secretary

2

of state for war – believing the regular army too small – made an appeal for volunteers for a 'New Army'. Men responded from every walk of life – city clerks, coal miners, farm and factory workers, university students. Soon, the members of 'Kitchener's Army' were encamped across the country, learning to be soldiers and itching to get to France and face the 'Hun' before the war reached its soon-expected conclusion. Among these men were many thousands from Ireland, including the 36th (Ulster) Division.

THE BIRTH OF THE VOLUNTEERS

Their story begins in the months leading up to the outbreak of European war, when Britain had been preoccupied with a dangerous crisis in Ireland. The problem centred around the Third Home Rule Bill, promoted by the Liberal government to give Ireland a limited measure of independence within the Empire, and due to become law in 1914. Backed by the Conservative and Unionist Party, the Protestants of Ulster refused to accept Home Rule, and prepared to resist fiercely any attempt to implement it.

Once indifferent to the Union, Protestants became its most loyal defenders, and viewed with mounting alarm the growth of Irish national feeling. In the three southern provinces, the demand for Home Rule was all but unanimous, and even in the nine counties of Ulster almost half the population was Catholic, and eagerly awaited the establishment of a Dublin parliament. Protestants, forming almost a quarter of Ireland's population but in a clear majority only in the north-east, believed that Home Rule would lead to their subjugation by a poorer southern Ireland. They feared that their religious freedom would be endangered, that the Dublin parliament would ruin the industrial north-east by heavy taxation and restrictive tariffs, and that Home Rule was merely the first step towards taking Ireland out of the Empire for ever.

Violence was rarely far below the surface in Ulster. South-central Ulster had been convulsed by sectarian warfare in the 1790s, and there were further incidents, as at Dolly's Brae and Garvagh, in the early nineteenth century. Seeking work in the industrial centres of Belfast, Derry and Portadown, the people of rural Ulster brought with them memories of past wrongs, and settled in distinctly segregated districts. Savage sectarian riots in Belfast had been the bloodiest incidents in Ireland in what had been a turbulent but comparatively peaceful nineteenth century.

Sir Edward Carson signs the 1912 Covenant in Belfast's City Hall
SOMME MUSEUM

In the new century, as controversy raged over the issue of Home Rule, Ulster seemed as volatile as any Balkan state. Unionists prepared to prevent the implementation of Home Rule by extra-parliamentary means. Under the leadership of the distinguished Dublin barrister and MP, Sir Edward Carson, a massive movement of resistance was organised, and the military wing of that resistance was to be the Ulster Volunteer Force. Hints of the birth of the force had come on 23 September 1911 at the first great demonstration of Ulster 'loyalty' – held at Craigavon, the residence of Captain James Craig, MP for East Down. On a platform overlooking Belfast Lough, Carson had addressed some fifty thousand people and had told them that they 'must be prepared ... the morning Home Rule passes ... to become responsible for the government of the Protestant province of Ulster'.[1]

Many of the men at Craigavon were members of the Orange Order or the more recently re-formed paramilitary Unionist Clubs. The Orange Order, dedicated to the strengthening of Protestantism, had its tradition of marching and its memories of battle and conquest, and was an ideal framework around which a citizen army could be formed. A band of Orangemen from County Tyrone, under the training of a Captain Ambrose Ricardo, had stood out from the others at Craigavon, due to its strict military discipline. It became a model for other Orange lodges throughout Ulster,

4

and soon, under the tuition of men who had been in the British army, members were drilling all across the province. As for the Unionist Clubs, they had always had a military emphasis, and many of their members held firearms.[2]

Throughout 1912 the plans for Home Rule pressed ahead and Ulster opposition stiffened. On Easter Tuesday Andrew Bonar Law, the Tory leader, addressed a vast crowd on the outskirts of Belfast and pledged his party's support for the unionists. 'You will save the Empire by your example,' he told his eager listeners, and he compared the Orange and unionist volunteers to Cromwell's Ironsides.[3]

In the autumn of 1912 a programme of meetings was planned to sweep across Protestant Ulster from Enniskillen to Belfast. Carson addressed crowds in one town after another, and men marched with dummy rifles, sometimes by torchlight and often to the sound of martial music. On 28 September – designated 'Ulster Day' – a 'Solemn League and Covenant' was signed, pledging Ulster loyalists to defend their 'cherished position of equal citizenship in the United Kingdom'. Many men signed in their own blood, and loyalist women put their names to a separate declaration. The total number of signatures was 471,414. So by the winter of 1912 the British government was faced with a menacing obstacle to its plans. Loyalists had pledged themselves to use 'all means which may be found necessary to defeat the present conspiracy to set up a Home Rule Parliament in Ireland'. To the Ulster Unionist Council – the umbrella body for unionist and Orange organisations, led by Carson and Craig – 'all means' included the formation of a coherent military force. The volunteers, who had been marching with their wooden rifles, were drawn together under one command and, in January 1913, the Ulster Volunteer Force, the UVF, was officially born.[4]

Almost all Catholics in Ulster gave their support to the nationalists – that is, the Irish Parliamentary Party led by John Redmond, a man who not only expected the imminent establishment of a parliament in Dublin but who also had a strong affection for the British Empire. As yet, only a tiny proportion of Ulster Catholics gave their support to the revolutionary Irish Republican Brotherhood.[5] For the present, Redmond had enough authority amongst his supporters in the north to prevent Home Rule counter-demonstrations to loyalist rallies, and placed his faith in Asquith's Liberal government. His brother, Willie Redmond, in an article specially written

The first signatures on a list of nearly half a million who signed the Covenant.
Some men are reputed to have signed in their own blood.
SOMME MUSEUM

for the *Irish News* on 10 February 1913, reminded Ulster nationalists of support throughout the Empire:

> If Ireland's claim for justice came before the tribunal of the Empire, there is no doubt as to the verdict. If Home Rule for Ireland depended upon the approval of the British Empire, Ireland would be immediately emancipated.

Willie Redmond was to be killed at the Battle of Messines four and a half years later, his body recovered from the battlefield by members of the UVF enrolled in the Ulster Division.[6]

VOLUNTEERS IN RURAL ULSTER

Often, there seems to have been a particular charismatic character, very likely an old soldier, who was the focus for the young Volunteers of an Ulster village or town. In the small market town of Ballynahinch, County Down, for example, an old soldier called Harry Gordon, who had a barber's shop in Main Street, was a key figure. Captain David John Bell was later to remember Harry's influence:

> ... he had been wounded (in his army days) and had a short leg. An accomplished violinist, he taught my brother Harper to play the violin and the two of them were in great demand at socials and gatherings all over the Ballynahinch area ... Harry's was a great meeting place for the boys, because at the back of his shop he had a hut in which he installed the first billiard table in Ballynahinch. He was an authority on British military history... Lord Clanwilliam was to raise and command a battalion in East Down, and Harry, being greatly interested in the movement, took an active part in organising the local company. I became interested too and eventually joined. Harry was Sergeant Major and I was appointed Captain.[7]

Conflict between landlord and tenant in Ulster – often bitter and violent in the late nineteenth century in Donegal in particular – had largely been resolved by 1913. The most wretched tenants had emigrated, the rise in agricultural prices benefited all working the land, and the Land Purchase Acts gave many title to farms for the first time. Local gentry often took the lead in actively organising the Volunteers. Westminster had deprived them

7

of many of their privileges in the nineteenth century, and yet they regarded the preservation of the Union as crucial to the maintenance of their remaining power and position. Protestant farmers, agricultural labourers and landlords combined to create rural battalions of the new paramilitary force. The estates of the chief landed gentry were to be used for training: locations such as the Duke of Abercorn's estate at Baronscourt, County Tyrone, or the estate of the O'Neills at Shane's Castle on the shores of Lough Neagh. The grounds of the local 'Big House' would be the training ground for each village, as at Crossgar, County Down, where the Clelands' estate, Tobar Mhuire, was put at the Volunteers' disposal. A fairly typical situation developed at Springhill House, near Moneymore, County Derry: not only did the owner, William Lenox-Conyngham, help to raise the two battalions of the UVF's South Derry regiment, but his wife was closely involved in the UVF Nursing Corps, arranging for eleven hospital centres in the area.[8] To the south west, in County Fermanagh, Castle Hume, on the shores of Lough Erne, was used for storing arms throughout the Volunteer years, and witnessed parades not just of the local battalions but of the highly drilled section of Volunteer cavalry, the 'Enniskillen Horse'.[9]

Historic backdrops were thus provided for many Volunteer meetings – the courtyard of the turreted Killyleagh Castle on the shores of Strangford Lough or the leafy grounds of Donard Park in Newcastle, where the Glen river plunges down from the bare slopes of the Mourne Mountains.[10]

In the rolling farmlands of the Waringstown area in County Down, the local Volunteers went out for route marches, sometimes ten miles in length and which they called their 'Sunday afternoon strolls'. On several occasions they had to put up with the remonstrations of a Mr Richardson, a Quaker, of Moyallen, who told them in no uncertain terms that they were breaking the Sabbath, even if it was for a 'fight against popery'.

As winter nights came, the men marched – when it was dry – with hurricane lamps at the fore and rear of their column. For those who seemed not to know the difference between their left and right feet, the story goes that they were told to put hay in one foot and straw in the other, and the call would then come: 'Hayfoot! Strawfoot! Hayfoot! Strawfoot!' On the march, a side-drummer would beat out a 'rattling good pace', and occasionally the men would sing Orange songs such as 'Dolly's Brae' and 'The Sash'. Blisters became fewer as the men grew used to marching.

County Antrim Volunteers being put through their paces. A local field often supplied a useful but uneven parade ground.
SOMME MUSEUM

Raising money for boots, overcoats and equipment was a key issue. One of the most interesting methods used was in the Waringstown area, where people would pay for poems to be written about themselves by a local rhymester. One girl, with two brothers in the UVF, was reputed to have paid five shillings for such a poem; considering that she received only £14 a year in wages, this was a considerable contribution to Volunteer funds.

Wealthy, sympathetic businessmen always contributed a good deal to the funds. One way in which a large shop in nearby Portadown helped out was by supplying turf and coal for winter heating, so that Orange lodges would not be financially crippled by the large number of Volunteer meetings in their halls. Harvest suppers continued into the winter months of 1912 as a means of raising money, and regular 'shindigs', held in Orange halls, were supplemented by ceilidhs, often in neighbours' houses, which might contribute a few shillings to the kitty.[11]

Interest in the UVF was by no means universal amongst Ulster Protestants. The Revd J.B. Armour, Captain J.R. White, Sir Roger Casement, Alice Milligan, Lord Pirrie, Bulmer Hobson and Joseph Campbell were well-known if untypical Ulster Protestants who continued to support Home Rule. Apart from the Enniskillen Horse, organised by the newspaper owner W.C. Trimble, recruitment to the UVF was slow in Fermanagh until the future of the county was hotly debated in compromise proposals in 1914. In the adjacent Clogher valley, however, the UVF made rapid headway.[12] Here, in south Tyrone, the nationalists were determined that their voice should be heard; a mass meeting at Donaghmore was presided over by the Revd Canon McCartan PP on Sunday 9 November 1913. The first speaker, J.P. Convery, an organiser of the United Irish League, denounced partition proposals and warned that under no circumstances would they allow 'Ulster or any portion of it to be taken from the map of Ireland'. More ominously, the next speaker, J. Skeffington, declared, as reported in the *Irish News* of 12 November 1913, that if 'a vote of nationalist Ulster was taken, they would fight on sooner than accept any form of Home Rule which would make the government of Ulster different in any respect from that which would obtain in the rest of Ireland'.

A fortnight later, on 25 November 1913, the Irish Volunteers were formed at a great meeting in the Rotunda in Dublin with the purpose of ensuring the implementation of Home Rule. Recruitment was particularly brisk amongst Ulster Catholics.[13] The prospect of a violent conflict between two opposing volunteer movements in Ulster loomed before a distraught British government in 1914.

THE 'DEAD-END KIDS' OF BELFAST

But the story of the Ulster Volunteers also begins in the city of Belfast. Life for young men growing up in the city streets was often tough and dull. Belfast had all the poverty and distress of any English industrial town, and also the sectarian bitterness that had been its hallmark for almost a century.

J. Hutchinson was born in a 'sensitive' area of east Belfast, so his first contact with soldiers was an early one:

> It was in 1907 a great strike was raging at the Belfast docks. I was a six-year-old then and one morning on my way to school in Comber Street, soldiers were on duty outside the Catholic chapel ... it was an event in our otherwise miserable lives, we were a collection of Belfast sparrows; poor, chirpy and barefooted. We carried what books we had with a string round them and in our pockets two slices of low-quality bread and jam wrapped in a newspaper. We called it a 'piece'.

Carrying rifles and performing military exercises in the UVF came as a thrill to boys like these, many of whose families had army connections. Very often, army life had been a way out of the squalor of a city that though containing the biggest shipyard in the world also contained dreadful slums.

> ... we were dead-end kids without hope. Sometimes in the school
> holidays we would wedge our way into the small Victoria Park which
> catered for the vast population of Ballymacarrett – and the nearby shore of
> Sydenham on Belfast Lough was our Shangri-La. Tuberculosis swept
> through the area, wiping out whole families.

To some, the Volunteers must at first have seemed like one step up from the very popular Boys' Brigade, which emphasised drill as part of its training and which, with its uniform, flutes and drums, must have given a touch of glamour to the 'dead-end kids' of Belfast.

And 'dead-end' many of them indeed were. A 'half-time' system operated whereby Hutchinson and his friends, from the age of twelve onwards, went to work in the flax mills on alternate days, working from 6.00 a.m. to 6.00 p.m. and going to school on the other days.

> ... on our schooldays we were so tired with our long hours and work of
> the previous day that we found it hard to concentrate on our lessons.
> The humidity at work sapped our energy and I suspect the half-time
> system caused the deaths of many of our young folks. In work we were
> sweated to death, and in school frozen to death.[14]

Home and family were not always a secure base, either. Hutchinson recalled how his mother was left a widow with four children and no pension to help her. Another east-Belfast man, Tommy Ervine, recalled how his parents were both heavy drinkers and 'didn't give a damn' about his education. As a result, Tommy hung around with people from the touring circuses, and learnt all about horses as well as picking up the skills of tap-dancing and playing the mouth organ and bagpipes.[15] To such boys, the emergence of the Volunteers gave new interest and meaning to life, as J. Hutchinson remembered:

> I recall our contingent in east Belfast wearing bandoliers and belts, they
> drilled and marched openly throughout the neighbourhood. One
> company drilled on waste ground just outside 'Ye Olde Princess Picture

Palace'. We had drama inside this pioneer cinema on the Newtownards Road and real drama on the spare ground outside.[16]

Hutchinson recalled how he attended the great meetings in Craigavon estate and sat cross-legged on the grass, listening to Carson and Craig. He and his friends initially followed the Volunteers on their route marches into the Castlereagh Hills. Apart from the thrills, though, Tommy Ervine witnessed the Volunteers unleashing sectarian feelings in the shipyards, where a number of Catholics worked within a predominantly Protestant workforce:

> I joined the Volunteers in 1912. I actually walked down the
> Newtownards Road with a rifle over my shoulder (you wouldn't be
> allowed to do that today!) ... I was only about seventeen or eighteen at
> the time – I thought it was very exciting. There was all sorts worked
> in the shipyards ... they started throwing nuts and bolts at Catholics and
> lookin' for them and so on. So I went and told a Catholic mate of
> mine that they might come an' get him. I was sorry about it.
> He had to leave ...[17]

In July 1912 a fracas took place at Castledawson when members of the nationalist Ancient Order of Hibernians attacked a Presbyterian Sunday-school outing.[18] When reports of this reached the shipyards in Belfast, apprentices and riveters' assistants called for the expulsion of all 'Fenians' and 'Home Rulers'. In the sporadic violence and intimidation that followed, some two thousand workers were forced out of the yards.[19]

ORGANISATION

The involvement of many of the younger men in the Volunteer movement was greeted by concern on the part of their families. In the Martin family, in Crossgar, County Down, Alexander Martin was a local blacksmith – his oldest son William was preoccupied helping his father run the business in the smithy overlooking the Glasswater river, but a younger son, John, who was a bicycle mechanic, joined the Volunteers along with his friend, Hugh James Adams. He kept the whole thing very secret as his mother was worried at the prospect of a son of hers carrying arms.[20]

In Lisburn, Hugh Stewart, then only sixteen, tried to join the platoon his

Two Fermanagh UVF men in uniform.
Many volunteers could not afford
to be so smartly dressed.
SOMME MUSEUM

father commanded, but his father would not 'hear tell' of the idea. Hugh promptly went off and joined another platoon, claiming that he was seventeen.[21] At the other end of the age range, men were supposed to be no longer eligible to join at sixty-five, but lies were told here, too.

So men whose ages might be half a century apart were banded together in an organisation that followed the model of the Territorial Army. Each village or townland with a sufficient number of loyalists made up its own platoon or company. As far west as Donegal town, small towns with enough Protestants were able to make up a battalion each. Belfast city contributed four regiments of unequal size depending on the distribution of loyalists and nationalists in each urban parliamentary division.

Recruitment was much more brisk in eastern Ulster than in the west of the province. In County Donegal, for example, the Presbyterians in the fertile north-eastern farmland appear to have resented the prominent role of Church of Ireland clergy and landlords. Even by the summer of 1914 the Donegal UVF had attracted only a minority of adult Protestant males in the county. In July 1913 the Royal Irish Constabulary county inspector reported to his superiors in Dublin Castle:

> One thing is certain and that is there is a very bitter feeling against Home Rule among the great majority of Protestants in the county; but I honestly believe that if Home Rule were passed tomorrow they would not be capable of doing anything to prevent it being operative and owing to the friendly feelings that genuinely exist between the Roman Catholics and the Protestants, the latter would not turn on their Roman Catholic neighbours for revenge.[22]

Protestant professional and business families played a major role in Donegal's economy, and these were reluctant to jeopardise their livelihoods by giving wholehearted support to the UVF. Belfast was therefore the most natural home base for the force.

In charge of the UVF was to be Lieutenant-General Sir George Richardson, aged sixty-six and with imperial experience that included the quelling of the Boxer Rising in China. By July 1913 he had established himself in Belfast and was firmly in control. By September a framework for a provisional government had been set up by the Ulster Unionist Council, and a Military Council had been established; an Indemnity Guarantee Fund was provided to compensate UVF members for losses suffered if they should have to fight for Ulster's cause; and a centre of operations for the force was located in the autumn in the Old Town Hall in Belfast's city centre. Among the most important appointments was that of Captain Wilfred Spender as assistant quartermaster-general; one of his tasks was to establish a committee to organise food supplies for the civilian population in the event of war. He was also responsible for the establishment of an equipment committee and a transport committee.[23]

Initially, the Volunteers had little in the way of uniform: belts, bandoliers and haversacks were the prime distinguishing features. By winter of 1913 the staff at UVF HQ had sent out a detailed list of addresses of suppliers in Belfast, together with the articles of equipment that could be purchased, including puttees, gaiters, belts, water bottles, army boots, rifle slings, waterproof groundsheets and greatcoats.[24] When a Volunteer joined the UVF, his first acquisition would be a small bronze badge emblazoned with the Red Hand of Ulster and the famous motto, 'For God and Ulster'.[25] He would also have a canvas armband with details of his regiment and battalion printed on it. As organisation progressed, he was encouraged to possess a personal store of emergency rations, and certain members of each company would be responsible for entrenching tools, maps and cooking utensils. One directive stated:

> Every volunteer should be urged as strongly as possible to keep always
> in his possession some food, such as tinned meat, sardines, chocolate, or
> potted meat, tea … which in addition to bread and biscuits … he
> may be able to collect at his home in case of emergency.[26]

Meanwhile, the autumn of 1913 provided further opportunities for the UVF to display its growing strength. Once again, Carson aroused his audiences at meetings and parades with his pugnacious oratory. Four thousand Volunteers paraded in the city of Armagh on Saturday 4 October – the procession included nurses, stretcher-bearers and cavalry. (There had been a marked increase in sectarian tension in the city in the period leading up to the parade – Armagh Urban District Council, controlled by a nationalist majority, had refused permission for displays of loyalist bunting, flags and posters – but in the event the day passed off relatively calmly.)[27] A vigorous campaign was launched to win over British public opinion, and UVF parades and demonstrations were reported regularly in English newspapers. The *Daily News*, the *Manchester Guardian*, and the *Daily Herald* condemned the loyalist paramilitaries, *The Times* sympathised with Ulster Protestants but was alarmed by the UVF, while the Tory press – such as the *Morning Post* and the *Yorkshire Post* – was full of warm approval. A review at Balmoral in south Belfast was reported in glowing terms by the correspondent for the *Liverpool Daily Courier*:

> Not since the marshalling of Cromwell's Puritan Army have we had
> anything approaching a parallel; as a body of men they were magnificent.
> The hardy sons of toil from shipyards and factories marched shoulder to
> shoulder with clergy and doctors, professional men and clerks.[28]

These displays of unionist strength elicited a variety of responses from the Catholic community, ranging from fear to ridicule. Belfast's nationalist daily paper, the *Irish News*, lashed the 'Carsonites' and their blustering threats of civil war, describing the Craigavon demonstration of September 1911 as an 'orgie of Ulsteria', and claiming that during Carson's 'dull, monotonous' speech, most of the audience was in fact squatting on the grass, smoking and talking loudly about football.[29] The Covenant of 1912 was to the *Irish News* 'a farce', organised by people 'who insist upon referring to "Ulster" as their own private cabbage garden'.[30]

Throughout 1913 the paper continued to hope that 'the whole thing will melt away' and that the Home Rule Bill would take its course, ushering in the 'Sunrise of Irish Freedom'.[31] Every opportunity was taken to deflate the pretensions of the UVF, one demonstration being described thus: 'a straggling wavy line of farm yokels, chauffeurs, grooms, and veterans of seventy winters stumbled forward in ragtime ... causing much hilarity to the onlookers'.[32]

Ulster Catholics clearly felt themselves threatened by the increase in sectarian clashes that accompanied the growth of the Volunteers in 1912 and 1913. In September 1912, for instance, just prior to the signing of the Covenant, an enormous crowd of Protestant football supporters converged on Celtic Park in Catholic west Belfast for a Belfast Celtic vs. Linfield match, waving Orange banners and chanting 'obscene versions' of Orange songs. Large-scale rioting, including indiscriminate shooting, broke out, with scores of injured being ferried to hospital once police reinforcements had re-established order.[33] In Derry in August 1913 the Orange com- memoration of the relief of the Siege of Derry in 1689 sparked off several days of vicious rioting during which the windows of Catholic churches were smashed, Catholic business premises were attacked, Catholics were intimidated on their way to and from work, and shots were fired at Catholic homes. In addition, a Protestant man was shot dead by police in the Fountain Street area. The *Irish News* recorded a trail of violence left by Protestants travelling to the Derry celebrations; in Dungannon, a shot fired from a train window had left a young girl with a severe leg wound, and outside Omagh a farmer had had to shelter from a fusillade of revolver shots from the Derry-bound train.[34]

The atmosphere in Ulster, always tense, was becoming increasingly manic, and there seemed to be a number of 'Carsonites' looking for any excuse to indulge in indiscriminate violence.

CAMPS OF INSTRUCTION

By the autumn of 1913 the Ulster Volunteers were certainly a force to be reckoned with, and in order to consolidate the military training, camps of instruction was held by various regiments. The Tyrone Regiment was the first to initiate such a camp – to be held at the Duke of Abercorn's estate in October 1913. Ambrose Ricardo, now a colonel in the UVF, had first mooted the idea in August, and when the duke's grounds at Baronscourt were offered, a camp was quickly planned. It was to be restricted to officers and NCOs of the fifteen battalions, except in a few special cases, and although the late harvest of that year caused problems for the farmers who were to be involved, Baronscourt's stables and several vacant cottages on the estate were turned over for billeting, and on Saturday 11 October the men began to arrive. The Ulster Menu Company had taken up residence on Friday to provide food, and two marquees had been set up to accommodate lectures on 'military topics'. As each man arrived, he handed over a £1 note and an admission ticket.

Reveille on the following day was at seven o'clock, and church and dinner was followed by a Sunday afternoon walk through the autumnal glory of the demesne. On Monday the party divided into six companies for instruction purposes. That afternoon Lieutenant-General Richardson visited the camp. On Tuesday there was musketry and infantry training, followed in the evening by a lecture on 'field defences' illustrated by blackboard sketches. The evening concluded with a sing-song. Wednesday featured a lantern lecture on the South African war and its lessons. On Thursday squad drill, musketry and battalion drill were followed by a lecture on scouting, and on Friday more advanced work was done on targeting in rifle fire, with an inspection of defence works at a nearby fortified farm – using trenches, sandbags and high-wire entanglements,

On Saturday the men marched to Newtownstewart railway station and departed. The keeper of records noted that they had consumed over a ton of potatoes and 1,470 pounds of beef. No man who attended would be

UVF men march from Newtownards to Clandeboye for a camp of instruction
SOMME MUSEUM

financially worse off – compensation for loss of wages would be provided where necessary.[35]

Among the memorable but unplanned incidents that occurred during the week was a fracas with some suffragettes who had arrived at the camp from England, complete with firearms. They raised a great protest when told that they could play no part in the proceedings, and finally Ricardo took their guns and marched them out of camp.[36]

Also memorable was the havoc caused when a practical joker interfered with two boxes of pills, one for the treatment of constipation, the other for alleviating diarrhoea. The labels were switched – with resultant indisposition.[37]

The UVF camp at Baronscourt formed a fascinating cross-section of society. Among the officers and NCOs attending were an auctioneer, a barrister, a chauffeur, a cooper, a fishery inspector, a French polisher and a watchmaker. The group included six clergymen.

Unquestionably, the camp would have enhanced the *esprit de corps* of the Tyrone UVF and, in some ways, would have improved its military efficiency, but many of the lectures were delivered by army officers whose experience of war had been in the outposts of the British Empire, and to men whose knowledge of fighting was nil. For example, the 'Lecture on Scouting and Intelligence Duties in the Field' had more relevance to the South African veld than to the lush fields of County Tyrone – the lecturer bade scouts to remember that 'a low thick dust indicates infantry while a light, high cloud of dust is raised by cavalry'. Some of the instructions seemed to be given with Zulu tribesmen in mind rather than Irish nationalists or the British army. The scout, the men were told

> … should carry his messages secretly… in a tobacco pipe already filled with tobacco, as his captors will probably seize it and smoke it, thereby themselves destroying the dispatch.[38]

Likewise, many of the manoeuvres, conducted against an imaginary enemy, can only have given a false sense of what war was about. Captain Bell, of Ballynahinch, has summed this up well when referring to a County Down UVF camp of instruction:

In 1914 I brought the Ballynahinch UVF company to Montalto for a week's training from Monday to Saturday. We were billeted at the farmyard ... Lord Clanwilliam took the company out for exercise and extended them from Montalto Gardens past Drumaness to the Spa Road. We advanced on the far wood, which is called Woodlands, on the other side of that large field. We leap-frogged across the field and when we came close enough to the wood, Lord Clanwilliam led the charge, and we took the wood without a casualty!

Well, almost without a casualty... for an old fellow called Tommy Gray, of Mulloughdrinn, put his foot in a rabbit burrow and broke his gun – they were wooden training guns – and finished up with only a barrel![39]

A MODERN ARMY

In some respects, however, the UVF had an undoubted modernity – which Captain Spender was to boast about in later years – and in no area was this more the case than in the organisation of motor transport. It is interesting to compare the 827 motorcars and 15 motorcycles that the British Expeditionary Force possessed at the outbreak of the Great War[40] with the 500 motor vehicles assembled by the UVF at Larne on the night of the *Clyde Valley* gun-running in April of that year.[41] By February 1914 Spender hoped that each county should be able to supply several complete squadrons of vehicles, to be co-ordinated eventually as a motorcar corps, province wide. A circular from the Old Town Hall stipulated that a squadron should be able to convey one company of the UVF or '100 refugees'. A removable UVF emblem should also be provided for each vehicle. Before long, a list was to be prepared of garages owned by 'reliable Unionists'.[42]

The motor squadron of the 2nd Battalion of the 3rd County Down Regiment, for instance, comprised in all thirty-one vehicles, including two charabancs. All told, the squadron could carry 212 people.[43] In an era when motor transport was in its attractive infancy, this squadron on manoeuvres must have presented a marvellous sight to loyalists – and chilling to nationalists – on summer evenings in the shadow of the Mourne Mountains, or snaking its way at night along the banks of Carlingford Lough with headlights blazing.

Well-armed volunteers with two UVF nurses in attendance
SOMME MUSEUM

By May all members of this squadron had received a series of careful instructions from R.S. Redmond, their commander. Each vehicle should carry ten yards of strong rope for breakdowns; when out driving, a companion should be taken; and 'in case of accident' there should be '3 short sharp blasts of your horn or whistle'. The directive insisted that all cars should carry arms, but that it was also advisable for passengers to keep a stout stick or baton.[44]

The UVF had its own communications system, for it became clear that the telephone and postal services were vulnerable to interception. A central 'Ulster Signalling and Despatch Riding Corps' was established, which provided a totally independent means of conveying secret information.[45]

The medical services of the Volunteer Force were also organised. A directive issued by the doctor in charge of the North Down Regiment, 1st Battalion, instructed that the battalion's First Aid Corps should be under direct control of a 'battalion surgeon':

> The First Aid and Stretcher Corps will accompany the battalion in the field, marching in the rear and will form a dressing camp. The wounded will be collected and carried back to the field dressing camp by the stretcher-bearers from whence they will be conveyed back to the nearest hospital.[46]

Each battalion's First Aid Corps would include seventy-two stretcher-bearers and eighteen stretchers.

One respect in which the UVF was a modern army was in the importance of women's roles within it. Many women were not content to be nurses and caterers – though some did these jobs and went on to nurse in the Great War. Women were also involved in the Signalling Corps of the UVF, and some, like Mina Lenox-Conyngham, of Springhill, found themselves out at night on hilltops signalling messages with a lamp to distant locations.[47]

Despite its modernity, and despite the organisation of back-up facilities and camps of instruction throughout the province, the UVF would pose an empty threat without guns and ammunition for the 90,000–100,000 men who had enrolled by the time entry was closed on the last day of February 1914.[48]

LEADERS AND ADVENTURERS

The Ulster Volunteer movement had its share of colourful leaders, and none among them is more intriguing than Captain Frank Percy Crozier.

Crozier came from an Anglo-Irish family with strong military traditions, but in 1896 he had been denied entry to the army because he was too short and too light, so in 1898 he made his way to Ceylon as a tea planter. In 1899 the South African war gave him his opportunity to join the British army abroad, where standards were less tight. He fought in the Boer War and then joined the West African Frontier Force, fighting Hausa tribesmen in Nigeria. Here, he acquired a drink problem and a bad bout of malaria. After treatment, he left for Canada where he helped raise a squadron of the Saskatchewan Light Horse, met the Antarctic explorer Shackleton, helped lay a telephone line through Manitoba, was almost killed in a hurricane, and, finally, became a teetotaller.

In the autumn of 1912 Crozier returned to Britain to find the Home Rule crisis well under way. It was an ideal opportunity for more adventure. In 1913 he joined the 'British League for the Defence of Ulster and the Union', and before long had accepted an invitation to join the UVF. On arrival in Belfast he was posted to the West Belfast Regiment, where his job was to raise part of a Special Service Section.[49]

A decision had been taken to raise such a section in the Belfast area – a

Sir Edward Carson – the 'great man'
whose personality cult was a feature of
the anti-Home Rule movement
SOMME MUSEUM

force of some three thousand men drawn from each of the four regiments
– who would be the cream of the Volunteer movement, well trained and
ready for swift action.[50] Crozier took great delight in raising and training
his quota of three hundred men. He would appear to have had some distaste
for his fellow officers, but had a healthy respect for his raw and fearsome
Shankill recruits who paraded on Monday, Tuesday, Wednesday and
Thursday nights at Forth River Football Ground.

Crozier, with the fervour of the reformed alcoholic, put the fear of God
into any man in his Special Service unit who abused drink. Any Volunteer
known to have been drunk whilst on duty would receive a personal call
from Crozier to indicate his dismissal. The culprit, according to Crozier,
would then have to suffer the humiliation of having women and children
shout after him in the street, 'Did the wee man tear the breeks off ye?'[51]

Carson addresses the UVF camp at Clandeboye, guarded by
a senior colleague on horseback
SOMME MUSEUM

A character from a different background who threw himself into the
UVF's activities was Robert Adgey, a pawnbroker at Peter's Hill at the foot
of the Shankill Road. Adgey had spent much of his youth on the Shankill,
where he was a milkman's boy before going to work for a pawnbroker. He
headed straight from work each evening to a working-men's club to 'get
educated'. By the time the Ulster Crisis was reaching its height, he was
doing big business for the UVF in the clandestine world of gun-running.

On one occasion, Colonel T.V.P. McCammon of the UVF told Adgey
that he wanted 100 Webley service revolvers for his dispatch riders. Could
Adgey get them to Belfast urgently?

That night Adgey and a friend went aboard the Liverpool boat with two
large suitcases, having drawn £200 in sovereigns from the Ulster Bank. The
next day they went to Webley & Scott Ltd in Birmingham, where they were
'well known', and received the consignment of revolvers. They returned to
Liverpool to catch the night ferry, and answered a railway porter at New
Street station, who complained of the weight of their suitcases, by saying that
they contained plumbers' brass fittings. The steward on the boat was, in
Adgey's words, 'an old friend', and the two men were locked in with their
suitcases in a single berth. Another 'friend', who supervised arrivals at the

Belfast quayside, ensured that Adgey and his accomplice got through untroubled. The guns were at the Old Town Hall, to the astonishment of McCammon, before noon – less than forty-eight hours after the request had been made.[52]

The Ulster Crisis was to throw together men of divergent social backgrounds in a way that rehearsed the social mixing that membership of the British army was to bring to so many in the Great War. The UVF had drawn into its network men whose roots were far removed from those of Adgey and his like, and who were to form the officer material for the Ulster Division before 1914 was over.

One of these was John Leslie Stewart-Moore of Ballydivity near Dervock, County Antrim, who had been educated at Rossel School in Lancashire, and graduated in 1913 from Trinity College, Dublin, with a BA in philosophy. Stewart-Moore was contemplating holy orders at this stage, but the gathering momentum of the crisis in Ulster, followed by the crisis in Europe, was to change that. At Trinity, Stewart-Moore had joined the Officer Training Corps, originally in the Army Service Corps area because he thought it might give him a chance to work with horses. His support for the UVF had been undiminished by his absence from Ulster, and he and his friends held concerts to raise funds for the Volunteers; the meetings they organised to plan the concerts were, with conscious irony, held in the rooms of the Gaelic Society.

In March 1914 the young men in the neighbourhood of Ballydivity went to their local clergyman to ask him to drill them. Being inexperienced, the clergyman asked for the help of Stewart-Moore, who had returned from Dublin for the Easter break. Stewart-Moore drilled the men in the local Orange hall, but then found considerable difficulty in trying to get his unit recognised, as recruitment to the UVF had officially closed at the end of February. On appearing with his men at a parade of the North Antrim Battalion on Easter Monday, Stewart-Moore was virtually chased off the premises by an outraged adjutant. Finally, the men were included in the Dervock company of the local battalion, and made their way proudly to a parade service in Armoy Presbyterian Meeting House on the following Sunday, dummy rifles clattering noisily against the pews.[53]

Another intriguing and influential figure who played a crucial role in the establishment of the UVF was Ambrose Ricardo, the great-grandson of the famous eighteenth-century economist, David Ricardo. This leading Volunteer had met his wife, Ella Herdman, in India, where she was visiting relatives, and returned with her to the Herdman home in Sion Mills. He had fought in the Boer War, but on coming to Ulster became a director of the family flax mill. The Ricardos had no children, but they led an active life, and amongst their many charitable activities they provided movie shows and concerts for the village children. Ricardo also organised a rose show in Sion Mills each summer, and a regatta with races between departments of the mill. He was a keen theatre-goer, too, and regularly produced amateur plays.[54]

Crozier's opinion on Ricardo was that he was 'efficient if verbose'.[55] He would seem to have possessed a warmth and culture that Crozier lacked, and no doubt he brought these qualities to the work he was doing for the UVF. Those who remember him recall quirky details – his early motorcar with no seat beside the driver, only a space to get into the back seat from the front; and his spoilt, rumbustious dog, called Cupid, who had a habit of running off with visitors' hats.[56]

A remarkable woman connected with the UVF was Monica Massy-Beresford, of St Huberts in the Fermanagh lakeland. She had been an adventurous girl from the start, helping to crew her father's yacht at the age of ten and driving his motorcar when she was eleven. In 1914 she would help her father drive to Larne to pick up the smuggled guns from the *Clyde Valley* gun-running operation. She often accompanied her father to shooting practise, and could target as well as any man. Sometimes, she hid guns in her skirts when the car she was travelling in encountered the Royal Irish Constabulary. Given this adventurous background, it is not surprising that when Monica Massy-Beresford later married a Dane and lived in Denmark during the Second World War, she became involved in the resistance. She was betrayed and died in a concentration camp in February 1945.[57]

CIVIL WAR LOOMS

By March 1914 the UVF believed itself to be sufficiently prepared to engage in a full-scale *coup d'état*, cutting off all lines of communication, capturing arms depots and closing the roads into and out of Ulster. It is doubtful if even the most optimistic of the commanding officers believed that all nine

A UVF company, prepared for the looming civil conflict. The man in civilian attire (lying on the ground to the right) could well be their chaplain.
SOMME MUSEUM

counties of the province could be thus sealed off, but they seem to have been confident that the predominantly Protestant and industrialised north-east could be seized. As it was unlikely that Catholics throughout the province would have accepted a UVF coup with peaceful resignation, Ulster seemed to be lurching closer to civil war.

Nationalists had few contingency plans, either political or military. No attempt was made to prevent UVF activity. In County Monaghan, for example, the 'Northern Battalion' held manoeuvres in the Leslie demesne and paraded through Glaslough in January 1914, while the 'Southern Battalion' gathered on the Murray-Ker demesne at Newbliss. The following month 125 men from Monaghan were given a fortnight's intensive training on the Earl of Erne's estate at Knockballymore. On 26 February 1914 the Ulster Women's Unionist Council met in the Assembly Rooms in Monaghan town to discuss the setting up of a field hospital should civil war break out. In the concluding speech, Miss Murray-Ker deplored the prospect 'of being placed under a Dublin Roman Catholic Parliament which will be under priestly influence and dominated – and this I fear most – by Mr Devlin's anti-Protestant Ancient Order of Hibernians'.[58]

While many Ulster Catholics continued to depend on the Liberal government's promises, others looked increasingly to the Irish Volunteers as a guarantee that UVF plans would be thwarted. In January 1914 a county committee was organised in Fermanagh and arrangements were made to establish eight battalions. The Enniskillen battalion, for example, contained 300 men who drilled once a week and kept what few arms they had in Joe Gillen's furniture store. In May the battalion obtained permission from the nationalist-dominated Fermanagh County Council to drill in the old jail.[59]

The Irish Volunteers were not established in County Donegal until February 1914 when Patrick Pearse, a member of the national executive, set up the first unit in Dungloe. The movement spread rapidly thereafter, and within weeks there were units in every part of the county, to the alarm of the Catholic bishop of Raphoe, Patrick O'Donnell. The bishop of Derry, Charles McHugh, was more sympathetic, and encouraged plans for a great demonstration to 'strengthen the hands of Mr Redmond and the Irish Party'. Bishop O'Donnell was horrified, however, and Redmond himself cancelled the demonstration planned for 14 March 1914 in Derry, pointing out that Carsonites 'would welcome an outbreak of riot and disorder in Ulster'.[60]

In east Tyrone, the Irish Volunteers seem to have been more militant than in any other part of Ulster. Here, even Catholic clergy were seen to be more radical than elsewhere, and the infant Sinn Féin had considerable influence under the guidance of Patrick McCartan, a medical student from Carrickmore. By 1914, however, McCartan had been so disgusted by the conservative sectarianism of so many of his co-religionists that he had resumed his studies. McCartan's impact in the area had, nevertheless, been very important in bringing recruits to the Irish Volunteers.[61]

Meanwhile, Asquith's government sought, with increasing desperation, to find a compromise solution in order to avert bloodshed. Redmond, somewhat unhappily, agreed to the exclusion, at least for a time, of some Ulster counties.[62] His Ulster followers pugnaciously rejected attempts to appease the unionists in this way.[63] A rift in the nationalist camp was prevented by Carson's intransigence: the Ulster unionist leader would accept nothing less than the permanent partition of all nine counties of Ulster, and this he knew the government would refuse.

The Liberal government decided to assert its authority in Ulster in March 1914. Troops were to be moved north, and the navy was to carry further reinforcements across the Irish Sea. On Saturday 14 March 1914, Winston Churchill, the first lord of the Admiralty, spoke at Bradford, saying:

First, I have greatly desired that we should not do the unliberal or hard thing to the Ulster community, mistaken though I think they are, and, secondly, and not less strongly, I have felt that we cannot let ourselves be bullied. (Cheers.) We cannot let ourselves be prevented by threats of force, or, let me add, by force itself from doing justice to the rest of Ireland and from making good arrangements for the future of the whole of Ireland and from maintaining the authority of the State.[64]

Joseph Devlin, MP for West Belfast, made a speech at Bradford the following day reinforcing Churchill's statement that unionists could expect no further concessions. *The Times* reported Devlin's speech:

The Nationalists had gone to the utmost limits to conciliate them. They would not go one single inch further. They had strained the feelings of their people in Ireland, and particularly in Ulster, almost to the breaking point.[65]

Indeed, Redmond and Devlin were roundly condemned by other nationalists for even contemplating the temporary exclusion of six of the nine Ulster counties. William O'Brien, speaking at the All for Ireland conference in Cork that weekend, declared that 'the proposal to exclude Ulster in whole or in part, permanently or temporarily, would be regarded by all genuine Irish nationalists with resentment and loathing ...'[66]

As British troops began to arrive in Ulster, and Royal Navy warships steamed from Spain and Portsmouth up the Irish Sea towards Belfast, the UVF in response prepared for mobilisation. The entire HQ staff took up residence at Craigavon, guarded by Crozier's Special Service men.

GUNS FOR ULSTER

Then on Saturday 21 March the news that officers of the British army at the Curragh camp had mutinied – having refused to participate in a 'betrayal' of Ulster – put paid to the government's plans for extensive suppression of the resistance to Home Rule. Directives for military action were withdrawn and tension was defused, if only by Asquith's abject capitulation. However, the unionist leaders felt they had learnt that the UVF was not properly prepared to take on the British army unless it was fully equipped with arms. Plans were made for a large-scale gun-running operation.[67]

It would, however, be foolish to imagine that the UVF had been reliant on wooden rifles until the spring of 1914. In many of the rural areas, the periodic threat of Home Rule over the previous decades had led to the presence of guns in cupboards or under beds in the houses of Ulster Protestants. In the Waringstown area, for instance, some farmers had regularly fattened extra pigs to get money for guns. Especially popular was a Webley that had been issued to officers in the Boer War.

The first semblance of training in the use of guns in the early volunteering days around Lurgan and Portadown was provided under the aegis of 'sporting gun clubs' when, of a Sunday afternoon, townspeople who were unused to guns could obtain training at the hands of farmers who were in the Volunteer movement and were well acquainted with the practicalities of shooting.

Some of the models that turned up in the early UVF days were mid-nineteenth-century muzzle rifles with gunpowder and ball and a high degree of inaccuracy. Other antique shotguns would prove equally inaccurate, and when modern rifles did begin to arrive, a more accurate standard of musketry had to be achieved.

Small-scale gun-smuggling was already going on before 1914. Guns came in on fishing boats to ports such as Kilkeel, and were hidden in boxes of herring. Colliers also landed guns, to be entrusted to someone specially delegated for the task on the quayside. Volunteers in the village of Waringstown, County Down, received rifles smuggled to the province in these ways, and then sent them by train to Lurgan; a carriage would be diverted down by Brownlow Terrace, from where there was easy access for a local lorry driver, who would then deliver the precious cargo around country areas.[68]

However, the number of guns getting through was inadequate to the needs of a massed army, especially now that a watch was being kept on key British ports following the discovery that gun-running had become a standard practice. So the go-ahead was given to an enterprising and influential figure in the Belfast Volunteer hierarchy, Fred Crawford, to endeavour to buy a very large consignment of rifles on the Continent, to ship them en masse directly to Ulster, and to land at some secret night-time rendezvous. Crawford, a former artillery officer in the British army, had been involved in the Volunteer movement since 1911, and had built up contacts with a

The *Clyde Valley*. One April night in 1914, five hundred motor vehicles waited in Larne for her consignment of smuggled arms.
BOBBY FOSTER

German, Bruno Spiro, that were to prove invaluable. The so-called 'business committee' of the UVF approved Crawford's plan to buy twenty thousand rifles and two million rounds of ammunition from Spiro in Hamburg, and to acquire a suitable steamer in a foreign port for bringing the weapons back to Ulster, perhaps with a secret mid-voyage transfer to some other vessel.

The gun-running was planned secretly and scrupulously. The operation was code named 'Lion'. On the night of 24 April 1914 there was to be a test mobilisation of the UVF under cover of which the County Antrim Regiment was to take over the port of Larne whilst the *Clyde Valley* docked there and unloaded. The motor corps of various UVF units would be assembled in Larne, and waiting, with engines turning, to collect their parcels of guns and deliver them to secret locations in their home areas.

In Belfast, Volunteers were to endeavour to draw attention away from the Larne operation: they were to march a contingent to the docks where the SS *Balmerino* would arrive in what would be a 'decoy run'; a great effort was to be made to frustrate the customs authorities in their attempt to search the vessel, adding to the suspicion that she contained arms for the waiting Belfast Volunteers.

On the night, all went according to plan. The UVF took control of Larne under cover of darkness, and column after column of vehicles approached the port, passing checkpoint after checkpoint. Men from local battalions had been placed at key points along the highways to guide drivers unfamiliar with the roads. At certain points, there were reserve supplies of petrol and tools for possible breakdowns. It was a cold, wet night at Larne, and many of the men involved had already done a day's work, but by the time the *Clyde Valley* had pulled into harbour, the headlights of five hundred motor vehicles were flaring in the County Antrim town. Lorry drivers were soon on their way with their clandestine cargo.

At Larne, two local ships were loaded with guns for Belfast and Donaghadee, and soon the *Clyde Valley* was heading for Bangor on the County Down coast, where a further, smaller consignment of guns and ammunition was unloaded. By 7.30 a.m., as Bangor awoke, the last cars were leaving the pier with their cargo, and at Donaghadee and Belfast, the guns had also been quietly slipped ashore. The *Clyde Valley* operation had been an unqualified success.[69]

The weapons were soon being secreted in stockpiles across Ulster. Stewart-Moore and his Volunteers had spent a disappointingly dull night guarding Stranocum village. They were to prevent police from entering the village, but there was no sign of the RIC through the night. At 4.30 a.m., tired and sleepy, they were ordered home. The next afternoon, Stewart-Moore drove to Stranocum House and found his uncle James, revolver in hand, organising a group of men who were loading a car with bundles of rifles done up in canvas. They had originally been delivered at 7.00 a.m., but a disturbing report had come through that there were five policemen fishing on the river nearby with only one fishing rod! It was decided swiftly that the rifles had better be distributed around the country for safekeeping. Stewart-Moore put a bundle of guns under a rug on the floor of his cart, stopped briefly at a neighbour's for afternoon tea, then returned home, where, with stifled excitement, he and his sister hid the rifles after nightfall in an unused loft above the scullery. Shortly afterwards, the guns would be handed out to his Volunteers for the first time.[70]

Outside Crossgar, County Down, Hugh James Adams and John Martin lay in a ditch along the main road, awaiting the guns from Bangor. When the weapons finally arrived, early in the morning, they were taken to Tobar

Mhuire for swift distribution to a variety of locations. Bundles were placed in carts and taken quietly to houses in and around the village, where they were hidden under the floorboards until further orders arrived.[71]

In Lisburn, Hugh Stewart, who had originally been forbidden by his father from joining the UVF, found his night's duties hard going, and as he lay out on the Moss Road, on guard, he fell asleep. However, the guns were safely brought in and stored in buildings around the town. Hugh recalled how he had got his old dummy rifle for 1s 6d and had been proud of it, too, but was keen now for one of the real guns and a shining bayonet.[72]

At Springhill, County Derry, the Lenox-Conynghams were instrumental in getting the guns to their area. Just a few days previously, Sir Edward Carson had visited them, sitting down to a dinner party around a damask tablecloth portraying the Siege of Derry, with a small wreath of laurels at Sir Edward's place. Mina Lenox-Conyngham was proud to be at Carson's side as he walked in the gardens, but she records that he told her: 'I see terrible times ahead – bitter fighting – rivers of blood!' Unflinching and defiant in his public utterances, Carson on occasion expressed in private conversation grave doubts about the consequences of his actions.[73] With political passions running high and two opposing paramilitary forces preparing for action, bitter fighting and rivers of blood seemed a likely outcome in Ulster before the year was out.

On the Friday of Operation Lion, orders came by dispatch rider for the Lenox-Conynghams to mobilise their men that night. In the dawn of the next day, the squadron of cars pulled into the motor-yard with their newly landed rifles. The women of the house had been up all night preparing food, and now a hot meal was ready for the drivers and their helpers who had motored the fifty miles from Larne.[74]

The guns that had been landed were mainly German Mauser and Austrian Männlicher rifles, and the majority went to Belfast, Antrim and Down, with some to Derry and Tyrone. There were also several thousand Vetterli rifles of Italian make, which were distributed in Armagh, Fermanagh, Monaghan and Derry. These Italian guns were to gain a certain unpopularity before long, because they were stamped 'annunciata', which was interpreted as meaning 'blessed by the Pope'![75] However, with or without a papal blessing, the Volunteers were soon drilling openly with their new guns.

Unionists in Britain, particularly the Union Defence League and others promoting the British Covenant, were impressed by the gun-running operation. Lord Roberts, the Anglo-Irishman who had led the retreat from Kabul to Kandahar and had been in command in the Boer War, had refused Carson's offer to head the UVF only on grounds of age. On hearing of the landing of arms, he is reputed to have said to Carson:

> Magnificent! Magnificent! Nothing could have been better done; it was
> a piece of organisation that any army in Europe might be proud of.[76]

The success of the episode, despite all odds, was seen as a sign of God's hand guiding the Ulster Protestants. Men such as Crawford, mastermind behind the gun-running, believed strongly in the rightness of their cause:

> I felt my responsibilities very heavily, but I believed that our cause was
> just and I believed in God Almighty. We were going to defend
> our faith and liberty.[77]

It was with this sense of achievement that the men of the UVF were to enter the British army and, eventually, the gun and shell fire of the Somme. They had had the verdict of military men that they could compare with any army in Europe in their organisation and strategy, and they had had 'evidence' that God was on their side.

Again and again, Ulster loyalists emphasised the righteousness of their cause. Even before the *Clyde Valley* steamed into Larne, the *Northern Whig* declared:

> There is a strong feeling in Belfast today, notwithstanding Mr Churchill's
> ferocity, Mr Lloyd George's vulgar bluster, and Mr Devlin's impotent
> boasting, that the worst of the battle is over, and that the cause of Ulster
> has been justified in the eyes of England, of Europe, and of the world.[78]

This confidence – and refusal to recognise that more than half the electorate of Britain had voted for parties promoting Irish Home Rule – was no doubt engendered by the fact that, while the UVF was armed, the Irish Volunteers were not. Sir Roger Casement and his friends, however, were already at work to redress that military imbalance.

Young Citizen Volunteer footballers pose with their comrades,
who are dressed in the distinctive YCV uniforms
SOMME MUSEUM

YOUNG CITIZEN VOLUNTEERS

The Ulster Volunteer Force was a diverse and complex organisation,
spanning rural and urban Protestant Ulster, stretching from isolated loyalist
outposts on the Atlantic coast of Donegal to the shipyard communities of
east Belfast in the unionist heartland. One of the most dedicated groups of
men, at first quite separate from the UVF, was the Young Citizen Volunteers
of Ireland (YCVs).

The inaugural meeting of this organisation had been held in Belfast City
Hall on 10 September 1912, just prior to the fervent days of the Solemn
League and Covenant. On the committee was Major Fred Crawford, and
the president was Robert James McMordie, Lord Mayor of Belfast. Each
member was to pay 2s 6d on joining the YCVs, and a further sixpence each
month; he was to attend weekly drills in order to learn 'modified military
and police drill, single stick, rifle and baton exercises, signalling, knot-tying
and other such exercises'. If possible, he was also to gain some knowledge
of 'life-saving and ambulance work'.

The YCV movement was, perhaps, aiming to fill a gap left by the
disbandment of the old militia and volunteers during Haldane's army reforms

of 1907 – which had been designed to make the British military system more economical and efficient – and also to extend the highly successful strategies of the Scout and Boys' Brigade movements to a somewhat older age group. The constitution of the YCVs insisted that members should not take part in any political meeting or demonstration. The organisation's objectives were stated as being 'non-sectarian and non-political', and the YCVs aimed

> ... to develop the spirit of responsible citizenship and municipal patriotism by means of lectures and discussions on civic matters ... to cultivate, by means of modified military and police drill, a manly physique, with habits of self-control, self-respect and chivalry ... to assist as an organisation, when called upon, the civil power in the maintenance of the peace.

Membership was open to anyone aged between eighteen and thirty-five who was over five feet in height and could present 'credentials of good character'.[79] There was little possibility, however, that the aim included in the constitution that the YCVs should be 'non-sectarian and non-political' could be realised, even at the outset. Some Catholics did indeed join, but the recruitment was overwhelmingly Protestant.

The YCVs planned to extend its organisation further afield than Belfast, but growth was limited as a result of the financial burden imposed by the organisation's membership fee and the costly uniform. There would be few young men in the YCVs who did not have a reasonably remunerative job or come from a fairly comfortable background. The *Belfast News Letter* of 11 September 1912 spoke in vivid terms of the enthusiastic launch of the organisation:

> The large banqueting hall was well occupied by fine specimens of the young manhood of the city.

To the sound of bagpipes played by a piper in 'picturesque Highland uniform', some two thousand young men turned up, eager for enrollment. The Lord Mayor told them that:

> In times of difficulty men had to carry their guns while they followed the plough ... the nation or the people that had lost the fighting instinct was sure to be swamped by others who possessed that instinct.

The secretary, F.T. Geddes, claimed that the organisation was unique, and expressed the hope that the YCVs would be fostered by the government. The treasurer, Frank Workman, went on to compare the situation in contemporary Britain with that in Germany, where

> men walked with military bearing through the streets of the towns
> because they had been drilled for at least three years in connection with
> the Army.

It would seem that the formation of the Young Citizen Volunteers was a response to both the German threat and the Home Rule threat.[80]

On Tuesday 10 December a meeting of the YCVs was addressed by Francis Forth, principal of the Municipal Technical Institute of Belfast. He extolled, above all else, the 'well-ordered and intelligent discipline' that 'expands the mind, exalts the faculties, refines the tastes, cultivates a spirit of patriotism'. Quoting from John Stuart Blackie, Forth went on:

> Let the old Roman submission to authority be cultivated by all young
> men as a virtue at once most characteristically social, and most
> becoming in unripe years.

Obedience, he claimed, was the link that tied everyone to their immediate superior in the pyramid of society, and sound discipline would be achieved not merely through self-discipline but through drills.

Several references in the lecture make evident an underlying unease. There was a prolonged passage on the recent loss of the *Titanic* – itself a great blow to Belfast's confidence – and to the way in which the city's grief was softened by the knowledge that many on board showed great discipline in time of peril. The Young Citizen Volunteers must do the same. They must show self-sacrifice and courage in these difficult times. The speaker also dwelt at length on a painting by Sir Edward Poynter in which a Roman soldier was standing at his post whilst in the background Vesuvius erupted. Here, Forth declared, was an example of real faithfulness and courage to stir the YCVs.[81]

In the course of 1913 the gathering momentum of the Home Rule crisis swept the YCVs into the arms of the Ulster Volunteer Force. Many Young Citizens were having difficulty finding money for the uniforms, and were paying off the costs in monthly instalments. An application for financial assistance in return for the placing of the YCVs at the government's disposal was refused. Absence of government recognition for the force as a 'territorial' unit proved hurtful, even if it were unsurprising in the circumstances. A large body of the YCVs advocated that they throw in their lot with the UVF, which, by April, had guns and prestige. There was much soul-searching within the YCVs, and resignations from the movement. But by May 1914 the majority remaining had decided that the cause of defending the realm and that of the Ulster Protestants was one, even if the government of that realm seemed intent on breaking the Union. The YCVs applied for membership of the UVF, and became a battalion of the Belfast Regiment.[82]

On Saturday 6 June the Young Citizens marched to the Balmoral Showgrounds with their new comrades, to be reviewed by Sir Edward Carson. A stream of people who had been thronging the Lisburn Road poured into the grounds when the gates opened at 4.00 p.m., and bathed in the warm afternoon sunshine. When the Young Citizens marched past at 4.45 a roar went up from the crowd of twenty-five thousand.[83]

Three Belfast newspapers gave their unreserved support to the loyalist cause and its military arm, the UVF: the *Belfast News Letter*, the *Northern Whig* and the *Belfast Evening Telegraph*. Of these three, the *Telegraph* was then the most stridently partisan; it endorsed the stand the YCVs had taken: 'Where indeed should they be, but with those who stand for civil and religious freedom?'[84] However, the *Irish News*, the nationalist paper and sole voice of Belfast's Catholics, had a different slant in its Monday-morning editorial, reminding the Young Citizen Volunteers that it had once claimed to be 'non-political' and 'non-sectarian'.[85]

Before long, the YCVs would have a chance to prove its military prowess in an arena far wider than that of Balmoral. The last hours of peacetime in Europe were swiftly ticking away.

THE BRINK OF WAR

In the month leading up to the outbreak of European war, Ulster's blood-pressure had remained at a high level. The Ulster unionists, with the support of most of the peers of the realm and the Conservative and Unionist Party, were committed to setting up an illegal provisional government of Ulster

Portadown UVF men on parade outside the town. Within a few months,
many of these men would have enrolled in the Ulster Division
and taken the first steps on the road to the Somme.
TOM ROBERTS

and preventing the introduction of devolved government to any part of
Ireland. The will of the Liberal government, the majority of Westminster
MPs, and the majority of the Irish people was to be resisted – if necessary,
by force; the UVF was fully armed with rifles smuggled in from imperial
Germany and with the Kaiser's tacit approval. Meanwhile, recruitment for
the Irish Volunteers was so brisk that the total exceeded 180,000.[86]
Committed to defending Home Rule from the menace of an armed UVF,
these armed Catholics were often living cheek by jowl with armed
Protestants across Ulster, where sectarian clashes were endemic even in the
most peaceful times. The north of Ireland was becoming an armed camp.
In a desperate attempt to prevent a bloodbath, Redmond demanded and,
with difficulty, obtained Irish Party control over the Irish Volunteers, which
were renamed the National Volunteers in May 1914.

For how long could young radical National Volunteers be made to
comply with directives from the elderly Irish Party leadership? For how
long could Carson and Craig – themselves defiantly flouting the rule of law
– restrain the passions of eager young loyalists? In a confidential report, the
RIC county inspector of Londonderry wrote that 'there is no doubt that

many of the lower element of the Orange Order' had joined the UVF, and he feared that they 'will be prepared to proceed to extremities'.[87] When the Home Rule Bill finally passed through the Commons and went up to the Lords for the last time, in May, it seemed as though apocalypse could not be far off.

But by 1 July the newspapers were beginning to manifest greater concern about the war clouds over the Balkans. The *Belfast News Letter* reported that in Austria

> an anti-Servian agitation has already commenced and it may bring about a war in that country at the first favourable opportunity. Then if Russia should support Servia all Europe will be involved.

Yet the front page of the newspaper for the same day presents a picture of a whole society still unaware of the possibility of an engulfing European war. Although Ulster was in political crisis, shops advertised their summer sales; the newly built 'picture theatres' promoted their silent films; the Grand Opera House advertised two shows a night; art exhibitions and agricultural shows awaited visitors; in the 'for sale' columns, there were early flowering chrysanthemums, fragrant bedding violets and blue-and-white lobelias to be purchased.

During July the Liberal Prime Minister, Asquith, tried to bring all the parties in the Irish dispute to some kind of agreement. On 20 July he announced that the king had called a conference at Buckingham Palace for all those concerned. In Ulster, plans were being made in some quarters for the evacuation of 'refugees' to England and Scotland. The UVF was primed, armed, ready to act.[88]

On 23 July a British government preoccupied with its internal troubles heard the news from Vienna that the Austro–Hungarian government – apparently sufficiently convinced of Serbian complicity in the Archduke's murder – had sent an ultimatum to the Serbs. On 26 July Austro–Hungary declared war. Four days later, Russia mobilised its army. Germany demanded that the Russians demobilise, and when they did not, the Germans declared war, first on Russia, then two days later on France. On Sunday 2 August Germany asked for free passage through Belgium and was refused. Suddenly, Britain, too, was on the brink of war.

Monday 3 August was a bank holiday. The *Belfast News Letter* carried an article that declared:

Europe is face to face today with the most awful calamity of war that has ever threatened – that which every nation has been dreading has come. On Saturday evening, Germany declared war on Russia ... we can only express the opinion that the prospect is very dark and that the probabilities are all against our government being able to steer the ship of state free from the dreadful cataclysm of war that has overtaken the continent.

A number of UVF parades and demonstrations had been held in Ulster during the weekend. At Sand Quay Hill, near Downpatrick, Viscount Bangor spoke to the local battalion of the UVF's East Down Regiment in words that proved strangely prophetic. He extolled the Union Jack ...

under which they were born, and under which, please God, they would die, and they would prove themselves to be brave, true men of County Down, of Ulster, of Ireland and of the Empire.[89]

The UVF stood now, on the brink of the Great War, as an organisation that had come a great way since its 'Hayfoot! Strawfoot!' days. It had become an armed and intricate body of soldiers, one of the first in the twentieth century to have recognised the varied role of women in warfare, the first to use the motorcycle dispatch rider and motorcar on a large scale, the first to introduce armoured lorries in street patrols. The UVF did not possess heavy artillery, but in other respects appeared formidable and modern. Certainly, the Volunteers were not lacking in self-confidence.[90]

Many were to remember what they were doing on that last Monday of peacetime. John Stewart-Moore took his UVF men by train to Ballycastle for a big parade on the golf links. In the early afternoon, a heavy drizzle came down over the coast and blocked out the beautiful view of Fair Head and Rathlin Island across the sea. The parade was curtailed, and as there was no train home until 4.30, the men marched to the Presbyterian meeting house and sat there to wait, damp and disappointed.[91]

The next day, Tuesday 4 August, Britain declared war on Germany.

2

'I AM THE SOLDIER BOY'
THE ULSTER DIVISION: FORMATION AND
TRAINING 1914–15

Rifleman Kirk of the
9th Royal Irish Rifles with a
Martini rifle and Boer War bandolier
that had found their way into the
Ulster Division training armoury
SOMME MUSEUM

THE CALL TO ARMS

Within a few days of the outbreak of war, the British Expeditionary Force had set sail for France. It was a small force, and although popular wisdom decreed that the war would be over by Christmas, Kitchener foresaw a long conflict with which the regular army could not cope, even when supplemented by the Territorial forces. Before long, parliament had passed a bill that permitted the raising of half a million men for his New Army. As news filtered back of the severe difficulties facing the British soldiers up against the power of the German 'war-machine', a surge of patriotism spread across Britain. Army bands played at the head of recruiting marches in the streets of every town; posters exhorted young men from walls in every city in the land; women waited on corners to give white feathers to those who were still in 'civvies'; politicians cried out for a united effort to defeat the German tyrant. The poet Rupert Brooke endeavoured to capture the mood of the period:

> Now, God be thanked Who has matched us with His hour,
> And caught our youth, and wakened us from sleeping,
> With hand made sure, clear eye, and sharpened power ...
>
> 'Peace'[1]

It was a surge of naive patriotism unique in its power and infectiousness.

This tide of fervour was to take two million volunteers into the forces before the horrors of war became fully known and conscription had to be introduced, as it was in early 1916.

In troubled Ireland, there were, understandably, mixed reactions to the call to arms. Just hours after hostilities commenced, both Carson, for the Ulster unionists, and John Redmond, on behalf of the nationalists, declared their loyalty to the British government in the time of crisis. Each assured Asquith that many of their respective followers would be prepared to serve in the defence of the country. Each presumed that a show of loyalty to the Empire would be a sure way of strengthening his claims to his political objectives when the war was over.

However, the unionists saw no evidence that the British Prime Minister was prepared to abandon the Home Rule Bill. In fact, on 10 August he announced his intention to advise the king to sign the bill. In all probability the Act would not come into operation until the end of the war, but that was likely to be only a delay of execution. The Ulster Crisis would still go on in the hearts and minds of Ulster people, although a much larger political conflict now seemed to demand their response.[2]

SHOULD ULSTER GO OR STAY?

Many officers in the UVF were being recalled to their army regiments for service. Some were busy encouraging enlistment – Ricardo immediately called for recruits at the army depot in Omagh. On 7 August he declared that when a man entered the barracks to join up, he would be welcome whether he came from the Ulster Volunteers or the National Volunteers.[3] On the following day forms were distributed to UVF units, on which they could sign up for service. Carson and Craig claimed that many of the one hundred thousand men were ready for some kind of service, at home or abroad:[4] after all, the UVF, despite its confrontation with the British government, had become involved in such a conflict precisely because it declared its loyalty to the British Crown and Empire.

In actuality, the UVF leaders at this stage mainly showed a willingness to engage in home defence rather than to serve abroad. Spender suggested to the Committee of Imperial Defence that the best way the UVF could help would be if the two British army divisions in Ireland were removed and the UVF given their job; the regular troops could then join the British Expeditionary Force in France. The unionist leaders greeted with some chagrin the news that Redmond had made a similar proposal for home defence on behalf of the National Volunteers, who offered to do such duties 'in comradeship with our brethren in the north'.

There were many Ulstermen who were very reluctant to give any help to the British war effort whilst Home Rule remained a problem. Some farmers were reluctant even to let their horses be requisitioned by the army.[5]

A remarkable feature of the first days of the war was the manner in which National Volunteers and the UVF joined forces in many parts of Ulster to give a rousing send-off to departing troops. For the National Volunteers, supported by the Irish Party – which in turn was in coalition with the ruling Liberal Party – this response to the government's call to arms was natural, especially as 'little Catholic Belgium' was the first victim of German militarism. The UVF, on the other hand, had been preparing armed rebellion against the Westminster government; it constantly proclaimed its patriotism and loyalty to Crown and Empire, and it would have seemed churlish to refuse to respond to the king's call when the Empire was in peril. As early as 6 August 1914 the *Irish News* reported:

> A great number of reservists left Belfast yesterday to join various
> mobilisation centres, and at night especially their departure was attended
> by large and enthusiastic crowds.

The four Hamilton brothers of William Street, Lurgan,
who enlisted in the 9th Royal Irish Fusiliers
ROYAL IRISH FUSILIERS MUSEUM

About six hundred men attached to the Irish Volunteers in Belfast were called up, and there was a great gathering to wish them God-speed and a safe return, when they departed yesterday evening for the regimental centres, quite a large demonstration attending the departure of one body, while at the same time a quota of the Ulster Volunteers were being seen off by a cheering crowd with a band and pipers.

In that instance, the two forces may merely have tolerated each other, but on 10 August the *Irish News* approvingly carried this report:

TYRONE'S FINE EXAMPLE. NATIONAL AND ULSTER VOLUNTEERS
MARCH TOGETHER. ROUSING SCENES.
The Ulster Volunteers and Irish National Volunteers united at Omagh on Friday night [i.e. 7 August] in giving a most hearty send-off to the final draft of the Army Reserve of the Royal Inniskillings, who left the town about half-past nine o'clock, and a scene of an unparalleled description was witnessed when the procession of both bodies of Volunteers and military marched through the town together ... Subsequently, as both bodies of Volunteers paraded the town, they met one another and respectfully saluted.

The report also stated that on the following day, Saturday 8 August, there was a similar scene in Strabane, with both bodies of Volunteers marching to tunes played by the brass and reed band of the Strabane Catholic Temperance Society. Captain Roderick Gallaher of the National Volunteers 'called for three cheers for the Ulster Volunteers, the call being responded to in a most spirited manner'. Captain William Smyth of the UVF in turn called for and obtained a rousing three cheers for the National Volunteers.

On Tuesday 11 August a large advertisement proclaiming 'Your King and Country Needs You' appeared for the first time in the *Belfast News Letter*; the *Irish News* had carried a similar recruiting advertisement the previous day. In the following days, news was carried in the paper of the new 'pals battalions' being formed in England, in which groups of friends enlisted together. Before long, there was news, too, of the fighting in Belgium and France. However, the letter columns of the same newspaper reveal the divided opinion in Ulster Protestant ranks. On Friday 7 August an 'elderly volunteer' had written:

> The Volunteers are to be asked tomorrow if they are willing to serve
> abroad. It may be assumed that those who will agree to do so will
> be the youngest and most efficient men. It is highly probable that many of
> them will never return. When the war is finished, and the Home Rule
> situation has to be faced again, the UVF will be without many of its most
> useful members, and as a fighting force it will be less formidable.
> Therefore I ask you, is it desirable that any Volunteer should offer
> himself for foreign service?

Another letter-writer, on Wednesday 12 August, also warned against Ulster Volunteers joining up, saying that the National Volunteers in his district were awaiting their opportunity to rise against England. The previous evening he had heard them returning from drilling and they were cheering for the Germans.

Other correspondents claimed that the only loyal response was to offer the Volunteers for foreign service, and some saw practical political value in this: 'our men will be thoroughly trained, if necessity arises, to fight for our liberties, later on'.[6]

If a large body of the Volunteers remained unconvinced throughout

August, a number who were impatient to serve in the army did join up – some of these joining the Scottish regiments that recruited vigorously in Ulster. Also, the Officer Training Corps at Queen's University was fostering new officer material, and by early September over one hundred young officers had been sent up for commissions in the New Army.[7] And, of course, many Ulstermen were already fighting in the field with the regular army. However, processes were now well under way to facilitate the creation of a division of the New Army out of the Ulster Volunteers.

The British top brass were well aware of the formidable qualities of the Volunteers; indeed, most of them were deeply sympathetic to the Ulster unionist cause. General Sir John Gough had travelled around Ulster in July, staying with Volunteer leaders, and he became well acquainted with the organisation of the UVF. He had been reported as saying that it could 'with experienced leaders be made equal to any force in the world'.[8] The new secretary of state for war had also known of the UVF's potential – indeed, who had not? A reading of the recent newspapers would have shown any observer that they were the best-prepared civilians in Britain to go into the army and train for battle. Two days after being appointed to his new job, Kitchener had sent for Colonel T.E. Hickman MP, president of the British League for the Defence of Ulster, to tell him: 'I want the Ulster Volunteers.'[9]

Hickman had recommended that Kitchener see Carson and Craig. He did so, but the meeting was not a smooth one. Kitchener and Carson argued about the Home Rule issue, Carson still keen to hold out for a political deal before fully supporting the war effort. If the UVF were to be thrown into the recruitment pot, Carson and his colleagues wanted to ensure that it would be kept together as a unit; also, they wanted the prefix 'Ulster' to accompany the number of the proposed brigade or division. Kitchener was initially ill-disposed towards all this bargaining. Throughout August the debate was to continue; only at the end of the month was a deal struck that enabled Carson to return to Ulster and invite his Volunteers to sign up in large numbers for service abroad.[10]

A guarantee was given that although the Home Rule Bill would pass on 18 September, it would not be made operative during the war. An amending bill would be introduced in the next parliamentary session to give parliament the chance to alter its provisions to accommodate the needs of Ulster. On 3 September Carson announced at an Ulster Unionist Council meeting in Belfast the formation of what was to be the 36th (Ulster) Division. Recruitment was to begin immediately at the Old Town Hall and at civil buildings all across Ulster. The men would be trained in camps in Ireland – at least initially – and they would be enrolled in territorial units formed out of the local Volunteer regiments. Already, Craig had put in an order in London for ten thousand uniforms, to be paid for by some of Ulster's 'rich English friends'.[11] Large camps were envisaged at Ballykinler, Clandeboye and Newtownards in County Down, and at Finner in County Donegal. Sufficient members of the UVF would be kept organised and alert at home whilst those who joined the 36th were trained and then sent abroad to fight. 'I and those who remain behind will take care that Ulster is no invaded Province',[12] promised Carson.

Everything that the UVF had provided by way of equipment and uniform would prove valuable in the first weeks of training. The scene was set for the Ulster Volunteers to express their loyalty to the Crown and their fighting spirit as part of the British army, with which, just a few months earlier, they had been preparing to do battle.

THE ULSTER DIVISION IS FORMED

From its newly acquired HQ at 29 Wellington Place in Belfast's city centre, the Ulster Division began the formidable task of organisation. Three infantry brigades, twelve battalions in all, were to be formed. Three field companies of the Royal Engineers, a signal company, and Royal Army Medical Corps personnel were to be recruited. Royal Army Service Corps, cavalry and cyclist sections were to be established in the division. Whereas all these bodies were to be formed primarily of Ulstermen, the Divisional Artillery was to be recruited in England: the UVF had no artillery and it was thought that considerable delay could be caused by raising and training an artillery in Ulster, so the 153rd and 154th Brigades, Royal Field Artillery were to be recruited from Croydon, Norbury and Sydenham, and the 172nd and 173rd Brigades were to be from East and West Ham. These four brigades of Londoners were not to join the rest of the 36th Division until the following year. In the absence of artillery recruiting in Ulster, many men keen to serve on horseback joined the mounted section of the Field Ambulance, which thus became a very impressive unit.[13]

The five Clarke brothers who enlisted in the 16th Royal Irish Rifles
ROYAL ULSTER RIFLES MUSEUM

In the business of organisation, Captain Spender and the now Lieutenant-Colonel James Craig were to transfer the considerable talents they had shown in the UVF to the building of the Ulster Division. Spender became a general staff officer and Craig the assistant adjutant and quartermaster-general. Sir George Richardson, because of the seniority of his rank, was unable to take command of the division, so Major-General C.H. Powell, a former Indian army officer, became the commander of the 36th.

Three infantry regiments had their territorial base in Ulster – the Royal Irish Rifles in the east of the province, the Royal Irish Fusiliers in the south, and the Royal Inniskilling Fusiliers in the west – and the 36th Division's infantry would be comprised of battalions from all three. Each regiment was licensed to create numerous supplementary battalions for 'Kitchener's Army', in addition to their regular and Territorial Army battalions. So the structure of the Ulster Division turned out as follows:

107TH INFANTRY BRIGADE

     8th Battalion Royal Irish Rifles (East Belfast Volunteers)
     9th Battalion Royal Irish Rifles (West Belfast Volunteers)
    10th Battalion Royal Irish Rifles (South Belfast Volunteers)
    15th Battalion Royal Irish Rifles (North Belfast Volunteers)

108TH INFANTRY BRIGADE

11th Battalion Royal Irish Rifles (South Antrim Volunteers)
12th Battalion Royal Irish Rifles (Mid Antrim Volunteers)
13th Battalion Royal Irish Rifles (1st County Down Volunteers)
9th Battalion Royal Irish Fusiliers (Armagh, Monaghan and
    Cavan Volunteers)

109TH INFANTRY BRIGADE

9th Battalion Royal Inniskilling Fusiliers (Tyrone Volunteers)
10th Battalion Royal Inniskilling Fusiliers (Derry Volunteers)
11th Battalion Royal Inniskilling Fusiliers (Donegal and Fermanagh
    Volunteers)
14th Battalion Royal Irish Rifles (Young Citizen Volunteers of Belfast)

PIONEER BATTALION

16th Battalion Royal Irish Rifles (2nd County Down Volunteers)

DIVISIONAL ARTILLERY

153rd Royal Field Artillery
154th Royal Field Artillery
172nd Royal Field Artillery
173rd Royal Field Artillery
Divisional Ammunition Column, Royal Field Artillery

ROYAL ENGINEERS

121st Field Company Royal Engineers
122nd Field Company Royal Engineers
150th Field Company Royal Engineers

DIVISIONAL TROOPS

Service Squadron, 6th Royal Inniskilling Dragoons
36th Divisional Signal Company Royal Engineers
Divisional Cyclist Company
Royal Army Medical Corps: 108th Field Ambulance
                             109th Field Ambulance
                             110th Field Ambulance
                             76th Sanitary Section RAMC
Divisional Train, Royal Army Service Corps
48th Mobile Veterinary Section [14]

Before long, six reserve battalions were formed to provide drafts for the division, as active service would mean depletion of the ranks.

Now the men of the Ulster Volunteers, despite their still unquelled doubts about Home Rule, had the opportunity to enlist, shoulder by shoulder, with their neighbours and friends in the local UVF company. All the comradeship and closeness of the 'pals battalions' from Newcastle, Liverpool, Bradford and Sheffield would be theirs, plus the aggression, resolve and basic training that the past two years in a military organisation had given them. However, these Ulstermen were now preparing to fight a Germany that could have been their potential ally. The *Clyde Valley* gun-running had provided them with German guns with which to fight the British army, and in the months leading up to the war, the Germans had shown some interest in the rebellion that seemed certain to break out in the north of Ireland, and in its potential to distract and debilitate the British if faced by a European war.[15]

Most ironically of all, the Ulster leaders had pointedly claimed that they looked on the Kaiser with favour. Craig, in January 1911, had said that the German ruler would be preferable to John Redmond.[16] Fred Crawford had said, less than a year later, that 'if they were to be put out of the Union … he would infinitely prefer to change his allegiance right over to the Emperor of Germany'.[17] To many, the Kaiser was a latter-day William of Orange – Protestant and resolute – on whom, if all else failed, they could call for assistance. A letter in the *Irish Churchman* of 14 November 1913 had said:

> should our king sign the Home Rule Bill the Protestants of Ireland
> will welcome this Continental deliverer as their forefathers, under
> similar circumstances did once before.[18]

Although the newspapers of the early months of the war were full of reports of German savagery in the captured areas of Belgium and France, and this must have aroused considerable fear and hostility towards the 'Hun', there can be little doubt that the Ulster Volunteers had had every encouragement to feel benignly towards the Kaiser in the months leading up to Sarajevo.

As it was, their 'Ulster Division' was to be an expression of Protestant Ulster power, pride and independence. Their aggressiveness and the fearful reputation they were to acquire as bayonet fighters were the outcome of the pent-up belligerence of those tense months of drilling, marching and gathering in large public groups. Their efficiency and *esprit de corps* were marks of the ethnic solidarity and separateness that they felt was being ignored by the British government's Home Rule legislation. Most of the men had signed the Ulster Covenant. They were a covenanting army, oath-bound and committed as much to the collective survival of Protestant Ulster as to the survival of the Britain they fought for and were part of. As one writer was to note:

> In compelling the War Office to admit a separate and complete unit
> bound by a special political oath – a course unfamiliar in modern
> armies since Cromwell's time – Sir Edward Carson had won
> a notable victory …[19]

RECRUITMENT GETS UNDER WAY

On Monday 7 September the Belfast papers reported the departure of the first men of the Ulster Division to their camp at Ballykinler. They had been cheered all the way through the city centre to the railway station. Ligoniel Brass and Reed Band had played 'Lead Kindly Light' and 'God Be With You Till We Meet Again' amid emotional scenes as the first soldiers boarded the train for what would be their new home. The *Belfast News Letter* made it sound like a holiday resort:

> Ballykinler Camp is situated in the centre of picturesque country, with
> the Mountains of Mourne forming an imposing background. On the edge
> of the camping ground, and within easy walking distance of the tents, is
> an arm of Dundrum Bay, and here the men will have swimming and
> bathing drills. Within sight of the camp is the beautifully situated
> demesne of Tyrella.

By Saturday, the papers were also reporting that Clandeboye was ready for occupation by the first detachments of men from Lisburn, Bangor and Holywood. The following week, the *News Letter* reported on the arrival at Bangor railway station of the first contingents, who then marched to Clandeboye, and encamped in the beautiful demesne of the Dowager Marchioness of Dufferin and Ava.

The men of the East Belfast UVF joined in large numbers. Tommy Ervine went marching down Templemore Avenue from Orangefield with his friends and colleagues, all on the way to join up. He broke off to recover his tools from the shipyard when they reached the bottom of Templemore Avenue. All the shipyard men shouted at him that he must be afraid to join up, but Tommy replied that he would be enlisting on the next Monday, which he subsequently did.[20]

J. Hutchinson was too young to be in the UVF or the army, but he remembered seeing the East Belfast Volunteers, now members of the 36th Division, assemble to travel to Clandeboye:

> One day I was on the Newtownards Road and saw men walking, in the
> direction of the waste ground opposite the Princess Picture Palace.
> When I reached the spot I saw hundreds of them forming up. It was a
> remarkable parade. Men from all walks of life. They were the East Belfast
> UVF. Some of my relatives were with them and their families had come to
> see them off ... they were soldiers of the British Army, soon to become
> the 8th Battalion of the Irish Rifles and known as 'Ballymacarrett's
> Own' ... an officer addressed the parade before marching to the station
> for a training camp. He told them that in camp they would receive
> uniform and equipment and would undergo a period of serious training.
> They moved out in columns of fours ... my heart went with them.[21]

In the west of the city, the 'Shankill boys' were also joining up, if with some initial reluctance, due to their fear of the Home Rule demon. Percy Crozier was later to call this condition 'political paralysis of the top storey'. His men, he said, 'found it difficult to set themselves free from insular and parochial associations'. To encourage the men to join, he inflated the enlistment figures.[22]

Crozier had welcomed the war as a relief from the tensions and uncertainties of the Ulster Crisis. Initially, he had received a message asking him to rejoin the Royal Irish Fusiliers in Dublin. However, in September he was appointed major and second-in-command of the 9th Battalion Royal Irish Rifles, the 'West Belfast Volunteers', and began the long process that he was to describe as 'knocking the beer and politics' out of his men.[23]

Immediately, Crozier went to London to send back as many good NCOs as he could find to take his 'Shankill boys' in hand. At three o'clock each day, he went to Horse Guards Parade where veteran NCOs of former

F. Percy Crozier – soon to gain a
reputation as a 'callous
and overbearing martinet'
DERMOTT DUNBAR

campaigns were on display as available for service. Many of them had lied about their age, but if they were good men, Crozier took them. 'Into this conspiracy against Anno Domini I enter with glee', he recorded.

Crozier returned via Glasgow and picked up some 'Orangemen' who wished to join the 36th Division. With scornful alliteration, Crozier later reported that he had never witnessed more 'blasphemy, booze and banners' than on the return voyage to Belfast. The captain of the ship ordered a hosepipe to be turned on the men to cool them down. They were badly hungover when they reached Belfast, and Crozier marched them to Victoria Barracks.

In command of the 9th Rifles was Lieutenant-Colonel G.S. Ormerod, aged over sixty, who had seen Burmese and South African service, and had also been an able cricketer in his day. Ormerod and Crozier motored to

Jim Maultsaid of the
14th Royal Irish Rifles, whose diary
sketches were to make him an
unofficial war artist
MICHAEL MAULTSAID

Newcastle, County Down and found their battalion under canvas at Donard Lodge alongside the 10th Rifles, the 'South Belfast Volunteers'. There they met the camp commandant, Colonel Bob Wallace, who had been an important figure in the establishment of the UVF in County Down.[24]

Meanwhile, the Young Citizen Volunteers of Belfast had been enlisting in the 14th Royal Irish Rifles. Many men who had not been in the YCVs were also to join the Rifles, including Jim Maultsaid, who was actually an American citizen. He had attempted to join up on 5 August, but the Inniskillings in Clifton Street had refused to have him. When recruiting started for the 14th Rifles in mid-September, Jim went with his Young Citizen friends and they all joined up. They did their first drilling in the yard of Davidson's engineering company on Mountpottinger Road, where Jim, an ex-Scout with a knowledge of Morse and signalling, was given

Billy McFadzean of the 14th Royal Irish Rifles. He was destined to earn a posthumous VC, the first of the entire Somme campaign.
BILL McFADZEAN

charge of a squad.[25] Another young man – who kept a diary of his experiences under the pen name G.H.M. – joined his friends, Joseph Hawthorne and James Russell, and enlisted on Monday 14 September at the Old Town Hall. In the evening, after tea, magistrates appeared for the swearing-in process, which was done in large groups. Each man signed on for three years or the duration of the war. G.H.M. remembered that first muster in the yard in east Belfast, and, in particular, how many of the men were wearing straw hats and carrying walking sticks – an indication of their social class. There was little fuss as the men assembled: they were intelligent and they were well organised under the initial leadership of men who had been their NCOs in the YCVs. Before the war, the YCVs had been in eight companies, labelled A to H; on joining the army, each man chose his own company, sticking with his friends where possible.[26]

Another recruit to the 14th Rifles was Billy McFadzean, who lived in Cregagh and whose father was a JP. Billy had not been a model pupil whilst at school, having been reprimanded no less than thirty-four times for bad conduct in his second year at the Trade Preparatory School. He was an apprentice to the Belfast linen firm Spence Bryson and Co. at a wage of £20 per annum. An ardent rugby player and keen member of the Young Citizens, he was destined to become the most famous member of his battalion.[27]

Within a week, the first men of the 14th Rifles had begun the rail journey to Finner Camp in County Donegal to begin their training properly. The sight of so many young men going off to war aroused emotions in those left behind. Civilians strove to support the lads who were leaving the recruiting offices across the land as servants of king and country. In Newtownards, each Volunteer on the way to be measured for his uniform was handed a stick of 'McClinton's Hibernia shaving soap' by a Boy Scout – the soap was a gift of John McClement JP, who also presented each Volunteer with a neatly printed card on which these words were inscribed in gold lettering:

> I would be True, for there are those who trust me.
> I would be Pure, for there are those who care.
> I would be Strong, for there is much to suffer.
> I would be Brave, for there is much to dare.
> I would be a Friend to All, – the foe, the friendless.
> I would be always Giving and forget the gift.
> I would be Humble, for I know my weakness.
> I would look up, and laugh, and love and lift.[28]

The *Newtownards Chronicle* published each week a patriotic poem designed to stir pride in those whose sons, brothers and fathers had joined the forces, and shame in those whose loved ones had not:

> A hundred years ago your fathers fought
> As you must fight for liberty today.
> Beside that heritage all else was naught,
> And shall you prove yourselves less staunch than they?
> The hour has struck, and Britain asks your vow
> Of loyal and ungrudging service – now!
>
> Think, from our cliffs the eye can almost see
> Fair Belgian home go up in smoke and flame.
> Unless you fight to keep your homeland free,
> She too must know the agony and shame.
> Then it may be, when Britain meets her fate
> Her laggards will arise – Too Late! Too Late![29]

Very often, recruiting space in local newspapers was devoted to an appeal to the 'women of Ulster', who were seen as exercising an emotional hold over husbands and sons to incline them to stay at home or to leave. One advertisement asked: 'Do you realise that the one word "Go" from *you* may send another man to fight for Ireland?' and followed with another question: 'When the war is over and your husband or your son is asked, "What did you do in the Great War?" – is he to hang his head because *you* would not let him go?'[30]

Meanwhile, Carson had returned to Ulster to make recruiting speeches all across the country.[31] His appeals seemed more necessary in the rural areas, where recruiting was unquestionably slower, than in the city. John Stewart-Moore, for instance, had considerable difficulty persuading the men in his UVF company in north Antrim to volunteer for service overseas. Only two or three came forward to join the 36th Division. One man had an argument with Stewart-Moore, and said: 'I'd like to go, but I wouldn't enlist.' They had the traditional belief that only the work-shy and the worthless enlisted. They had heard stories, too, of the bad old days when soldiers arriving home from the wars could find no employment or prospects. Meanwhile, Stewart-Moore himself applied for a commission with the 12th Royal Irish Rifles (Mid Antrim Volunteers), but his parents objected that he had not the health for the job, and a local doctor refused to pass him fit, probably under his parents' influence. Stewart-Moore went to Dublin and got a clean bill of health from a doctor there, then on 18 September, his twenty-third birthday, he went to Ballymoney Town Hall and was enlisted in the 12th Rifles.[32] Meanwhile, in Ballynahinch, County Down, David John Bell, captain of the local UVF company, enlisted with thirty-three of his men. He was soon posted company quartermaster sergeant in C Company under the command of Robert Perceval Maxwell, of Finnebrogue, in the 13th Rifles (1st County Down Volunteers). The age limit for joining was thirty-five; Bell was thirty-seven, but he told a lie and enlisted as aged thirty-four years and nine months.[33]

Lies were told at the other end of the scale, too. In Crossgar, County Down, John Martin went off to join the 13th Rifles, and like so many under the legal limit of nineteen, he lied about his age. But his parents heard immediately of what he had done and went to the recruiting office at once to fetch him back, revealing his true age to the recruiting sergeant. However, many men who joined the 36th Division were under age but were never apprehended.[34]

John Martin was one of only a handful in the locality who were keen to join the Ulster Division. Hugh James Adams, John's close friend, was later to estimate that perhaps only seven or eight out of every hundred young men in the Crossgar neighbourhood joined the 36th.[35] In the Lisburn area, however, where men were joining the 11th Rifles (South Antrim Volunteers), the response was much better.[36] Albert Bruce, of Lambeg, was one of 250 volunteers who marched in a group to the centre of Lisburn and joined up. Hugh Stewart, who had fallen asleep on duty on the night of the Larne gun-running, was another who enlisted:

> On the 12th of September the recruiting stations were packed. The
> Lisburn Assembly Room's stairs were hivin' with young men on that day,
> a Saturday. With a quick medical, which included an eye and ear test,
> and check that you'd got good reflexes and no ruptures ... they gave their
> first shillin' to you and you'd sign on.[37]

The 11th Rifles had the prestige of including in its official ranks Captain Charles C. Craig, MP for South Antrim and brother of James Craig, the unionist leader.

In rural Armagh, the recruiting process took place more slowly. As one Volunteer was to put it in later years: 'You cannot get up and leave a farm the way you can walk away from a loom in a factory.'[38] However, some Armagh farmers did make their way into the 36th Division, and their local battalion was the 9th Royal Irish Fusiliers. One such man recalled:

> We were called up in groups from the same part of the country. Each lot
> going down was like a 12th of July outing ... There was one Lurgan man
> I knew very well, Hobbs, a butcher from Union Street. He was seeing
> some relations off. I shouted at him ... he shouted back at me that if I
> could sell the same amount of bad beef to the Germans as I had sold him
> over the past years, the war would be over by Christmas.

One boy, living in the vicinity of Bleary, was to remember vividly the experience of seeing his father leave home to join the 36th. He and a neighbour had both joined up, and another friend of the family called for them on a pony and trap to make the journey to Lurgan station. To the sound of receding hoofbeats on a country lane, one boy's father disappeared out of his life.

Another boy, living in Mill Street, Lurgan, had similar recollections:

We walked to the station, and my mother was crying all the time ... I remember my father telling my mother to dry her tears for he would be back in next to no time ... On the platform I saw Father squeeze my mother's hand and give her a sort of a kiss ... It was lonely that night without my father ...[39]

When the County Armagh men reached Belfast, they found that very few of them knew their way around – it was a confusing experience to leave home for the first time and to gain a new identity.

They took us to a big hall near the Old Town Hall ... we put all our clothes in a large paper bag and wrote our names and addresses on pieces of paper and they sent them home ... we climbed into the lorries again and was taken to the barracks near Bangor.[40]

There were to be many arguments, at the time and in the future, about the recruitment figures from the Protestant and Catholic communities. Numerous, seemingly incompatible, statistics have been bandied about. Carson himself was to claim loudly that the recruiting figures were evidence of Ulster loyalty. The *Belfast News Letter* in April 1915 was to quote figures proving that up to that date 35,000 recruits had come into the army from Ulster, and only 15,000 from the other Irish provinces.[41] According to Ronald McNeill, making a sympathetic study of Ulster unionism in 1922, the recruiting in Belfast was better than in any other city in the United Kingdom, with 305 soldiers recruited per 10,000 population during 1914.[42] (His figures came from the Annual Register for 1914.) But the less sympathetic Alice Stopford Green turned up figures in 1918 which indicated that the northern counties often fell behind the southern ones. She quoted from the Viceroy's report of 14 January 1916 to show that only 1.36 per cent of the population had volunteered by that date in counties Antrim and Down, whereas 1.7 per cent had done so in Kilkenny, Tipperary, Waterford and Wexford.[43]

T.J. Campbell, writing his nationalist-orientated history of Ulster in 1941, was to indicate that, according to his figures, there were actually just as many National Volunteers as Ulster Volunteers in the New Army by the end of 1915 – 27,000 to 28,000 in each case, including those in the reserve battalions. Not only this, but as early as 1 November 1914 more than 16,000 National Volunteers had already enlisted. Campbell went on to state that of the 49,400 Irishmen who actually died in the war, 39,400 were from the south, and 10,000 from what was to become Northern Ireland.[44]

A proper analysis of these controversial figures will reveal a clearer story some day, but there can at least be no doubt that men from John Redmond's National Volunteers did join the 16th Division, and fought and died on the same battlefields as the 36th – occasionally alongside them. There were also many splendid Irish regiments in the regular army: the Irish Guards, the Connaught Rangers and the Dublin Fusiliers to name but three of those that recruited in southern Ireland.

However, it is equally clear that it was in the Ulster unionists' interests to portray Ulstermen as rallying to the Empire's defence in throngs whilst the mutinous Catholic population sat unmoved and unpatriotic at home – even though this is certainly a falsification of the diverse reactions to the war from within both the Ulster Protestant and the Irish Catholic communities.

The pride about recruitment figures, whether justified or not, indicates the way in which Ulster unionists saw the 36th Division as proof to the British government that the Scots–Irish, for all their mutinous display of opposition to Asquith's Home Rule Bill, were the one truly dependable people in Ireland. Surely England would remember Ulster's loyalty in her hour of crisis? A popular poem of the period expressed this sense of anticipated contract:

> What of the men of Ulster?
> Hark to the armed tread,
> As they turn their backs on the Province,
> And face to the front instead;
>
> The sword half drawn on her own behalf
> In Ulster's Red Right Hand
> Will leap from the scabbard and flash like fire
> For the common Motherland.

And wherever the fight is hottest,
And the sorest task is set,
ULSTER WILL STRIKE FOR ENGLAND
AND ENGLAND WILL NOT FORGET.[45]

CLANDEBOYE

Like many another division of 'Kitchener's Army', the 36th was noticeably enthusiastic in the early days of training. Its infantry was formed on perhaps the most strictly territorial basis of any of the Kitchener divisions, and so companies and platoons were like large families. A disadvantage of this was that many NCOs were relatives or friends of men they commanded, and orders, which should have been issued with military brusqueness, came out, often enough, as friendly requests. To counter this, some NCOs were changed about so as to be in charge of men with whom they were not so familiar. Another problem was that many men were stationed close to their own homes and could not understand why they were unable to 'go home' on a Sunday. Absence without leave was therefore a frequent problem.[46]

Powell, the divisional commander, had been in the Ghurkas and was a well-known mountain-climber in the Caucasus and Himalayas, and he laid great stress on physical training – to be achieved partly through long route marches. As full equipment had not yet arrived, the infantry marched with Alpine rucksacks on their backs, full of stones, or nuts and bolts from the shipyards. There were, Spender noted, grumblings about Christian under his burden of sin in Bunyan's *Pilgrim's Progress*. Inspecting generals, meanwhile, deigned not to notice machine guns and rifles borrowed from the UVF to supplement the 'drill purpose' rifles the men were using in the early days.[47]

The camp nearest to Belfast was Clandeboye and there the 108th Infantry Brigade was to train. The wooded demesne contained the beautiful Helen's Tower, built in memory of Lady Dufferin by her son. No sooner had the troops arrived than a wet autumn made living under canvas impossible, and hundreds of men were swamped out. Hugh Stewart and the 11th Rifles were sent back to Lisburn to train; many of the country lads in the battalion had to be billeted around the town, but Hugh could now live at home. (The billeting process was to cause a lot of headaches for the divisional staff, who had already practised a scheme for billeting the division, taking Lisburn to experiment on. Billeting parties had gone from house to house, chalking on doors the imaginary number of horses and men allotted there. Next day, a deputation of the nationalist inhabitants had come to HQ to complain that the number of men billeted in Catholic homes was outrageously large.)[48]

Hugh Stewart trained each day in his home town, until huts were built at Clandeboye and he could return there. When he did so, he was issued with new supplies and, of course, his weekly pay.

> Now we had toothpaste and soap and a razor but I didn't need mine
> because I didn't have a beard yet. We spent our money on
> ciggies … I remember the Song about Woodbine –
>> Five cigarettes in a dainty little pack,
>> Five cigarettes that cost 1d.
> I recall, too, I used to forge Carson's signature on paper to make passes so
> people could get leave … On one occasion … a friend and I got ourselves
> out and made a beeline for Scrabo and on over to the Comber straight so
> as we would outwit the 'redcaps'. There we met a horse-drawn bread cart
> and got a lift to Belfast, lying down under the tarpaulin. We leathered
> into the stale currant bread lying in the back!
> … We got seven days for defaulting. But our fatigues only consisted of
> working in the officers' mess, and I can tell you we got some of the best
> food of our lives![49]

The note of independence and rebelliousness in a lot of the men was observed by Spender, who had heard of an incident when an orderly officer had been going round camp and had come upon a brilliantly illuminated tent. He ordered those inside to put the lights out, and was met with the reply: 'Stop making that noise outside or I'll jolly well come out and put out both your lights.'[50]

For the inexperienced, less confident country fellows from Armagh, the experience of Clandeboye was, at first, frightening and strange.

> The first night I was away from home was the worst of all. I was brought
> up in a Christian home and we always knelt down to say our prayers …
> I was in a dither. I wanted to kneel down and say a prayer but I was
> afraid the others would laugh at me and think it childish. However,

I took my courage in both hands and said, 'Look boys, I always say a
prayer at night and if any of you would like to join me, you're
welcome.' I started to say the Lord's Prayer and at least half the others
said it with me. The rest kept silent. There was no tittering or laughing.
Now and again some of us got together and had a prayer-meeting
in the corner of a hut. We had some unforgettable moments
when we felt God's presence.

The religious convictions of the men were noted by a Church of
England chaplain who visited the 36th Division and sent a letter about his
observations to the Presbyterian chaplain, Revd McConnell.

One thing that really impressed me was the number of men who actually
read their Bibles, and in such odd corners as the guard room or when
having a cup of tea, in the mess or sitting in their huts ... It did my heart
good to be present at their 'wee meetings'. What I learnt from these
was that the simple approach – almost childlike in a way – they had to
the ways of salvation, was better, by far, to the teaching of any
theological college.

Good country wisdom characterised many of these Armagh men, as
well as simple religious sincerity. One useful tip was: 'A wisp of hay in
each boot'll keep your feet warm as long as you have a good pair of boots
that'll keep out the wet.' And as winter drew in, the Armagh boys used to
get a dozen yard lamps and turn them up as far as they would go – which,
although it caused a smell, gave considerable warmth to the cold huts at
Clandeboye, often so damp that water would run down the inside of the
windowpanes.

As well as the weather, there was the discipline to get used to –
administered often by quaint and memorable NCOs.

At Clandeboye there was a sergeant who had been a bricklayer before
joining up. He used to shout at the men, 'Keep that line straight as a row
of bricks!' ... This sergeant was not a very fluent reader ... he read out
loud ... [but] blindfold he would strip down a rifle or any firearm
used by his men and put it together again faster than we could do it
with our eyes open.[51]

John Leslie Stewart-Moore.
He had intended to take holy orders,
but when the war came, he joined
the Ulster Division
DERMOTT DUNBAR

Some of the wealthier young men in the ranks resented the fact that they were under the orders of men who were a social class beneath them; but occasionally, such middle-class recruits were selected for possible training as officers. One young man of social rank to arrive at Clandeboye had been John Stewart-Moore, newly enlisted in the 12th Rifles. He had had a tremendous send-off from a cheering crowd at Ballymoney station, and on arriving in camp had been glad to find all the tents pitched, and food, water and blankets waiting. On the first night, Stewart-Moore made friends with Johnnie Giles, son of the manager of Ballycastle coal mine. They were packed in a tent with seven or eight other men; the atmosphere was electric and no one slept soundly. On the following morning, the company was divided into platoons and later subdivided into sections. Stewart-Moore found that the first days were taken up with long marches over rough ground in the Clandeboye demesne – an exercise designed to discover the unhealthy. One man, who had been a tailor all his life and had spent his working hours on the floor with his legs crossed, was soon found unfit to continue as a soldier.

Another feature of the early weeks was the fervently Orange atmosphere. Stewart-Moore missed the diversity of thought and opinion he had enjoyed in Trinity; here, no such debates were possible because everybody thought alike.

> The tents were decorated, many of them, with Union Jacks and Orange
> emblems and at night the overflowing enthusiasm of the men found its
> outlet in song. For the first week or so, I went to sleep every night to the
> strains of Orange ditties such as …
>> Come back to Ireland those who are over the sea
>> Come back to Ireland and fight for liberty.
>> They are flying the flag, the harp without the crown
>> So come back to Ireland and keep Popery down …
> and when I woke up in the morning they were still singing, apparently
> they had never stopped all night.

In these early days, Stewart-Moore and Giles joined Harry Macnaghten and another officer for a game of bridge. This familiarity between NCOs and officers was soon strongly reprimanded. At this stage, the officers were still not in uniform as they were technically civilians until their commissions had been 'gazetted' in the *London Gazette*.

Stewart-Moore had applied for a commission; he soon received it and got into his uniform made by Marshall's of High Street, Belfast. He transferred to the 11th Rifles, encamped only a few hundred yards away, and was posted to A Company, sharing a tent with a man called Wilson, son of a Presbyterian minister. In the 11th Battalion, Stewart-Moore also met Arthur Samuels, a Dublin barrister whom he had known well in Trinity College OTC and with whom he had played many games of tennis in the grounds of Samuels' home on Howth Hill. Stewart-Moore had bought his brother's motorbike by this stage, and when off duty travelled in style to have lunch with Bishop d'Arcy at the See House on the shore of Belfast Lough (later to become the Culloden Hotel). The training, meanwhile, consisted of 'imaginary battles against non-existent foes … in which we

A very early scene at Clandeboye camp. Food is being prepared in large 'dixies' for soldiers who as yet have no uniform and little sense of battalion structure.
SOMME MUSEUM

advanced in open order across the hills and woods'.

When Clandeboye was flooded and the battalion moved to Lisburn, Stewart-Moore stayed with his cousin, Jim Reade, on the outskirts of the town, and went with great reluctance on the arduous route marches into the countryside. It was a relief when, shortly before Christmas, he was sent on a course of instruction at Queen's University.

> I do not think that we learnt much that was useful but the course
> provided an opportunity for one or two pleasant tea parties with Harry
> Macnaghten and several others in a restaurant in Donegall Place.

Stewart-Moore had been conflicting badly with Lieutenant-Colonel H.A. Pakenham the battalion's commanding officer, and he took an opportunity to ask his cousin, Colonel George Ford-Hutchinson, who was in charge of the 15th Rifles, if there would be a place in that battalion. The changeover was agreed to, and after a short break to recover from a typhoid inoculation, Stewart-Moore left for Ballykinler.[52]

Meanwhile, David John Bell was busy organising C Company of the 13th Rifles at Clandeboye. His men were from the country towns of Newcastle, Castlewellan, Downpatrick, Rathfriland, Ballynahinch, Dromore and

Hillsborough and the countryside surrounding them. His job, as men arrived at Clandeboye, was to ensure that each one obtained food and accommodation. Eventually, Bell was promoted to the job of regimental quartermaster sergeant for his battalion, and had the additional responsibility of being quartermaster for Clandeboye camp as a whole. He was a jack of all trades, responsible for rations, equipment and stores, and in charge of such assorted personnel as cooks, butchers, tailors, shoemakers and sanitary staff. Rations were drawn every day and distributed from the quartermaster's stores. One of the most exacting jobs Bell had to face was the preparation of identity discs, stamped with each man's name and number, his religious denomination and the battalion he belonged to. Each letter and number had to be punched individually onto 1,350 discs:

> I didn't trust anyone to do even part of it. I started on Monday morning
> in my own room and for seven whole days I wrought from early
> morning till I was dead beat at night and just lay flat on the top of my
> bed with a blanket over me till next morning.

As Christmas approached, Bell was especially busy, preparing the provisions for a festive dinner, as Christmas leave had been cancelled in mid-December following the German raid on Scarborough.[53]

J. Hutchinson was observing the progress of the 36th Division with envy, for he was still too young to join, but an excellent chance was afforded to watch his heroes in training at Clandeboye. He was friendly with the son of the property agent for whom he worked, and at the weekends he would help him with cattle the family owned and which grazed on land adjacent to the Clandeboye demesne.

> [I] would wander towards the camp, and from a gap in the hedge would
> watch the troops training. There was drill with rifles, marching, squads
> doing PT, bayonet fighting, stabbing at stuffed figures suspended from a
> sack … there were high wire frames over which men hurled grenades like
> tossing a cricket ball.

Hutchinson also met men from his neighbourhood who came back on leave, looking smart in uniform, and with colour in their faces due to all the training and fresh air.[54]

Gradually, the Clandeboye camp was eased of the burden of the entire

108th Brigade. The 12th Irish Rifles and the 9th Royal Irish Fusiliers moved to the nearby town of Newtownards. Early in December the North Antrim men arrived in the town and encamped at the new huts in the Ards Recreation Society's grounds.[55] A few days later, the assembly room of the town hall was put at the soldiers' disposal for relaxation and recreation. As Christmas approached, concerts were staged for them, and the assembly room was made habitable and seasonal: 'Bright and cheery fires made the room most comfortable and the profusion of flags on the walls added to its cosy appearance', reported the local paper.[56]

As the old year drew to a close, the men who had trained at Clandeboye had had to face little more demanding than the rigours and blisters of twenty-mile route marches through the familiar beauties of the Ulster countryside. The year ahead would bring a very different kind of existence, on the Western Front. The contrast between life on either side of the New Year was to be unwittingly captured by the *Newtownards Chronicle* for Boxing Day 1914, copies of which lay, no doubt, in many huts at Newtownards and Clandeboye. In it, side by side, were two articles: one was an item on the beauty of the Mountains of Mourne, in which the writer waxed lyrical about 'the rush of the mountain stream … the grey of the granite, the purple of the heather, the black of the peat'. Alongside this evocation of County Down's beauty was an article on 'siege warfare', explaining about trenches, barbed wire, machine guns and other chilling facets of the new age. Sinister names, that soon would be all too familiar, were scattered through the article – the Menin Road, Zonnebeke, Ypres … Within a few inches of newsprint could be measured the vast distance that the Ulster Volunteers must travel.

FINNER

Meanwhile, on the west coast of Ireland, Finner was the training camp for the 109th Brigade of the Ulster Division, made up mainly of Inniskillings from the west of Ulster, but with the addition of the 14th Rifles – the YCVs – who were drawn mainly from Belfast.

John Kennedy Hope arrived at Finner and found it to be 'a godforsaken place – as bare as a golf ball'. At Ballyshannon, he picked up two old South African rifles for training, and as there was no horse transport available yet,

Finner Camp in Donegal; 'bare as a golf ball' is how
one soldier described the landscape.
SOMME MUSEUM

he had to help carry a share of the battalion equipment and stores on the
march to Finner from Ballyshannon station. More arduous work had to be
done when the men got settled in at the camp. The 'meat safe' was on a
nearby hill, and several recruits were delegated to carry bits of carcass down
to the 'store tent'; Hope felt himself unfortunate to be on this duty.

It was fourteen men to a tent, initially, and Hope struck up a good
acquaintance with a Jew called Cecil Marcus. Hope was not fond of the
cooks, who seemed to him to be mainly impudent old soldiers serving up
an interminable supply of stew. As there was no hot water, the 'dixie' was
wiped out with sods of earth that never quite removed the grease, leaving
it to spoil the tea the next time the dixie was in use. Chloride of lime in the
water tank was another taste that intruded everywhere. Not surprisingly,
there were stomach upsets, as one joke celebrated:

Sentry – Halt, who goes there?
Phantom – Diarrhoea.
Sentry – Pass diarrhoea, all's well. Light activity on the Finner front!

Hope was dismayed by the way the officers were called 'gentlemen' by
the colonel – 'And we wonder what we are', he brooded. Captain Wake,

70

who gave the men their first field manoeuvres, was little better – 'a blueblood with white horse and gammy leg'. When forced to do a fatigue that meant working in the officers' mess, Hope complained about 'washing up after these scalliwags … Who the hell are they anyway?'[57] Certainly, the officers attempted to dine well despite the rudimentary conditions. The dinner menu for the officers' mess on 30 September was as follows:

> Tomato soup
> Roast leg mutton
> Onion sauce
> Cauliflowers and potatoes
> Blancmange and apricots
> Dessert
> Coffee[58]

What was to amaze the men of the 14th Rifles, born to the relative sophistication of Belfast's streets and avenues, was the primitive condition of the west coast:

> We halt one day beside a house well off the beaten track, and go to
> explore the place. The primitive state of the dwelling amazes us.
> A woman appears, apparently in a state of terror, and we ask for a drink.
> She has no bread but proceeds to make scones like pancakes, baked
> on a flat affair over some burning twigs in the open hearth. Not a word
> does she say. Has she heard of War? Probably not. Maybe she thinks
> the country is invaded.

The cold Atlantic winter set in, and after a fall of snow in December, Hope moved with most of the battalion to the Great Northern Hotel in Bundoran. But on dry days, the long marches continued throughout midwinter. Sometimes, as the men looked from vantage points on the cliff tops, they could see breakers rising fifty feet high on the exposed coastline.[59]

For G.H.M., the Sunday before he had left for Finner had been a special one, when he had taken a long and thoughtful afternoon walk between Morning Prayer and Evensong, both of which he attended. Then, on Monday 21 September, he arrived at Belfast's Great Victoria Street station for the 10.00 a.m. train that would take him to Donegal. To G.H.M., it seemed not unlike a Sunday-school excursion, with everyone enjoying the view of

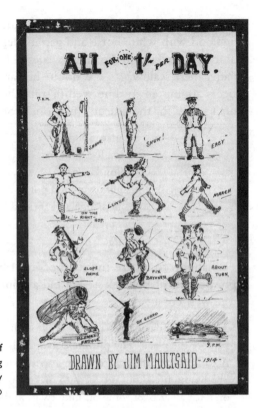

The new recruit's view of army life – all for a shilling (5p) a day

MICHAEL MAULTSAID

the countryside on the 114-mile journey westward. When he had marched to Finner, he noted the eighty bell tents set out in eight orderly lines for the Young Citizens. Palliasses were issued by the quartermaster and filled with straw. G.H.M. later discarded his – it was bulky and uncomfortable, and a waterproof groundsheet on the earth proved more satisfactory. He also received a set of primitive cooking and eating utensils that looked as if they had been around since the South African war, and maybe long before.[60]

One of the more enjoyable features of the camp was a special canteen that was soon opened and doing business, serving such pleasant extras as currant cake and ginger ale. Occasionally, there were campfire concerts around a large flickering fire; sometimes, a great sing-song would continue into the night, and one of the favourite performers was Private Tom Burrows, whose renderings of 'The Minstrel Boy' and 'I Hear You Calling Me' would linger in the Atlantic darkness with a piercing sweetness. On the route marches, singing was a popular pastime, and one of the great favourites was to do with that dreadful drinking water:

> And we won't drink chloride of lime!
> We won't drink chloride of lime![61]

Each day began at 6.30 a.m. with reveille; a cup of cocoa was drunk and toiletries were performed before the men fell in at 7.00 a.m. and headed out for a quick or double march through Bundoran and back to the camp. G.H.M.'s views on the training and the NCOs were rather more favourable than Hope's:

> There was no sarcasm, the NCOs being always polite and cheerful … it
> can be said with truth that training was always given in a leisurely manner.

G.H.M. also noted with favour that Lieutenant-Colonel Spencer Chichester always addressed his men as 'Young Citizens' when speaking to them on parade.

One of the pleasures of Finner was the opportunity of bathing, but that could be dangerous: once, G.H.M. swam out too far and would have drowned had he not been rescued by the battalion's champion swimmer, Ralph Cole. G.H.M. also enjoyed travelling to church in Bundoran and singing with the church choir on Sundays. In November came the move to the Bundoran hotel, to great relief and excitement: 'The boys kept milling round the corridors like dogs just released from the leash.' But, as Christmas approached, it became apparent that only half or so of the YCVs would get leave over Christmas Day. The other men would have to stay in Donegal and return home over the New Year period.[62]

A change was on the way, though. Shortly, only the 10th Inniskillings would be left at Finner to endure the wild Atlantic storms – the 11th Inniskillings had already moved to Enniskillen, and soon the 11th and 9th Inniskillings and 14th Rifles would all move to Randalstown, fairly close to Belfast.

On 6 January 1915 the Young Citizens occupied fine new huts, equipped with stoves, set in Castle Demesne at Randalstown, where they were to learn rifle and bayonet skills, dig trenches and sleep regularly in the open. Field manoeuvres and night marches were undertaken. Disillusioned as ever, Hope resented the new officer in charge of his company – Captain C.O. Slacke – 'a roundfaced fat-bellied gentleman with a cynical smile' –

and observed with relish how often the men made a mess of their drill under his command. By this time, some of his soldier neighbours were beginning to grate on Hope's nerves, and tempers were no doubt frayed by the quagmire of mud that developed at the Randalstown camp when heavy rains came. One objectionable fellow soldier was the son of a solicitor; he had been in Queen's University OTC and made sure he let everyone know it. He was untidy, had long hair, and got unkindly labelled 'bucket-mouth'. The occupants of Hope's hut gradually developed into two groups: those who liked listening to the gramophone and those who liked to play cards. Two of Hope's fellow card players with whom he got on well were not Ulstermen at all: 'Scotty' Wilson from Kilmarnock and Walter Cross from Lytham in Lancashire. After lights-out, there were frequent disturbances from people playing tricks on one-another's beds, and the early morning was also occasionally disturbed.

> Our hut is near the row. We hear all kinds of noises. The farmers are removing the contents of the swill barrels and other receptacles. The carts rattle past and some wit says in half sleep 'ships that pass in the night'.[63]

Meanwhile, G.H.M. was beginning to notice a degree of rivalry between the Young Citizen Volunteers and the Inniskillings. On one occasion, the brigade was on manoeuvres in the County Antrim countryside, and having reached Drumdarragh Hill, twelve miles from Randalstown camp and where they took part in a mock battle, Colonel Chichester arranged for his boys to get a train back to camp. The 14th Rifles thus returned home early, and considerable ill feeling was aroused in the other battalions who marched back later. There were numerous cries that the Young Citizens were soft. So, the 14th Rifles decided voluntarily to undertake a repeat march from Drumdarragh Hill to Randalstown, just to prove to the Inniskillings that they were competent and hardened soldiers. By May the Young Citizens were further outnumbered by provincial battalions as the 10th Inniskillings marched across Ireland to rejoin their brigade.[64]

Although many of the horrors of the Western Front were by now fully apparent to the British army – including the first use of gas warfare at Ypres early in 1915 – there was still a leisurely spirit in the training that much of the Ulster Division, and many of Kitchener's other battalions, underwent in 1914–15. The emphasis on physical fitness made it seem not unlike the

KITCHENER'S ARMY in the Making at NEWCASTLE (South, West, and North Regiments, U.V.F.).

Donard camp, where the Belfast brigade was based
prior to its move to Ballykinler
SOMME MUSEUM

preparation for a big sporting occasion, and no doubt there was a willingness to see the sports field and the battlefield as similar realms of human endeavour. The vision of Colonel Chichester allowing his men to take a train back from their mock war on Drumdarragh Hill epitomises, perhaps as well as any incident, how indulgent the training actually was. To men like John Hope, it may have seemed a harsh enough environment in which to exist, but no lives were lost in the 'Battle of Drumdarragh Hill', and there was hot food and a sound sleep to be had on returning to Castle Demesne.

BALLYKINLER

On the south coast of County Down, the 107th Brigade had been undergoing training. This was the Belfast Brigade, and it contained many tough, rebellious characters. As at Clandeboye, there was a problem of weekend absence without leave. Crozier was later to comment: 'The 107th … was under the distinct disadvantage of receiving its early training in close proximity to the locality in which it was recruited.'

Initially, Crozier had been under canvas with his own men and the 10th Rifles at Donard Lodge, but by December the entire brigade had been assembled in Ballykinler, in the 'tin camp'.[65] Since the 1890s, troops had used Ballykinler as a training ground. There were two parts, known as 'World's End Camp', near Tyrella beach, and 'Central Camp', with a view over the bay to Dundrum's ancient castle, but it was the name 'World's End' that stuck to Ballykinler for men who regarded it as the ultimate in isolation from the big city.[66]

Crozier was delighted at the prospect of instilling 'intellectual discipline' into his men. In an incredible display of sustained verbosity, he lectured his junior officers for six months, five nights a week, on the process of 'hardening' that they must undergo, and must make their men undergo also. His approach was more realistic and aggressive than that of Colonel Chichester. 'You must lose your gentle selves. You must steel your hearts and minds and be callous of life and death. That is war.'

Crozier went on his Christmas leave to London, and was pestered by a lady in Coventry Street who presented him with a white feather on seeing him in civilian clothing. Crozier choked down his rage and went on to the Alhambra theatre to book seats for the evening's performance.

The New Year saw a rigorous stepping-up of the training. Looking back on this period, Crozier was to comment that the whole object of this stage of training was to create 'blood-lust'. Bayonet fighting was coupled with propaganda about German atrocities, and there was plenty of martial music – drums, Irish pipes, bands, marching songs. Crozier makes the atmosphere seem markedly different from that in the YCVs:

Sacred and artistic music is forbidden, save at church and even then the
note of combat is struck. The Christian churches are the finest
blood-lust creators that we have and of them we made free use ...
everything we do is faultless, everything the Germans do is abominable.
It is the only way in war.

Esprit de corps and a sense of regimental history were crucial weapons, and Crozier thought them essential in helping the individual soldier transcend his sense of personal fear. For this reason he, and others, were to object to divisional HQ when a 'Red Hand' hat badge was authorised for the men of the 36th Division. After the protest, this was replaced by the usual regimental badge, the harp of the Royal Irish Rifles, representing many years of military endeavour on numerous battlefields of the world, rather than the immediate conflict that the 36th Division had been created to meet.[67]

But Crozier would have been wrong to see the Christian Churches as concerned only with creating 'blood-lust'. At all the camps, groups such as the YMCA helped provide recreation facilities and spiritual help for the young men who were thrust into new and difficult circumstances by the war. At Ballykinler, one of the Sandes' Soldiers' Homes had been in existence since 1901, formed by a Miss Sandes, who had aimed to create a 'home from home' for young soldiers – a Christian environment where men could enjoy an alternative form of recreation to drinking or gambling. She gathered a group of women to work with her, and their job was increased in scope and importance on the outbreak of war. To many in the 36th Division, Sandes' Home was a place of comfort:

> Ballykinler was a hutted camp and dreary beyond words ... However
> there was one haven for us in the dark and cold nights, the Miss Sandes'
> Soldiers' Home. This stood outside the camp in those days as you walked
> down the road that led to Dundrum Bay. It was a bungalow-like building
> ... the women would play endless games of chess and checkers. She [Miss
> Sandes] had grown old and looked not unlike Queen Victoria ...[68]

To the women who worked there, the men of the 36th Division whom they served were like 'Cromwell's Ironsides'; many had a strong Christian faith: 'I verily believe they would all die in defence of the Bible', said one Sandes' lady.

For these women, it was rewarding to see many men declare their faith in God as they faced imminent departure to the battlefront:

> At the watchnight service in 1914, a young Ulster officer faced a crowded
> room at midnight; he spoke in ringing words – 'Men, before this
> time next year we may all be killed; but to a Christian, death is only
> beginning to live.'[69]

One soldier wrote home to Tandragee a few days later, his mind on less spiritual matters:

> Third time in Newcastle since coming to camp. Got a great tea in Aunt
> Maggie's cafe. Wouldn't take any money. First good food since
> Christmas. Weather cold. Frost at night. Snow on the mountains ...
>
> Harry[70]

But if midwinter was a grim time at 'World's End Camp', spring was more attractive, with the countryside coming to life all around.

> Sometimes the heat mist would cover the Mountains of Mourne and then clear at midday. With the clear evenings we would ramble over the dunes and along the shore ... my haunt was Dundrum Bay. I often went there alone ...[71]

Also enjoying the spring of 1915 at Ballykinler camp was John Stewart-Moore, who had transferred to the 15th Rifles with considerable relief. He had a room to himself in one of the huts, bought himself a deck chair for greater comfort, and installed his gramophone, a modern HMV with a large horn. The officers in the 15th were from all over Britain, and so not so clannish as those of the 11th. The atmosphere was much more informal, but the men nonetheless wore stiff white collars, instead of their daytime khaki shirts, for the evening meal. There was always an enjoyable outing to look forward to, as well:

> One evening I joined a party of three or four officers who went up to Belfast for a Gilbert and Sullivan opera ... a day or two after this I was approached by two young bloods, Hogg and Chandler, little more than schoolboys, and I suppose the youngest of our officers. The D'Oyly Carte company, they said, were moving on to Dublin for a week at the Gaiety Theatre and Hogg and Chandler, having become keen on two of the chorus girls, wanted to follow them there. They could hire a car and driver, leave after lunch on Saturday and return to Ballykinler on Sunday evening. The car would cost £5 – would I join them in sharing the expense? I agreed willingly, for as Hogg and Chandler knew, I loved Dublin and the idea of going there by motorcar by road was something exciting and unique ... I stayed the night with a friend in Trinity and went to another Gilbert and Sullivan at the Gaiety. Next day Chandler and Hogg picked me up at the Trinity front entrance in College Green and we were back in Ballykinler in time for supper. How Chandler and Hogg spent their time in Dublin I did not inquire but we had all enjoyed ourselves thoroughly.

On another occasion, Stewart-Moore visited Ardglass Castle – not far from Ballykinler – where the famous antiquarian F.J. Bigger lived, and saw

Trench-digging practice, possibly at Ballykinler
SOMME MUSEUM

Bigger's collection of ancient artefacts and souvenirs. Returning to the overnight camp that the men were making on Ardglass golf course, Stewart-Moore, always the gourmet, called at the harbour and found that a fishing smack had just come in with a full catch. There were 'scrumptious fresh herrings' for breakfast next morning.

Among the exercises that the 15th Rifles carried out was a march across Dundrum Bay, on a ford visible at low tide, to the grounds of Murlough House, where the men performed nocturnal manoeuvres. It was at the mouth of Dundrum Bay that some men had said they had seen the periscope of a German submarine. For a week or so, enthusiasts spent their time on top of sandhills, trying to get a sight of the enemy.

One of Stewart-Moore's duties was to take turns as orderly officer: inspecting the men's dinners, receiving complaints, and going the rounds of the sentries in the evening to see if they were alert and knew their duties. The orderly officer wore a sword as a badge of office.

> Nobody owned a sword but one was kept for the purpose and handed on
> from one officer to the next. Our overcoats were made with a special slit
> through which the hilt of the sword stuck out. If I ever had been
> involved in a fracas I suppose I was meant to draw the sword but I would

Training at Ballykinler. The sandbag full of straw was attacked with a
fixed bayonet, to simulate close-quarters combat.
ROYAL ULSTER RIFLES MUSEUM

not have known how to use it or what to do with it. For those who were
of a pugnacious turn of mind there was bayonet practise. A row of
dummy figures made of sacking stuffed with straw was hung up from a
sort of gallows and instruction was given by NCOs ... as an alternative I
had bought myself an automatic pistol and I had some target practise with
it in the sandhills which bordered the sea.

Occasionally, the officers' mess would have visitors, and one such distinguished guest was Spender, whom Stewart-Moore remembers talking
lucidly about philosophy (and, in particular, about Kant's *Critique of Pure
Reason*).[72] Such learned discourse was a long way from the experience and
conversation of the ordinary private in the ranks. One such was Tommy
Ervine, soldiering with the 8th Rifles – 'Ballymacarrett's Own'.

I mind Ballykinler. It was all sandhills full of rabbits. We built trenches
and we actually thought the Germans would come up from Dundrum!
There was a big dog belonged to one of the officers and one night he
came into our tent and we thought it was the enemy! I remember that
tent with candles. Eight to a tent and our heads leant out the canvas, and

Relaxation at Ballykinler.
As the spring of 1915 drew on,
many men enjoyed outdoor
life in the beautiful
coastal location.
ROYAL ULSTER RIFLES MUSEUM

boys-oh, you might get a kick! The uniforms too didn't arrive too soon –
I lent my uniform to a friend who'd got none as he wanted it to go
home in for the weekend ... Then we made drains to get the rainwater
away, then we built huts. My friend Billy Mills and I had a great
way of harmonisin' together as we worked on the huts – up on the roof,
say ... so we put together a song called 'The Gentleman's Son and the
Outcast'. We made a stage at Ballykinler and there were concerts there.
We saw the cinema too at Ballykinler and they came and took a
film of us working there and then I saw myself in the film when they
showed it in the cinema a bit later.

Tommy Ervine also remembered the men's excursions into Newcastle,
when misbehaviour and fighting were common. Tommy, although one of

the smallest men in the battalion, had been a boxer, and so he was chosen to be a military policeman for these trips. He had some rough customers to deal with:

> There was a tough guy called Chuck Patton, and there was no prison at Ballykinler so we fastened him to a pole in the marquee. Some NCOs showed him to some visiting friends one Sunday but he reared up and nearly pulled the tent down. He escaped once and, in handcuffs and all, he got a horse and cart and steered as far as Clough before they caught them.

Tommy was a piper in the battalion band. He had brought his pipes back to camp one weekend and an officer had asked him and six others to be the nucleus of the band that was being formed. He had a busy time, as the band headed recruiting marches in Belfast:

> We went all over Belfast different nights, recruitin', and left our gear in the Unionist hall off Cregagh Road. Men joined up behind us, then the band was thanked for the work done … We gave a fellow drowned in Ballykinler Bay a military funeral too. Fell down steps into the water, he did, and his mate was too drunk to save him. I played the 'Dead March' from *Saul* and saw all the women cryin'.[73]

Gradually, each battalion was acquiring its own band and its regimental marches. In the battalions of the Royal Irish Rifles that were part of the Ulster Division, the following songs were chosen:

10th Battalion, South Belfast Volunteers: 'The Rose'
11th Battalion, South Antrim Volunteers: 'Let Erin Remember the Days of Old'
12th Battalion, Mid Antrim Volunteers, and 9th Battalion, West Belfast Volunteers: 'King William's March'
13th Battalion, 1st County Down Volunteers: 'The Mountains of Mourne'
14th Battalion, Young Citizen Volunteers: 'St Patrick's Day'
15th Battalion, North Belfast Volunteers: 'Billy's March'
16th Battalion, 2nd County Down Volunteers (Pioneers): 'The Royal South Down Militia'[74]

By the spring of 1915, the three main bodies of men in the three infantry brigades were ready for overseas service, or at least as ready as could be expected. But to many of the men who joined up believing they would be in Berlin by Christmas, the fact that they had got no further than Ballykinler or Clandeboye was a disappointment and a frustration.

BACK-UP UNITS

Supporting the infantry battalions were various specialist units. In November 1914 a new battalion had been set up, the 16th Royal Irish Rifles, subtitled the 2nd County Down Volunteers, to be based at Brownlow House in Lurgan. A Captain Platt arrived in Lurgan on 10 November with several civilian clerks from the Old Town Hall, who began taking the names of those who would be the battalion's first members. The men's quarters were in Wellington Street and in Brownlow House itself.[75] Many of the men to join the 16th Rifles were country lads from County Down. John Martin, of Crossgar, whose original attempt to join had been frustrated by his parents, made a second attempt with the 16th Rifles, and this time his parents did not feel able to stand in his way. Hugh James Adams went with him, and by Christmas 1914 they were in training in the grounds of Brownlow House. Several hundred men from Lurgan's spinning mills joined the battalion,[76] and a large number of the original Young Citizen Volunteers would also appear to have been drafted into it.[77]

On arriving in Lurgan, these Volunteers found a number of young nationalists loitering about the streets to 'exchange shouts' with the soldiers on their way to Brownlow; but they had to try to ignore them – from now on, they would be busy men, taken up in arduous work. In January the battalion was upgraded to pioneer status, at twopence a day extra for the men, and this meant that the 16th was responsible for trench digging and maintenance, road and hut construction, and other practical aspects of war engineering.[78] A lot of hard work began with picks and shovels: trenches were dug in Lurgan Park, and roads were built along the shores of Lough Neagh, many of them constructed with timber from the woods of the Montiaghs.[79] There were also the statutory route marches, accompanied by the battalion's splendid pipe band.

One soldier in the pioneers was to remember Christmas 1914 at Lurgan

The pipers of the Pioneer Battalion, the 16th Royal Irish Rifles,
on the march
ROYAL ULSTER RIFLES MUSEUM

especially clearly, for it was then that he met his future wife for the first
time. He had seen a 'slip of a girl' standing at the head of Victoria Street
when he was marching up and down the road. Then, when a local family
took him into their house for Christmas tea, he found the same girl there
at the table – she was a niece of the host:

> I was nineteen at the time and she was sixteen. When I got back to the
> castle [Brownlow House] I wrote again to Mr Hopps to thank him
> for the day out. Then before I left Lurgan this girl sent me a pair of
> hand-knit gloves and a packet of Woodbine. We started to write
> to each other ...[80]

The other units of the division were training at a variety of locations in
the province – the Royal Army Medical Corps at Newry, for instance. The
RAMC was to be equipped with motor ambulances presented by the people
of Ulster, and each ambulance had inscribed on its body the name of the
town or area from which it came.[81] These vehicles, which cost around
£500, could accommodate four patients lying down or twelve seated. They
had such modern gadgets as Thermos flasks, special lamps and fire-
extinguishing apparatus, as well as tanks that could hold five gallons of
water.[82] The Army Service Corps provided training for jobs such as a driver,

chauffeur, clerk, fuel organiser, wheelwright and smith; cooks and canteen staff learnt the art of preparing hot food, on the march, from mobile field kitchens. The Royal Engineers, training initially at Randalstown, learnt to build and use pontoon bridges, dugouts and gun emplacements. The signalling company trained at Downpatrick, and the cavalry squadron was stationed at Enniskillen. Many farmers who had joined up but turned out to be poor shots or to have bad feet were drafted into positions where they looked after horses and mules.[83] The Cyclist Company was an attraction to those who had been keen cyclists before the war, but some were posted to ride bicycles because they could not handle horses. Tommy Jordan, from Ballynafeigh in east Belfast, recalled:

> We got the train down to Enniskillen. Some of us got a go at a riding
> school but there were fellas gettin' on the horse facing the tail!
> Some fella in charge would make a noise and they'd make a movement!
> So the man says, 'You, you and you' to the ones that was able, and
> those ones got working with the horses. The rest of us was the Cyclin'
> Corps. We went up to Magilligan. Then the corps was cut down,
> so we came down to Belfast and were told a new unit was being
> formed in Lurgan.

The new unit that Tommy joined was, of course, the Pioneers.[84]

George Lindsay, from County Derry, joined the Cyclist Company in February 1915. He had had no connection with the UVF but had a great love for cycling. He trained initially in Bangor – where he was based at the 'Cripples' Institute' – then went on a recruiting tour. The men got new bicycles with jointed frames that could be folded and put on the cyclists' back. They then travelled up to the north coast and down through Strabane to Enniskillen, where they completed more training, with rides out into the beautiful Fermanagh countryside. The rest of their time was spent at Magilligan on the Atlantic coast.[85]

GOODBYE TO ULSTER

Throughout the first months of 1915 the entire Ulster Division was striving towards war-readiness, but its links with the rest of the UVF were not forgotten. Recruitment had brought in men who were not Ulster Volunteers, such as George Lindsay, and, indeed, a number of Catholics had joined. However, the division was very much the cream of the UVF's fighting strength. The Volunteers who were left still continued to operate and to have manoeuvres on a regular basis; and Sir Edward Carson made visits to the province and extolled the need for home defence of 'the shores of Ulster'.[86] As the time of the 36th's departure to the front seemed near, local UVF companies held meetings in Orange halls, and presented gifts to those from their number who had joined the army. Local 'comfort committees' of women in the towns and villages of Ulster organised collections of socks, mufflers, mittens and helmets for their 'lads'. Spiritual concern for the souls of those about to face death and suffering also produced a series of 'mission services'. In late May and early June a week of mission services was held for the Fusiliers and Rifles stationed at Newtownards, and an average of seventy soldiers came along each night.[87]

As better weather came, brigade sports' days were held at the camps, and in June Shane's Castle camp at Randalstown staged a day of activities that included obstacle races and sack races, sack fights, tug o' war and wrestling on horseback.[88]

There was also a continued effort to recruit for the division. Captain David John Bell remembered visits to the hiring fair in Ballynahinch:

We had a meeting on the Wednesday evening, a parade on Thursday through the fair, and the band played some selections ... We left Ballynahinch on Friday for Clandeboye with fifteen new recruits for the battalion.

Also during the final months, the men learnt to 'entrain' – to board and disembark from a train in an organised way. Rows of seats would be set in an open field to represent a carriage, and the men would be marched out in companies and ordered to left-wheel or right-wheel into the 'train'.[89]

The highlight of the final months was on 8 May when a grand parade of the entire division was held in Belfast: having been inspected by Major-General Sir Hugh McCalmont at Malone, the men were to march along a bunting-strewn route to the City Hall. For days beforehand, relatives and friends of men in the division had been planning their trips to Belfast by special train excursions, so as to see their loved ones on parade. On the morning of 7 May Stewart-Moore set out from Ballykinler by

The 16th Royal Irish Rifles make their way through dense crowds past the City Hall the Ulster Division bids farewell to Belfast on 8 May 1915
ROYAL ULSTER RIFLES MUSEUM

road, and reached Ballynahinch with the men of the 15th Rifles by late afternoon, having halted on the way for sandwiches and water from their water bottles. At Ballynahinch, Stewart-Moore slept on his camp bed in a room over a shop. Next morning they made an early start and reached Belfast before midday.[90]

The Young Citizen Volunteers had also moved off from their base on 7 May, and arrived that evening at Wheatfield House in north Belfast, where they cleaned up and prepared for the big day. That night men from the Young Citizens went into the city centre to see the famous Miss Phyllis Dare at the Belfast Hippodrome. Her most famous song captured the mood of the hour ...

> Oh, we don't want to lose you,
> But we think you ought to go;
> For your King and country
> Both need you so.
> We shall want and miss you
> But with all our might and main
> We will thank you, cheer you, kiss you
> When you come back again.

After the performance, three representatives of the 14th Rifles presented the singer with a bouquet of flowers. That weekend – one of the most dramatic in the history of Belfast – the city was full of soldiers from every part of Ulster, as the entire division assembled. Only the men of the 9th Inniskilling Fusiliers were absent: they had to be quarantined at Ballycastle due to an outbreak of *German* measles![91]

At 12.30 p.m. at Malone the seventeen thousand troops of the 36th Division were brought to attention and a bugle call signalled the start of the inspection. At 1.15 the men began to march to the city centre, where there had been crowd trouble and fire engines had had to be placed across Donegall Place as a barrier. At 2.30 the mayor and mayoress together with Carson and his wife arrived at the City Hall, and at 2.45 General Powell and his HQ staff rode past at the head of the division. Then came the cavalry – the Inniskilling Dragoons – followed by the Cyclist Company wheeling their bicycles. Four field companies of engineers and the signal company followed, and pontoon and field equipment was carried past as part of the display. The 107th was the first of the infantry brigades to appear at the City Hall, with the 8th Rifles, the East Belfast Volunteers, heading the march. The 108th Brigade followed, with the fifes and drums of the County Down Volunteers' band winning special applause for a rendition of 'The Mountains of Mourne'. Then came the 109th Brigade – the measles-stricken 9th Inniskillings replaced by the 16th Rifles – and the Young Citizen Volunteers making an especial impression with their military elan. The procession was completed by the appearance of the Army Service Corps with over a hundred horse-drawn transport wagons; the butchers and bakers; and the Royal Army Medical Corps, its field ambulances and equipment. When the entire division had passed, the crowd sang 'God Save the King', and slowly dispersed.[92]

In later years, the sight of that enthusiastic body of men, as yet untouched by the war, was to haunt the memories of those who had watched. For an hour and forty minutes, eager young men had marched past the City Hall, naive and proud.[93] Although the provincial papers of the following week were full of news of the sinking of the *Lusitania*, there was room for description of the parade and the men of Ulster's own division who were so proudly assembled in Belfast on that May weekend. There were reports of how shops and works had closed for the day, and how

The soldiers leave Clandeboye
camp for the last time,
on the way to the railway station,
en route to England
SOMME MUSEUM

schools had given time off to their pupils. Young boys had vied for the best view of the parade:

> Sammy and I looked for the best vantage point and decided on a narrow window ledge of Robinson and Cleavers' famous store ... both of us balanced on the ledge for hours until the parade ended ... Their bearing was magnificent for they were being honoured by their own folk ... The crowds that May day gave their souls to our soldiers ...[94]

The newspapers referred to the men of the 36th in romantic and heroic terms. To them, the soldiers were 'the counterparts of the knights in armour who thrilled us with their deeds at King Arthur's court'.[95]

Saturday 8 May was Ulster's official farewell to the 36th Division and to the UVF from which it had been formed. It was a proud climax to all those great unionist and Volunteer rallies that had preceded the war.

As summer approached, the sunshine brought varying reactions in the men. At Randalstown, many soldiers slept out of doors in the warm June nights, and sat basking in the daytime sunshine. Ornamental flower beds outside their huts were coming up in bloom. The mud had gone.[96] But Private R. Dynes felt a melancholy stirred up by all this waiting. On a postcard, he wrote to his sister:

> Hope to get home Sunday week. Come down and we'll all go to Church like old times. On a march last week. Saw a ditch of primroses like the ones outside school. Happy and sad thoughts.[97]

The authorities realised that as the Twelfth of July approached, it would be undesirable for the men to remain in Ulster during the Orange celebrations. Early in July the soldiers were told to send home all their personal and private belongings.[98] They were to be shipped across the Irish Sea to complete the final part of their preparations in the south of England. 'Carson's Army' would finally have made its break with home, to become just another unit in 'Kitchener's Army'.

THE MOVE TO SEAFORD

John Stewart-Moore was pleased to make the move to England, and particularly glad that the quartermaster made no objection to him taking his gramophone with him. His battalion left Newcastle by train to Dublin, boarded the Holyhead boat and arrived in the Welsh port at midnight. There followed a long delay on the pier, and the men did not board their train until dawn. The rail journey was broken by a stop at Crewe, where Stewart-Moore enjoyed a delicious basketful of bacon and eggs. At midday the men reached their camp at Seaford in Sussex, in blazing sunshine and heat much stronger than anything they were used to in the north of Ireland.[99]

Most of the men seemed to find Seaford a pleasant place. Although it was wartime, minstrels were still performing on the beach. The men took the opportunity of a cool bathe in the English Channel, and there was the chance, when off duty, to visit Eastbourne and Brighton. The manoeuvres that the troops performed on the open expanse of the South Downs were appreciated for the beauty of the Sussex countryside, and a number of the men enjoyed watching the local shepherds and their well-trained sheep-dogs.[100] John Martin and Hugh James Adams greatly enjoyed their Sunday afternoon walks over the hills into Eastbourne, even though they had hardly a penny in their pockets to spend.[101]

There was plenty of evidence, at last, of the war they had come to participate in. On calm days, when the breeze was in the right quarter, they could hear the guns in France. There was a dirigible airship over Beachy Head, and aeroplanes regularly passed overhead. However, Seaford was very much an Ulster colony. Married officers were allowed to live out of camp when not on duty, and quite a few brought their families over to furnished rooms or houses.[102]

The accommodation at the camp proved reasonable, although men of the Young Citizen Volunteers discovered that the foundations of their huts were infested by ants.[103] The weather did not remain perfect throughout July, and a number of south-westerly gales blew in from the sea, and chilled and soaked the men.[104]

The majority of the Ulster Division were unfamiliar with England and the English, and, equally, the inhabitants of Seaford had little prior knowledge of Ulstermen apart from what they had heard during the Ulster Crisis, so many of them had been dreading the arrival of 'wild Irishmen'.[105] Soon, however, the Ulster Division made some favourable impressions. The Young Citizens battalion was referred to by Spender as 'the battalion of city clerks which was especially favoured by the fair sex of Sussex on the report that they were all sons of ministers of religion'.[106]

The men attended local churches on Sunday, and one clergyman came to the camp in midweek to say that his offertory box had been broken by Ulster soldiers. This caused initial consternation, as sacrilege should be the last crime attributable to young men of noted religious devotion. But the clergyman went on to explain that he had purposely not taken up a collection when he had seen his pews crowded with troops, and that the alms box had been broken by the weight of coins stuffed into it as the soldiers left the church![107]

On another occasion, the division had been engaged on night manoeuvres, and it was discovered at dawn that a deep trench had been dug across a valuable gallop belonging to a racehorse-training stable. However, the owner, rather than complaining, expressed pleasure that his ground had been of use to the division, and went on to offer his jumps to the mounted units and young officers for practise.[108]

Relations with the local inhabitants were probably put to an early test when the Ulstermen celebrated the Battle of the Boyne on 12 July. At dawn, Stewart-Moore was awakened by the skirl of bagpipes, and looking out of his window, saw the whole battalion, less the officers, marching around the parade ground led by a soldier representing King William on a white horse. The band was playing Orange tunes. Not being an Orangeman, Stewart-Moore left his men to their celebrations and took advantage of a holiday trip to Portsmouth to have a meal with his aunt.[109] Meanwhile, the locals had to endure the procession of a very amateur band through the streets of the town during the course of the morning. Later in the day, crowds of anxious townsfolk gathered to see a more organised procession complete with banners. Then, at 6.30 p.m., in the YMCA recreations rooms on Arundel Road, a large crowd heard a speaker from the London branch of the Orange Order express the hope that

> when July 12th came round again he would have the privilege of addressing them on their own beloved soil and that Germany would have received a sound thrashing by then.[110]

In due course, special military Orange lodges were established during the sojourn in Sussex. The Masonic brotherhood was also very strong in the 36th Division: a Pioneers' Masonic lodge, no. 420, was established at Seaford, and held its first meeting on 3 August.[111] The creation of such ties helped keep the sense of home alive in the soldiers during the first months of absence from Ireland. Meanwhile, in Ulster, local newspapers carried reports from Sussex to supplement the letters and postcards being received. The *Newtownards Chronicle* of 7 August boasted that the 36th Division was, in numbers, 'nearly equal to the entire British force which Wellington had at his disposal at the Battle of Waterloo', and that, in the words of one officer, the men were 'hard as nails, fit as fiddles, and simply spoiling for a fight'.

On 27 July Kitchener made a visit to inspect the men. By now, there had been changes in equipment – rucksacks and belts from UVF days were not standard army pattern, and they were soon replaced.[112] The day of

Kitchener's visit was a sunny one, and at 11.00 a.m. the inspection began. The general impression would appear to have been that the 'great man' was in a hurry – he mounted a horse that was not intended for him, and dashed off at speed to make his inspection. To the men, it appeared that he was there for a very short time. 'He did not stay long', remarked one soldier, 'and we felt a bit let down for most of us got little sleep the night before getting everything ready for him.'[113]

A cause of both pride and annoyance from Kitchener's visit was that he thought the personnel of the field ambulances to be of far too fine a quality for the RAMC. 'You will have to give me some of those men for the artillery', he said. Subsequently, 150 men were transferred to the artillery, and the majority of them, although flattered, were grieved to lose their chance to serve in the Ulster Division. Kitchener would appear, for all the swiftness of his visit, to have been impressed by the 36th, and shortly afterwards told Sir Edward Carson that it was the finest division of his New Army that he had yet seen.[114]

Carson and his wife were also to inspect the division in Sussex. The men marched some twenty miles into the countryside, where they assembled for Sir Edward, and as Spender later remembered it, the scene was a fine one:

... the top of one of the highest downs – Firle Beacon – raised its head
above the mists into the sunshine, and there stood Sir Edward Carson
with a little group behind him.

Their old leader came round to meet the infantry as they lay resting on the turf. The men rose to their feet and cheered as he approached. It was Carson, not Kitchener, for whom they felt most love and respect: they were still 'Carson's Army' first, and Kitchener's second.[115]

Being adjacent to London, many of the men had an opportunity for their first visit to the capital. Stewart-Moore found travelling by underground a great experience, and enjoyed seeing the sights of the big city, dining in style at a Soho restaurant and completing his happiness with yet another visit to a Gilbert and Sullivan opera, in a theatre near the Kensington Oval.[116] The train journeys to and from London were not without incident. On the way back from the capital, a soldier called Paddy Wallace pulled the communication cord and stopped the train. As a result. the train arrived half an hour late, the connection was missed and hundreds of men had to march several miles back to camp. Paddy Wallace was not a popular man.[117]

A picture postcard for separated lovers. As the time for departure to France drew near, many men treasured photographs of loved ones left at home.

The temptations of the flesh proved too much for many a young soldier on a visit to London. Crozier knew of one young officer who had to go into a private hospital to have an operation because he had injured himself in a 'high-class' brothel. To try to deal with the problem of venereal disease, Crozier arranged with his medical officer to ensure that all his soldiers 'had access to disinfectants after indulgence in sexual intercourse, free of charge'.[118] The precise nature and effectiveness of the disinfectants is not recorded.

BORDON AND BRAMSHOTT

One of the repercussions of the Kitchener visit had been a decision to move from Seaford to Bordon and Bramshott, where more intensive musketry training could be carried out. Sir Archibald Murray, deputy chief of the general staff, had pointed out to the secretary for war that the division was not yet ready for France, as neither musketry nor machine-gun training had been thoroughly undertaken – nor, indeed, had the Divisional Artillery been properly trained. As a result, Kitchener gave orders for the artillery to join the division, and for urgent training in musketry to be given to the infantrymen. So plans were made to leave Seaford and assemble at Bordon and Bramshott on 2 September. In all the months they had been soldiers, most of the men had barely fired a shot, due to shortages of ammunition and the absence of adjacent rifle ranges in Ulster and Sussex. This would be the opportunity to learn.[119]

When the advanced party arrived at Bordon, they found it a mess. The men of the 22nd Division, whom the Ulstermen were replacing, had received marching orders at short notice, and many items of belongings were left behind. Sadly, the Battle of Loos was to take place in September, and the 22nd Division was hurled into the fray, only to lose very heavily.

Stewart-Moore was stationed at Bramshott, and found the whole business of training on the rifle range time-wasting and tedious. There was an early start each morning, then a rail journey to a station north of Aldershot, and from there the men marched along a track to the range:

> Marching along the sandy track raised a cloud of dust very unpleasant for
> those who were in the rear of the column. We spent our days lolling
> about on the rifle range, each man waiting to fire the specified
> number of rounds which would qualify him for service overseas ... so
> many rounds at each of the prescribed distances ... and then home
> again to Bramshott in the evening. All this travelling took up
> quite a lot of time and effort ...[120]

The training was also disheartening due to the poor quality of the American ammunition, which made accuracy almost impossible.[121]

> After a very bad day at the butts when the ammunition was worse than
> usual, you got real mad at yourself for ever joining up at all. I don't
> think the British meant to swear at us but it seemed they were.
> They seemed to think we were blaming our poor results on the bad
> ammunition instead of allowing them to put the blame on us
> for being poor shots.[122]

No wonder Tommy Jordan, with the 16th Rifles, was to relate that most of the soldiers went away feeling they 'couldn't hit a cow on the back with a bakeboard'. Another of his comrades was to comment: 'Men who could shoot the eye out of a blackbird at fifty yards using a UVF rifle now found themselves missing the targets.'[123]

Other aspects of the training were of poor quality, too:

> In our battalion we did very little training with the barbed wire. They put a few rows before the trenches we dug and we crawled about under and over them, but all we got was cuts and scratches.[124]

The officers were also dismayed by the scanty training of the Londoners who comprised the artillery. To the amusement of many of the country boys in the infantry, the Londoners frequently proved to be quite afraid of their horses![125] Their training was intensified during the month of September, but generally it is clear that the training in all aspects of gun usage – from artillery through to rifle and machine guns – was too little too late.

Preparations were now being made for France, and senior officers were being sent there for courses of instruction. In September General Powell was told of his replacement as commanding officer by Major-General O.S.W. Nugent, who had already served in France and was in a better position to help the division adapt to war. Powell was banished to Vladivostok in charge of the British Red Cross, having been consoled with a knighthood.[126]

On Thursday 30 September the division was reviewed by the king in the company of Kitchener. Any inadequacies in training were not apparent as the men made their final complete appearance before leaving British soil for good. Cyril Falls – an officer in the division who later wrote its official history – was to describe his feelings:

> None of those who saw them is likely to forget the physique or the bearing of that splendid body of men. It is hard to think without emotion of what the Division was that day and the fate that awaited it …
>
> His Majesty warmly congratulated General Nugent, and, turning to Sir George Richardson, who was present, told him what a fine Division had been given by his Ulster Volunteers. As the King's motorcar overtook some of the troops marching back to camp the men burst out into cheering, so that the car swept along a loud roaring line – an unrehearsed spontaneous exhibition of loyalty.[127]

Ulster soldiers catch up on sleep in a trench at Seaford. The war zone was now just a few miles away, across the English Channel.
SOMME MUSEUM

ACROSS THE CHANNEL

By now, advance parties were in France preparing for the arrival of the division. David John Bell, of Ballynahinch, helped organise the shipment to Le Havre of one thousand men and 750 horses connected with the transport corps. He was responsible for forage and rations for the journey. The ship was the *Lapland*, a huge cargo carrier that had been one of the vessels to come to the assistance of the *Titanic* in 1912. The crossing of the Channel from Southampton was made in total darkness.[128]

On Sunday 3 October Stewart-Moore and his mother went to a Communion service at 8.00 a.m. in Grayshott church. She had come out to see the royal review and to say goodbye. That evening, the 15th Rifles marched out of the camp and down the Portsmouth Road to Liphook station, to entrain for Folkestone. It was a calm, dark night on the English Channel.[129]

Crozier, too, had the company of his mother – together with his wife and child – for the last few days in England. He glimpsed them standing under a tree, watching, as he marched at the head of half of the 9th Rifles to Liphook station.[130]

Arthur Samuels and his cousin C.J.H. Samuels, both officers of the 11th Rifles, left St Lucia Barracks, Bordon, on the afternoon of 4 October. As they marched to the station, they were struck by the apathy of the civilians;

> There was no cheering, waving of handkerchiefs, or kissing of hands;
> even the children making mud pies on the side of the road did not
> trouble to look up … so it was that as we marched down the short road
> to Bordon station, we felt that we were only going on our business, and
> that those plain clothed civilians – many of them young and physically fit
> men – were going on theirs. At Bordon station the somewhat
> questionable spirit of the men was revived by large cups of excellent tea,
> brought round by ladies.

At 9.35 p.m. the 11th Rifles departed on the transport ship *Onward*. Also on board were men from other regiments, and every inch of the vessel seemed packed and stuffy on this warm autumn night. On deck, it was impossible to walk from one end of the boat to the other. Smoking was strictly forbidden, but few culprits could be caught in the crowded darkness. The sea was smooth as glass.[131]

On 5 October the Young Citizen Volunteers made their crossing to France. The last thing Jim Maultsaid heard at the dock was a voice shouting 'Go on the Blues!' They boarded the vessel, an old Isle of Man paddle-steamer called the *Empress Queen*.[132] Billy McFadzean wrote to his family:

> You people at home make me feel quite proud when you tell me 'I am
> the soldier boy of the McFadzeans.' I hope to play the game and if I don't
> add much lustre to it, I certainly will not tarnish it.[133]

While journeying across the Channel, G.H.M. was detailed to peer through the darkness on one side of the ship for submarine periscopes. As morning broke on 6 October the *Empress Queen* crawled into Le Havre, and many of the men saw a large hospital ship getting ready to make the journey the other way. It gave food for thought to all who watched. Training days were over: now it was the real thing for the entire Ulster

Division. Many would not return, or if they did, it would be aboard such a hospital ship.[134]

The journey that the Ulster Volunteers had made from the days of enlistment, a year previously, to this day of disembarkation on French soil was a journey from one kind of warfare to another. They had been involved in a citizen army whose cause was home and family. Theirs had been a cosy, intimate warfare, involving nocturnal gun smuggling and games of bluff with a perplexed but benign British government. It was a war with scarcely a drop of blood shed in its campaigns. The massive military marches and open-air rallies of the Volunteers had been what Orange demonstrations and marches have always been – a form of psychological offensive, designed to scare the enemy with the rattle of sabres and the boom of big drums.

Now the Volunteers were caught in a monstrous fight to the death between rival empires for the domination not just of Europe but of the world. They were pawns in a very big and ruthless game, and there was little that the individual soldier could do to alter his own destiny. In this modern warfare, the participant, above all else, felt helpless, without a clear sense of why he was fighting, killing and being killed. This war was futile, savage and for real. If Carson had hoped that the creation of the Ulster Division would be a weapon in the fight to defeat Home Rule, he had been ignorant of how easily his men would become a much more disposable tool in a more lethal struggle for imperial status and wealth in the modern world.

3

'A FAR, FAR CRY TO MY OWN LAND'
THE ULSTER DIVISION IN FRANCE 1915–16

A group of Inniskilling soldiers make their way up a shallow communication trench to
the front line. Note the traverses, or 'zig-zags', in the trench design.
ROYAL ULSTER RIFLES MUSEUM

> It's a far, far cry to my own land,
> A hundred leagues or more …
> A candle stuck on the muddy floor
> Lights up the dugout wall,
> And I see in its flame the prancing sea
> And the mountains straight and tall;
> For my heart is more than often back
> By the hills of Donegal.
>
> 'It's a far, far cry'
> Patrick MacGill[1]

By the time the Ulster Volunteers crossed the English Channel, the European war had expanded to take in large sections of the globe. The Middle East, Africa and the Atlantic Ocean were theatres of conflict; the high seas were one of the most dangerous areas for the British war effort, for here the German U-boats were sinking the ships on which the British Isles depended for so many basic supplies. In the Near East, a campaign was under way to capture the Turkish peninsula of Gallipoli, open the sea route from the Mediterranean to Russia, and maybe even force Turkey, Germany's ally, out of the war. This campaign was to prove a costly and ineffective sideshow: the main theatre of war continued to be Europe, and the main threat to the Allies was still Germany, which seemed quite capable of sustaining a war on both Western and Eastern Fronts.

The Russian armies were not short of men, but they were disorganised and poorly equipped, and therefore easily containable by the Germans. Meanwhile, in the west a general stalemate had developed once the initial German push towards Paris had been halted at the Battle of the Marne. Germany was content to hold on to the land it had gained – it was the French who were honour-bound to expel the 'Boche' from their soil, but they could make little progress in pushing the Germans back.

The Allied armies faced the Germans along a line that stretched from the Belgian coast to the Swiss border. For most of that distance, the rival soldiers confronted each other from the relative safety of fortified trenches across an intervening strip of earth known as no-man's-land. The British held the northern sector along with the Belgians; the longest part of the line was held by the French.

Any attempt to break through the enemy lines seemed doomed to failure, each offensive being met by a reinforced counter-attack. New weapons were being invented so as to enable the incisive impact needed for victory. The Germans were the first to try poison gas – at Ypres in April 1915 – but its effect was diminished by the difficulty of using it without hampering the progress of one's own men, and by the creation of functional gas masks. The British envisaged tanks as a means of advancing across shell-churned ground, but they were only in the experimental stages. Aeroplanes were proving useful for scouting, and a spectacular aerial warfare was going on above the encamped armies in their trenches, but as yet the planes were much too light to carry effective bomb loads.

So the Western Front was dominated by the trenches and the heavy artillery, with greater and more fearsome guns being produced to try to pound the enemy into the earth. The latest failure to break this horrible deadlock had been at the Battle of Loos, resulting in fifty thousand British casualties and no significant progress. Such was the situation that the Ulster Division and the other New Army soldiers inherited on arrival in France in the early winter of 1915–16.

They were to discover an increasingly sophisticated maze of trenches on the British front line. The foremost trench, facing directly onto no-man's-land, ran roughly parallel to a second 'support-line' trench, and in the rear was a third line, the 'reserve' trench. Most of the trenches were floored with wooden duckboards, and the only shelter or accommodation was afforded by dugouts and holes scraped in the trench walls. Communication trenches, running at right angles, connected up the main lines. Most trenches were dug in a zig-zag pattern of short bays, rather than in a straight line, so as to minimise casualties from shell fire or from machine guns pointed down a trench. Sandbags and barbed wire helped fortify the defences, and out there, beyond the rows of wire, lay no-man's-land, which could be anything from half a mile to a few yards in width. Spasmodic warfare was maintained on even the quietest sectors of the front. German artillery sent over a range of shells, from the lighter 'whizz-bangs' to the heavy 'Jack Johnsons', and the British replied in kind. Snipers were ready to shoot at the obtruding head of any soldier, and where trenches were close enough, grenades could be lobbed across. Raids on the enemy's lines were undertaken, usually at night, to ascertain facts about the foe and to keep everyone on their toes.

A vast amount of monotonous physical labour was needed in a war where transport was only beginning to be motorised and mechanisation generally was primitive. The trenches were, therefore, on every account a horrible place to be, synonymous to future generations with the misery and degradation that warfare brings.

The 36th Division was to be drafted to the Somme sector, which was in the southern area of the British lines, and was part of the historic French province of Picardy, in which the cathedral city of Amiens was a central feature. Nearer the front was the town of Albert, with its basilica, above which rose the damaged golden statue of the Virgin Mary, visible for miles around. It had been, and to a degree still was, a rich, pleasant countryside. Small woods dotted the landscape, and the Somme, and its tributary the Ancre, had wide, marshy valleys that ran through the fields. It was, all in all, a fairly quiet sector, and large parts of it were used to a 'live and let live' routine. The Ulster Volunteers might have hoped for a smooth acclimatisation to war, but, nonetheless, the first few steps onto French soil on an autumn morning proved, for many, quite a shock.

FIRST IMPRESSIONS OF WAR

For Crozier, the landing of the 9th Rifles was, in fact, an ordeal. Several of his men were accused of having stolen alcohol from the ship's bar. The men were lined up on the quayside and reprimanded; the cost of the stolen drink would have to be deducted from pay. Crozier signed for the stolen goods and left Boulogne for Amiens with his 'Shankill Boys'.[2] When the 11th Rifles (the South Antrim Volunteers) landed at Boulogne (somewhat more soberly), Hugh Stewart noted the distinctive sound of the local voices; the first Frenchmen he met were selling apples to the soldiers. It was wet, and the men marched to a nearby camp before entraining for Amiens.[3]

Captain Arthur Samuels was to record the wet weather, the darkness, and the misery of marching to this rest camp to await the train:

> … the streets were wet and slippery, the men heavily laden with blankets
> and equipment and the road to the Rest Camp led up a steep incline …
> A few, mindful of the landing of the Expeditionary Force, and the ever
> famous 'Tipperary' stories, burst into song, but the Frenchman retires
> early to bed, and with the exception of one long thin arm fluttering a
> pocket handkerchief from a top window, we saw no sign of life
> in the deserted streets. After a very steep climb of about two miles we
> came to the Rest Camp, and a series of gasoline flares lit up the
> muddy flats on which the tents were pitched.

The following day, before their departure from the railway station, the men were to encounter numerous women and children wandering outside the railings of the camp and shouting out for bits of biscuit and bully beef. It seemed that France must be starving.[4]

The Young Citizen Volunteers had also arrived on French soil. G.H.M. had a chance to practise the language by asking a local boy, 'Quel est votre nom?'[5] When the men entrained, the journey turned out to be a slow one: Jim Maultsaid recalled that 'you could have got out to pick flowers along the line. We sat with our legs swinging out …'[6] Some soldiers even got out of the train and ran alongside at the edge of the track to stretch their legs. At a siding, they had a chance to disembark and have some refreshment, but many were astonished to find there was no tea – only strong black coffee.[7]

Stewart-Moore, with the North Belfast men, was swift to note that the soldiers were actually being carted off to war in 'horse boxes'!

> The train was made up of covered wagons marked 'Hommes 40, chevanx en long 8' – for the officers there was an empty first-class carriage with rounded doors and windows reminiscent of an 18th century mailcoach … we saw a French ambulance train and one of our officers named Hogg who was an incorrigible joker and had a very lively imagination … tried to make our flesh creep by telling us that he saw bandaged limbs with blood dripping.[8]

When they arrived at Amiens, the Ulster battalions had to make long marches to the villages where they were billeted. The South Antrim Volunteers travelled by train from Amiens to Flesselles, and then marched twelve kilometres to Rubempré. As the march began, Samuels noted that it was a lovely autumn evening, but he could hear an ominous sound on the breeze from the east: the rumble and growl of the big guns at the front.[9]

The march was something of a disaster, as the troops were heavily laden and too fast a pace was set for the clammy evening. Many men were hungry and thirsty, and still wore damp clothes. A number collapsed and had to be taken in mule-drawn wagons. As the men marched east and the night grew darker, the lurid flashes of gunfire became more noticeable. After eleven months of training, the Ulster Volunteers had arrived on the threshold of the 'Great War' at last.[10]

Many battalions were none too happy with the billeting arrangements in the villages to which they had been allocated. Often, confusion reigned. Captain David John Bell, of the 13th Rifles, had gone to Rainneville in an advance party to make arrangements, but after a night's sleep, he awoke to discover that his Down Volunteers were waiting outside the town, a day

HOW YOU FELT AFTER
30 KILOMETERS SLOGGING.

JIM. MAULTSAID
— 1916 —

FROM MY SKETCH BOOK

A portrait of the artist
with sore feet – a sketch
by Jim Maultsaid
MICHAEL MAULTSAID

earlier than expected. There had been no time to make proper arrangements, so Bell 'fixed the men up' as best he could.[11] The 9th Irish Fusiliers were also in Rainneville, and the official war diary recorded that the accommodation was scanty, the village too small for two battalions, the barns unrepaired, and the water supply poor.[12]

Stewart-Moore, in Vignacourt, found the situation equally primitive and dirty, and he suspected that conditions had not changed much since the Middle Ages. On arrival, he possessed a map but absolutely no instructions about where to go in the town. Relationships between soldiers and villagers were to grow rather unpleasant in the subsequent confusion.[13]

When the South Antrim men reached Rubempré, at eleven o'clock at night, trying to find billets in the pitch darkness was a horrendous task. The village seemed to consist of a long series of barns with barred and bolted

Stewart-Moore with his friend
I.W. Corkey, a medical officer,
shortly after arriving in France
ROYAL ULSTER RIFLES MUSEUM

doors. The men had anticipated beds and comfort. At last, the doors of locked barns were broken open, and despite protests from irate owners, the men piled in, up to thirty occupying a barn.

> At length on straw and hay, on floors hard and soft, everyone found a
> bed, and tired as they were, one or two were heard to mutter,
> Orangemen though they might be, that they wouldn't mind a bed even if
> the picture of the Pope himself hung at the head.

Within a day or two, billeting was more carefully organised, and the Ulstermen got a chance to look around them. Many were appalled by the dirtiness of the Picardy villages. The absence of French adult males – many of whom were at the front – meant that maintenance and upkeep of the dwellings was poor: 'the yards were swimming with filthy water from great heaps of manure that were piled up in front of each house'.[14]

Also difficult to take was the suspicious hostility of the French, who had had a variety of troops billeted with them and were heartily sick of their rowdy guests. Sometimes, the behaviour of the Ulstermen did not endear them to the locals, as Hugh Stewart indicated:

> The old boy who drove his calves out of the barn to let us in was upset because we got up on the scrake of dawn the first day and ate all the luscious pears in his orchard – they were like jelly! It done my heart good to get them![15]

Over the next couple of weeks, there was the routine of training; two or three brigade field days and a divisional field day were due to be held.[16] But everyone's mind was on the first, brief, statutory visit to the front line, which was about to take place.

On 18 October Samuels and his men left Rubempré. As he and his men neared the line, the gunfire grew menacing, and they saw tiny puffs of white smoke in the sky from German anti-aircraft guns. The soldiers halted some three and a half miles from the front trenches, then marched towards Mailly-Maillet, and past several lines of heavily wired trenches, which made long white streaks across the otherwise brown landscape. The little town at which they arrived had once been a fine place, with a chateau that had an elm-lined drive. But now there was not a pane of glass anywhere; many houses were without doors, and some were pierced by large shell holes. This was the region of war and utter desolation. A battery of howitzers nearby shook all the window frames, and every so often some slates would tumble down. The town was already crowded with troops, and the South Antrim men were an extra battalion, so their billets were poor outhouses with little straw.

On 21 October men of the South Antrim battalion were sent up to the 'Toutvent' trenches. Samuels was attached to a company of the Royal Warwickshire Fusiliers, whose HQ was in a dugout known as the 'Catacombs' – twenty yards long and seven feet wide, in trenches built originally by the Germans. Making his way to the front trench, Samuels grew silent. Under a full moon, he looked out to see what he could on his first night in the battlefields; but mostly there were just dark shapes. The two armies lived in extraordinary proximity. Although the enemy lines were parallel at a distance of approximately one hundred yards for most of the way, there were a number of saps – trenches running out into no-man's-land at right angles to the main front line. These had originally been German communication trenches, and extended as far as the present German lines, so the Germans occupied one end of the same sap as the Ulstermen. Sandbag emplacements separated the two sides, and the enemies were at times only fifteen feet from each other! Samuels recalls the first dawn in the trenches:

> Gradually, out of the darkness, things began to take upon themselves their proper shapes ... A maze of misty barbed wire, some in loose coils lying on the ground, some draped from stumps and stakes driven in at all angles, some in shell holes, all in a shapeless and indescribable jumble ... Then there is that desolate and shell-pocked strip of land which terminates with the German wire ... behind ... is the rolling country out of which the sun now begins to rise ... the 22nd of October promised to be the most lovely day.

There was the usual desultory rifle and machine-gun fire that started off each day in the trenches, but no real sign of what was to come. Samuels was having breakfast in the Catacombs with a couple of other officers when, suddenly, two whizz-bangs landed at the door of the dugout and there was a terrific explosion. The officers rushed out and up the communication trench to the front line, past a man who was rushing back with blood pouring from his shoulder and arm. Then, about ten yards in front, another shell exploded. Samuels was lifted clean off his feet and thrown flat on his stomach on the ground. The whole side of the trench fell over on top of him:

> I remember saying to myself aloud: 'I wonder when this is going to stop.' Still the earth kept falling, and the weight on my shoulders and the small of my back became oppressive. One thing was pleasing, there was dead silence underground. I began to heave with my shoulders and took a deep breath. There was no difficulty in breathing as the earth seemed full of air. On the second heave I felt I was more able to move, and after what seemed ages I got my head and shoulders clear.

When he had struggled free, Samuels helped his comrades out of the fallen earth, and as all were uninjured, they rushed on to the front trench and tried to marshall the men in the line, many of whom were still sleeping in their 'funk-holes' – scooped out of the front wall of the trench – despite the din. Gradually, the men were organised, and reinforcements filed into the front trench. Bayonets were fixed and ten rounds put in the magazines of their guns for the anticipated infantry attack that might follow such an unusually heavy bombardment. Samuels seems to have exhibited a remarkable clarity of mind, despite the obvious possibility of instant death or mutilation:

> I watched with fascination, a sheet of corrugated iron, blown from the
> roof of a dug-out, which flew about in the air like a card, and dashed
> hither and thither before finally coming down with a great slant on … the
> bay next to where I was.

Gradually, the British artillery started to retaliate. At 11.30 the bombardment began to die down, and soon it was over. No infantry attack came. Two men had been killed and sixteen wounded (although none of the mortally or seriously wounded would appear to have been Ulstermen). It was merely 'morning hate' on the Western Front. One gruesome effect of the explosives had been that corpses, previously buried in the earth, were exposed, and many men engaged in the grotesque practice of 'souveniring' buttons and badges.

That night, another trench was dug under another full moon in an eerie landscape of shell holes. The rest of the first few days' duty in the line passed more quietly for Samuels and his company. On Sunday 24 October they got their opportunity to hold the line alone, with their host company going back in support. The following evening, the men marched back to their billets in Mailly-Maillet, relatively unscathed – physically if not emotionally – by what they had experienced.[17]

Even before arrival in the front line, the prospect of it took a toll on some men in the form of heavy drinking. In the Shankill battalion, Crozier discovered several warrant officers drunk and absent from parade when the battalion assembled for the first march to the trenches. They were tried by court martial, reduced to the ranks and got a spell of imprisonment with hard labour.[18]

When they arrived at the front for their initiatory spell, the men often found unexpected terrors awaiting them. G.H.M. was daunted by the sound of rats squeaking in the dugout on his first night in the front line. In fact, the rat problem was so bad that one of his comrades hung his mother's food parcel by a cord from the roof to prevent the vermin from getting at it; but by morning they had rifled it![19] John Kennedy Hope also found the rats appalling. He took his bread from his haversack and kept it in a mess tin, 'so that those boys won't eat the heart out of our quarter loaf'. The beds were comfortable enough, and the dugouts spacious, but Hope found there was a constant dripping of water from the roof, so he covered himself with a rubber sheet.

But there was time in that first tour of duty with the Royal Warwicks to look around and see the particular features of this part of the line – the wickerwork sides of the trenches, built in French style; the elaborate dummy artillery guns behind the lines; and the trees in the wood nearby all wired together so that if a shell hit one tree it would not fall and deplete the camouflaging effect of the wood.[20] To Jim Maultsaid, night time was fascinating, with star-shells bursting over the front in a variety of eerily beautiful colours.[21]

When Stewart-Moore moved up to the trenches with his men, he was intrigued to see for the first time a German aeroplane, with its black Iron Cross markings. The trenches his battalion occupied were in first-class order, the weather was reasonable, and the Germans quiet, so all was fairly well.

> Looking across no-man's-land we could see the roads of Gommecourt village just behind the German wire. It was here that I saw a German shrapnel shell exploding in mid-air … we also noticed how the trees stood dark and black, deprived of their foliage by the bombardments.

When their first spell was over, Stewart-Moore and his fellow officers arranged for a hamper of provisions from Fortnum & Masons to be sent to the officers of the Warwicks in return for their 'hospitality'![22]

All through the winter of 1915–16, the men of the Ulster Division were to renew their experience of the trenches and to become used to the routines of manning the front line. They would get accustomed to the daily episodes of 'morning hate' followed, hopefully, by a quiet day. In the evening, there might be a repetition of the 'stand to' and 'hate' of the morning, and then by night there would be rations and stores to fetch from the battalion transport, and repairs to be made to the barbed wire or the trenches, sentries to be increased, and patrols sent out into no-man's-land to reconnoitre. Sentries were relieved at intervals of every two or three hours.

When a battalion was on front-line duty, two of its four companies would be in the front trenches, a third company would be in the support line, and a fourth would be in the reserve trenches. A battalion might expect to spend four to eight days in the front line before relief. The period regularly proved exhausting, even if no serious attacks from the Germans were experienced. Sentry duty at night was a particular strain on the men, as Stewart-Moore recorded:

> It gave one an eerie feeling to get on to the firing step and talk in
> whispers to the sentry while he stood there with his rifle at the ready
> peering into the darkness through our barbed wire entanglement.
> Once I found a sentry asleep. It was an offence punishable by death, but
> I did not report it hoping that the man would be so scared that he
> would never do it again.[23]

The weather conditions were also trying, as the men were gaining their initiation into trench warfare in the winter months. One rural Ulsterman described the front-line duties 'like standing in a peat bog, only you did not move about as much as you do when stripping the bank and at least the cutting keeps you warm'. Initially, it was rain rather than cold that presented the problem, although according to one soldier, the weather was less vicious than in Donegal.

> … here the rain was warmer and without a strong wind blowing, it did
> not seem to get through your clothes as quickly as it did in Finner so that
> it took longer to get soaking wet in France than it did at home.

The shelter of the dugouts was a dubious relief, for they were very claustrophobic:

> … there was always a smell in them. On a good spring day it smelt like
> the earth smell you get when digging potatoes. Usually they were
> musty and stank like a midden. I did not smoke, and, mind you, when
> you got half a dozen fags going … the place became a hell-hole.

Very often, the men learnt more about the practical skills of comfortable survival than about killing the enemy:

The most important thing I learnt in that first few days in the trenches was how to open a tin of bully beef with a bayonet without taking the edge off the bayonet or getting oil in the beef.

Unquestionably, though, there was for some men a sense of purpose informing the first months in the trenches – that would be gone later in the war – and that helped make the privations and dangers endurable.

There was a feeling of excitement and of getting things done as quickly as possible, as best you could, like doing a bit of late ploughing after a bad winter, working from daylight to dark to make up for lost time.
As you plough you know that there is always the harvest at the back of your mind. Them early days was like that ploughing; it was something that would get results later on and you put your back into everything you did.

Many men, however, would find their first few months in France taxing. Even when retiring from the trenches, the soldiers were not only busy but still uncomfortable. Although they obtained a wash and clean clothes, the rain and snow they experienced whilst training or building huts would leave them as soaking wet as they had been in the line.[24]

WINTER IN THE TRENCHES

In late October most of the division moved back towards Abbeville, with their HQ at Domart-en-Ponthieu. However, in November the Belfast Brigade, the 107th, was parted from the other two infantry brigades and transferred to the 4th Division – the 12th Brigade of the 4th Division joining the 36th in return. The Belfast men were to get their full share of trench warfare with the 4th, occupying a sector astride the Mailly-Maillet–Serre road and, later, a sector stretching south towards Beaumont-Hamel. Their typical six-day tours of the line, undertaken throughout the winter months, were a less comfortable option than the life experienced by the rest of the division – much of whose time was spent preparing accommodation for troops in villages throughout the Somme area.[25]

Cyril Falls was to record in his history of the 36th Division that the transfer of the 107th Brigade was part of a policy of training the New Army brigades alongside experienced soldiers, but Crozier was to tell a more complex story. The trouble, according to him, began with several acts of indiscipline in the Belfast battalions, especially looting. One incident especially annoyed the divisional commander, Nugent: four NCOs got drunk on brandy in an *estaminet*, and were absent from parade. Tried by court martial, they were reduced to the ranks and got long sentences of imprisonment. Nugent met the officers of the 107th Brigade in a village schoolroom and gave them a severe telling off – an experience Crozier said he would

> ... always treasure in my mind as the complete example of what can be
> said by the powerful to the powerless in the shortest space of time
> possible, consistent with the regulations of words and space for breathing,
> in the most offensive, sarcastic and uncompromising manner possible.

The sentence, according to Crozier, was 'banishment' to the 4th Division. As a result, the experience of the trenches afforded by joining the more seasoned soldiers was, in his view, a tremendous asset. Although Cyril Falls was adamant that the men of the 107th were 'most anxious to return', Crozier's jaundiced verdict was that they were quite happy to stay with the 4th Division for ever.[26]

In any case, the Belfast battalions learnt a lot of new lessons, especially about the understanding and use of the weapons of war. If one thing mattered in trench warfare, it was to keep your rifle clean, well oiled and free from rust. The NCOs and men were issued with the .303 Lee Enfield rifle, to which a bayonet could be attached. There was also the very useful hand grenade, which could do more damage than rifle or bayonet, and was more likely to be used. It was called a Mills bomb and was the subject of many cruel jokes and tall stories. Hugh Stewart remembered:

> The Chinese who were in the labour corps were supposed to be intrigued
> by this Mills Bomb which was just like a big goose's egg and I heard tell
> of one who took the pin out and held it up to his ear to hear the fizz –
> there wasn't much left of him![27]

The German hand grenade was of a different design, with a handle for effective throwing, and it was curiosity to examine this weapon more closely that took Stewart-Moore out into no-man's-land one night, just opposite

An Ulster officer wades
in a flooded trench
ROYAL IRISH FUSILIERS MUSEUM

Beaumont-Hamel. The Germans had made a sortie towards the Ulstermen's lines, and when they beat a hasty retreat, they left behind two or three stick bombs in a position that could be seen from the Ulster trenches:

> I coveted one of them so I got my batman to come with me and cover me with his rifle … There was no danger in doing so because they were lying in a position from which one could not be seen by the Germans though there was doubtless a German sentry within a stone's throw. The bombs were roughly made, rather like a Cocoa tin on the end of a short wooden handle. They had a string to pull so as to light the fuse just before you threw the bomb …[28]

Most men were not so eager to go out into no-man's-land, and grew to resent those officers who sent out regular patrols. However, the wire often had to be fixed and gaps in it closed. Sometimes, 'gooseberries' could be used – balls of barbed wire three or four feet in diameter that could be rolled out silently into position – and corkscrew stakes, to strengthen the wire, could be screwed into position rather than being noisily hammered into the earth. More dangerous were the patrols when men were sent crawling about on their stomachs across no-man's-land with the object of bringing back a bit of German wire to prove they had reached the enemy lines, or some tangible evidence to show which German battalion was opposite. There was always the chance of meeting a similar German party and bringing back a prisoner. Many officers and men felt that these patrols were purposeless, but Crozier was very keen on them. According to Stewart-Moore, it was from a false motive:

> Colonel Crozier … was particularly keen on sending out such patrols to
> no purpose except to show off. He had the reputation of being a callous
> and overbearing martinet.[29]

During the night, each side would send up flares and star-shells to see if they could spot men moving around no-man's-land. If a soldier was taken unawares, he had to freeze absolutely still, as the slightest movement could lead to death. There was also the danger that he might lose his way and not be able to locate the gap in his own wire through which he had emerged. The wire itself was another danger:

> The wire, no matter how cannily you handled it, cut and scratched
> your own flesh. I've seen many a man lose a finger or a hand or part of
> an arm because gangrene set in the cut caused by the wire.[30]

Some frights experienced in no-man's-land had their comical side, as Hugh Stewart found out:

> We was out in no-man's-land and a German sap was right and near us and
> we were scared to move or breathe for fear of getting caught. Anyway
> didn't we start to hear this fustling noise beside us and a tin can rattling or
> something. Our hair stood right on end. I reached and touched my mate
> on the foot. We listened again. So I whispers, 'Will we let a blarge and run
> for it before the Jerry artillery gets openin' up on us, or should we maybe
> wait and risk a grenade on top of us?' The sweat soon broke on me. Well,
> actually it turned out it was a rat scrapin' around inside a beef tin![31]

On other occasions, what had begun as a routine patrol had a dramatic ending. The soldier who tells of the following incident felt himself to be good on patrol, as he had been a poacher at home and had good night sight, but perhaps he was too confident:

> I used to guide the patrols to the 'gates' – gaps in our own wire which we wired in such a way that the wire could be easily pushed to one side to let our patrols out and in … one night we got completely lost in the darkness and instead of going to our own lines we found ourselves close to the Germans. There was a couple of Englishmen with us who were good at bombing and they lobbed half a dozen bombs right into the German trenches. There was complete silence for about five minutes after the bombs went off, then all hell broke loose from both sides. To crown it all when we got back to our wire I couldn't find the opening, so we had to stay out in no-man's-land till next morning. You'd have thought the officers would be glad to see us back but No. Me and the two Englishmen were going to be placed on charges until the Brigadier heard about it. We didn't get any medals for the stir we caused in the German lines but none of us landed in the guardhouse either …[32]

Gradually, the men did learn a sense of direction and a stealth that made them better soldiers. If there was an officer with them who understood German, a patrol would sometimes go right up to the edge of the German trenches and try to listen in, to pick up what the enemy were saying to each other. Useful information might be gleaned. Needless patrols, however, incurred ire among the rank and file of the Belfast Brigade, directed at the officers who seemed wasteful of human life in their planning:

> It was easy for some staff officer to order a junior to send out a patrol or to take one out while he sat … in some comfort and safety. It was our pals he was killing for no good reason. It was different when we were sent to probe the German lines with the aim of taking prisoners … If a friend was killed on this type of patrol then his death was not in vain …[33]

Tommy Ervine, of the East Belfast Volunteers, was a skilled man with the bayonet, and was useful to any patrol that was going to make contact with the Germans. He would blacken his face for camouflage, and take a supply of Mills bombs as well as rifle and bayonet:

> I was a PP man [permanent patrol] and one night I went out with Jack McVicker [an ex-boxer] and a fella called Skates. I was bayonet man on the raiding party – I went in front – each man had his duty. We went along this traverse of a German trench but we made noises in the water with our waders. Skates jumped up on the parapet and went along and took the pin out of a grenade and threw it ahead at a bunch of Germans round the next corner. We came round and found them – aw, it was a pitiful sight to look at them! Then there was a dugout with sixty or seventy steps down into it. Someone threw a couple of Mills bombs down before they could get out and they were cut to pieces down there. Well, three or four was alive and could walk and we got them to bring back. We didn't like to shoot them. We couldn't just go and murder a man. But we had to get away quick because the noise of Sammy's bombs alerted them. They sent up flares after us but we got back …[34]

Tommy's attitude illustrates the way in which a code of conduct still prevailed about whom one could kill or could not kill in wartime. To bomb a dugout was right and proper, but to shoot those who survived was entirely wrong. Ethical discrimination must have become increasingly difficult as many different new ways of killing the enemy were developed.

One of these methods was 'mining' – digging vast underground chambers beneath the enemy lines, which would be packed with explosives and then detonated. The Redan, near Beaumont-Hamel, was the main place where the Ulster Division was involved in mining. It was a source of much extra work for the soldiers, who had to carry sandbags full of the chalky soil sent up by the miners. Sometimes, the Germans would blow a mine and sometimes the British: when it blew, the men could feel the ground lift slightly and rock as if there had been an earth tremor.[35]

An even more sinister weapon was gas, and an essential part of training was the 'gas school', where the men learnt to use their masks in a gas chamber, and then when marching for a mile or more. The masks were still primitive, without even a proper mouthpiece, and things were made worse by particularly vicious instructors who insisted that the men keep them on for long periods of time.[36]

Gas warfare on the
Western Front,
as illustrated by
Jim Maultsaid
MICHAEL MAULTSAID

There was this thing like a small flour bag with two bits of glass in it which you were supposed to see through, but as often as not they were above or below your eyes and you'd stumble along like playing blindman's buff. After going a mile with a gas mask on I've seen the fittest man in the company lie down fairly gasping for breath. The first [gas masks] were little or no good at all. I've seen men coming out of the gas chamber where we tried them out in as bad a state as if they had no mask on at all.[37]

Those soldiers in the Medical Corps, or involved with stretcher-bearing duties, had to learn how to deal with a gas victim. Hugh James Adams, of the Pioneer Battalion, was told to think of the gas victim's lungs as a bottle. If the bottle was lying down, half full of water, there would be virtually no

Royal Irish Fusiliers wearing the primitive gas masks that
were in use in the early years of the war
ROYAL IRISH FUSILIERS MUSEUM

space at the neck, but if the bottle was sitting upright the water would be
well away from the neck – the same with the soldier's lungs half fall of gas.
He had to be left sitting upright, not lying down like other casualties. The
effects of severe exposure to poison gases were, of course, horrendous,
bringing about a painful, choking death, or, if the casualty recovered,
wreaking permanent damage to the respiratory system.[38] Hysteria about gas
was understandable when the Ulstermen first entered the trenches:

> When we first went into the trenches the orders about gas were alarmist –
> anyone smelling chlorine gas immediately to give the alarm by shouting
> 'gas', whereupon everybody was to put on their gas helmets and pass the
> alarm on to their neighbours further along the line. Gongs, made of
> empty shell cases hung up for the purpose, were to be rung and church
> bells behind the lines were to be tolled. Up to that time chloride and lime
> was used as a disinfectant in the latrines, and chloride and lime gives off
> chlorine gas. That being the case it was only a matter of time before
> someone smelt chlorine and panicked. This happened one evening ... we
> all put on our gas helmets immediately and waited to see what would
> happen. After five minutes we began to lift the corners of our helmets and

sniff the air, and as we could smell nothing we took them off. It was a still evening and behind us in the village of Mailly-Maillet ... we could hear the church bell tolling away and someone said to me, 'Just think of Padre Quinn running about Mailly-Maillet in a gas helmet!' I suppose it wasn't a very funny remark but it helped relieve the tension ...[39]

This burlesque aspect of gas warfare was short-lived. By December 1915 the relatively inefficient and detectable chlorine gas was being supplanted by phosgene – eighteen times more powerful and quite invisible. The victim who had inhaled a fatal dose did not realise till some time afterwards. He would die within two days of sustained and horrific retching and coughing in which up to four pints of yellow liquid would be brought up from the lungs in any single hour. Little wonder that poison gas became a source of such dread.

IN THE FRENCH VILLAGES

For the other two infantry brigades, the dread of horrific death was much less pressing. During a substantial part of November and December, the South Antrim Volunteers, for instance, were joined to the 12th Brigade at St-Léger-les-Domarts and Buigny l'Abbe, learning a lot about marching discipline, along the adjacent country roads, and also about the various modes of infantry attack. When staying in a village, the men might be engaged in work parties undertaking practical tasks to help improve the drainage or the roads. Billets varied in quality, but could sometimes be comparatively luxurious, as in St-Mauguille, where two companies of the South Antrim battalion were based in December 1915: hot and cold shower facilities were available for all the men. C Company had its mess in the home of Monsieur Vivien, manager of the local phosphate works, and Arthur Samuels found the house most comfortable and warm. He also enjoyed his time off duty when he could visit the nearby historic town of St-Riquier, whose ancient abbey had been founded by Irish monks in the sixth century.[40]

However, while officers occupied houses, very often the men were billeted in barns and outhouses, which were not so pleasant or comfortable, especially in colder weather. Barns were nearly set on fire sometimes when men tried to warm themselves by building extra fires in their braziers late

A French farmhouse behind the lines at Mesnil, where several officers of the 15th Royal Irish Rifles were temporarily housed
ROYAL ULSTER RIFLES MUSEUM

in the night.[41] Soldiers occasionally had to build their own beds in any available barn, cutting trees in lengths to fill the appropriate spaces. The 'springs' consisted of a tightly drawn stretch of one-inch rabbit wire held in place by staples.

Often, the men were busy with all kinds of tedious, menial tasks. At Beauval, the YCVs had to work under the guidance of a forestry expert, cutting down trees, making the branches into parcels of brushwood and binding them with wire rope for use in filling shell holes and gaps in the front line.[42] If it were raining or snowing, life seemed as bad as at the front itself. Divisional exercises in co-ordinated attack were sometimes undertaken in driving rain, sleet or snow, to the misery of all concerned. The building and maintenance activities also proved difficult for those with no great experience of handiwork:

The tradesmen used to give off something awful – 'It's not straight, Sammy! You'll never get mortar to stick to a dry stone wall – you'll have to wet it first! ... Ye're holding the float the wrong way!' It went on and on. We used to get our own back on them. By bending a piece of wire into a thing like an old-fashioned starting-handle ... and putting these in their palliasses. Many's an uncomfortable night they must have had trying to sleep![43]

This spell in the winter of 1915, spent in French villages, also gave the Ulstermen plenty of contact with the local people. There had been a lot of initial fear that the Catholic French and the militantly Protestant Volunteers would not mix well. Before leaving England, men had been lectured about the need to respect the numerous crucifixes, religious statues and shrines that they would encounter.[44] But according to Spender, the Ulster Division's relationship with the Catholic French was very good. He explains that the local population of Picardy had, indeed, been fearful of '20,000 wild Protestants' descending on them. However, it would seem that the Ulstermen endeared themselves to the Catholic clergy, who in turn wrote to the Vatican explaining their mistaken apprehension. Spender records (somewhat implausibly) that the 36th Division then received medals from the Pope, with an expression of his thanks for their treatment of the local Catholics! One of these medals was apparently presented to the senior chaplain by the local priest.[45]

If the relationship between French Catholic and Ulster Protestant was mellower than had been anticipated, it was also a matter for banter and humour. Tommy Ervine remarked that the fleurs-de-lis decorating the Roman Catholic chapel at Mailly-Maillet were in fact orange-coloured. Orange lilies were the Ulster Protestant's symbolic flower, and so Tommy and his friends had great fun trying to point out their 'mistake' to the local people.[46]

In practice, the unhygienic and awkward behaviour of a crowd of raw soldiers was an even greater source of friction than were any religious allegiances:

We used to dirty their wells by putting the greasy old dixies down them to clean off the grease and food ... [so] they used to hide the windlasses of the wells so we couldn't get at them.[47]

Before long, however, many of the prejudices built up in the early weeks were overcome, and a friendly relationship eventually developed, particularly between the rural Ulster battalions and the French farming families. Some even saw similarities with the Ulster character. The French farmers

> ... were like ourselves and we felt more at home with them than we did with the English folk ... the people were like the Ballymena folk, looked after the pence ... you found that they were shy at first but soon we became great friends and many's a bottle of wine we drank together. The one thing we noticed – they were jealous of their women and there was not many of the lads did any courtin' at all.

In the end, even the most fearful Orangeman made his visit to a French house, and found that the human contact overcame the previous sense of alienation:

> It was the first time I had ever been in a Frenchman's house for we thought them a bit heathen with all the idols they put up alongside the roads ... There was this girl about eight or nine years old, she had the nicest eyes I've ever seen. And she sat on my knee and pulled my side whiskers. I'm sure she broke many a man's heart before she married.[48]

The same benevolence was not felt towards the French army, however, who were regarded as poor soldiers. Hugh James Adams said of them, 'The French was a nervy type of people. They were all right goin' forward but no good goin' back.'[49] According to Tommy Russell, from Newcastle, County Down, 'a lot of our women on crutches would have been better than the French'.

One of the most deplored aspects was that the French kept their trenches in a poor state for the British who may have had to take them over. 'They'd have left their trenches filthy', said Tommy Russell. 'They didn't bury their dead properly. Just stuffed them into the wall of their trench', recalled Tommy Ervine.[50]

Perhaps a story from Stewart-Moore gives an amusing if macabre slant on this problem: it concerns 'a Frenchman who had been buried so hastily that his feet stuck out, so the British used to polish his feet every morning as a mark of respect!'[51]

HEALTH UNDER STRAIN

As the Ulster Division's sojourn in Picardy continued, it was gradually acknowledged that the conditions of warfare were a far more formidable problem than the actual enemy. For weeks together, trenches could be knee deep in flood water, and even if the water was shallow there would be thick mud. One communications trench near Mesnil, called 'Jacob's ladder', was infamous, in Cyril Falls' words, for making the men feel like 'flies in treacle'.[52]

There was also the cold: men's hands grew chapped and hacked; the trigger of the rifle was often so cold that it stuck to the finger. The frost and ice of midwinter were very severe:

> You'll hardly believe this but I've seen men frozen to the ground; boots frozen into the mud, after a couple of hours on the firestep.[53]

A bad snow could prevent rations from getting through to the front line, and hot food was least available when needed most. Hard biscuits and bully beef might be all the men got, and good drinking water might be unavailable, so they sucked the ice that formed on the trenches, and this gave them stomach upsets. One awfully cold spell prompted G.H.M. to write in his diary:

> Very cold winter night. Snow coming thick, everywhere white. I am in a rotten billet … heavy snow fall. The cold is intense. My section had to move to a new billet. The old billet was simply snowed out … The night is dark and I am far from home.'[54]

Sometimes, under bad conditions, the walls of the less-well-built trenches would collapse. For a rural battalion, handling of spades was a familiar thing, but for the city battalions it might be less so:

> They were all from the backstreets of Belfast, tradesmen whose lives had been spent working in the shipyard and linen mills so they were unskilled in handling spades and shovels. Throwing sticky mud up out of the trench is no easy task especially when you have to keep your head down for fear of German snipers … Next to us was a battalion of the Royal Irish Regiment from Wexford and the South-East of Ireland. Suddenly our Brigadier-General turned up and took in the situation at a glance. 'Come on now,' he said, 'stick to it Ulster, don't be disheartened, there's a Southern Irish regiment just around the corner, they're watching you, don't let them see Ulster giving way.'[55]

Needless to say, clothing became sodden, damp and filthy, and on reaching billets, men tried to dry out their uniform and scrape off the mud that had accumulated in their hair, fingernails and buttons.

When the thaw came, there would be fresh flooding. In the words of the Armagh Volunteers' war diarist: 'everywhere slush and dripping rooves'.[56]

Of course, the weather was not the only 'natural' enemy: there were also the vermin. Rumours spread about rats that were larger than cats and would go for you when you were asleep. A rat bite was, indeed, a serious thing: one officer in Crozier's battalion had to be evacuated due to blood poisoning brought on by a rat bite on the nose, inflicted while the victim was asleep.[57]

Lice, fleas and other parasites added to the horror. An effort was made to clear the men of their 'unwelcome visitors', but not always successfully, and the joke was heard that the fleas enjoyed the bath even more than the men did! When lice gathered in the men's puttees, they were instructed, somewhat fancifully, to take them off over puddles of water so that the lice would fall in and drown. The powder given to the soldiers to help kill the vermin often brought out large, red, itchy blotches on the skin – even more of a torment than the lice themselves.[58]

General bad health was a serious problem for the Belfast battalion during these winter months. Older officers were susceptible – Ormerod, commander of the West Belfast Volunteers, developed ill health in midwinter, a situation not helped when the roof of a dugout fell on him and a beam landed on his back, trapping him to his bed.[59] Even fit men succumbed: Hugh Stewart, who did not have too taxing an exposure to the trenches, developed bronchitis and had to spend time in No. 11 Station Hospital at Rouen.[60] Many men suffered 'bouts of trembling and fever'. If it was bad, they were moved to hospital; if not, the patient had to stay in the dugouts for a day and swallow plenty of 'a bitter tasting white powder that dried your mouth up'. For an upset stomach, there was 'a thick black stuff like treacle'. When stomach disorders were prevalent, the sergeant would give out the medicine to everybody, day and night. Unfortunately, his method of distribution was none too hygienic, as he used the same spoon for everyone. Many a young man must have felt that he was a long way from home and mother's loving care.[61]

Soldiers who had had indoor jobs before the war were subject to swelling of the hands and feet. One County Armagh soldier was given a bottle of

Troops being treated for foot rot – the result of hours spent
standing in water-logged trenches
ROYAL ULSTER RIFLES MUSEUM

horse liniment by an English soldier, and he soon found that it took the pain
and stiffness from his joints. Perpetual standing on wet, cold ground or in
flood water, wearing socks that stayed wet, brought about 'trench foot' – a
complaint in which the skin became tender and started to peel, leaving 'raw,
sore bits that stung like a nettle sting'. In the Ulster Division, it was known
as 'foot rot' and regarded as a curse. John Kennedy Hope's feet felt like
'wrinkled tripe' – only clean, dry socks and plenty of ointment had any
beneficial effect.[62] Pig's fat was often used as a remedy, though not always
in the orthodox manner:

> The only man in our lot who never complained of 'foot rot' was the
> sergeant. This old fellow fought in the Boer War and farmed one of the
> worst pieces of land in Ireland. No matter how long he was in the
> trenches and no matter how cold and wet the weather was he never had
> foot rot. We used to ask him why, just to hear him bellow –
> 'By the Lord Harry, youse put that pig's fat on your feet. Look at me!
> The fittest man that ever walked out of Rathfriland. Now me,
> I spread the pig's fat on me biscakes and it works better from the inside
> than it does from the outside!'[63]

Heavy marching was to play havoc with feet, and the situation was often exacerbated by ill-fitting boots and by socks that had been very badly darned by the men themselves. Thigh-high gumboots were issued, and proved a boon, as did the waterproof capes distributed in wet weather, although these items were sometimes in a bad state of repair. Hope thought that he looked like a sewer-man in his gumboots,[64] and the Armagh Volunteers also had reason to curse them when on 14 November they had to wear them to march twenty-nine kilometres to Punchevillers on freshly fallen snow. Hardly a man in the battalion failed to experience excruciating pain as a result.[65]

Toothache was another problem for the soldiers. Tommy Jordan remembered, with considerable unhappiness, a dentist called McKinley. Although he was 'so knock-kneed that a kick on the leg would have knocked him over', he was strong enough to pull out a bad tooth with a pair of huge pliers – and without the help of painkillers.[66]

Against the winter winds, the men had precious little protection. At this stage, there was no tin hat – that would be issued in 1916. Puttees were worn around the ankles and calfs, and if wound too tightly caused bad circulation. In the worst weather, warm sheepskin waistcoats were issued. One officer in the YCVs was unimpressed by these, and on first seeing them being worn, remarked: 'Well, "C" company, you look like a lot of London prostitutes. Dismiss.'[67]

On the march, the soldiers each had to carry more than sixty pounds of equipment. A man's haversack contained emergency rations of bully beef, tea, sugar and biscuits, plus utensils. In his valise would be spare clothing, greatcoat, blanket, and a hold-all containing such items as toothbrush, razor, comb, shaving soap, washing soap and a spare pair of braces. The infantry men also carried rifle and ammunition, clasp knife, gas helmet, iodine, water-proof sheet, mess tin, bayonet and scabbard, entrenching tool, water bottle and various other items, including the 'small book' in which one's name, number and corps were written together with a record of service to date in the army. The book also contained information useful to a soldier during his period of service – such as how to salute various officers, how to make an official complaint, and 'how to prevent sore feet'. Also included was a will form.

For men to lose any of their equipment was a serious misdemeanour, and they had to pay the penalty. Hope lost a pair of goggles that had been issued to minimise the effects of tear gas; in a subsequent kit inspection, he was reprimanded and the item – cost 1s 1¾d – was deducted from his pay. It made a considerable hole in the basic remuneration of a 'shillin' a day'.[68]

Among the useful items the soldier dare not lose was his knife. Arthur Samuels had a splendid one, containing a marlin spike for splicing ropes, button hooks, and special spikes for 'hoking out' stones from the feet of mules and horses; and, of course, there was a blade to cut open the ever-present tin of bully beef.[69]

Luxuries occasionally made life more pleasant for the soldiers, and gifts from home helped. Sometimes, presents arrived from institutions to whole battalions, as when the Irish Fusiliers received one thousand handkerchiefs from the Queen Alexandra Field Force Fund. The same day, over fifteen thousand cigarettes arrived from Messrs Vickers and Sons, and from the provincial newspaper, the *Armagh Guardian*.[70]

The medical system at the front had developed along certain lines for dealing with those who were ill or wounded according to the severity of their condition. A casualty would be taken first to the regimental aid post, usually in or near a trench, where very basic assistance could be given. If need be, he was then sent back to the advanced dressing station, where wounds could be properly dressed, morphia given and cigarettes lit. If there was a severe problem, the casualty would then be evacuated to the main dressing station, which was a temporary hospital where some surgery could be performed. From there, the cars of the motor-ambulance convoy could take him to the casualty clearing station and thence to a base hospital.

> Not until I went into the trenches with the 107th Brigade did I get the
> first shock of how badly a man could be shot up and still be alive … in
> the first-aid posts there was somebody coming and going all the time. The
> types of things we treated on the spot was minor injuries. Cuts, bruises,
> sprains, small burns, blisters and that sort of injury. Eyes we seldom
> touched except to wash them out and cover with a clean pad if we had
> one and tried to get the soldier back to the hospital.

If emergencies required 'life or death' attention, the doctor would be sent for urgently, or a stretcher would be used to rush the casualty to the dressing station; in the early days, there were no field telephones to facilitate

A scene every soldier dreamt of – a return to Blighty with a
survivable injury and the comfort of a hospital bed
SOMME MUSEUM

the process of obtaining the appropriate help. When a big patrol was going
out or an enemy attack was expected, a complete medical team came to
the locality. A doctor would be on hand, too, if there was severe shelling.

The ordinary soldiers admired the men of the Royal Army Medical
Corps (RAMC) for their courage when they had to go out into no-man's-
land with nothing but a stretcher and a few dressings to tend to the
wounded, and for their continual acts of mercy in the aid posts in the face
of immense suffering and horror. But they also envied the medics when the
troops were on the move:

> We marched everywhere but they went in style in the motor ambulances.
> They could brew up a pot of tea any time they felt like it. We went cold
> and hungry – they had plenty of blankets and warm food.

Occasionally, there would not be enough orderlies about, and an
infantryman might have to help out as a stretcher-bearer: the job could be
very difficult:

> There was one night four of us was carrying back a wounded man and the
> doctor was walking beside us trying to keep the arm of the wounded man

as steady as he could … the four of us was slipping and sliding about in
the mud and cursing and swearing for all we were worth. All of a sudden
the doctor said, 'Don't look at the mud, look up, men, look up at the
stars.' Many's the night when I was up to my ankles in mud I
remembered what the doctor said and I looked at the stars and I forgot
all about the mud.

Inside the aid posts was a stock of blankets, antiseptic ointments,
bandages and dressings, quinine powder, ether, chloroform, tourniquets,
morphia and opium, spirit lamps and stoves for sterilising scalpels,
hypodermic needles and syringes, and 'sealing irons' for dealing with stumps
when limbs were amputated. Stretchers were piled against a wall.

Stretcher cases coming in were normally treated where they lay. There
was a bucket of dried sand or soil to throw over pools of blood that would
form, and then the floor would be scraped clean with a spade. Shock,
lockjaw and gangrene were terrible killers of those with bad wounds, since
medical care really was primitive. There was no such thing as blood
transfusion. One member of the RAMC, who was transferred to the infantry,
said the transfer was like entering another world because 'For the Infantry
orders were orders … in the Medical Corps everyone was encouraged to use
their wits and treat the wounded and the sick as best he could.'

The Medical Corps also supervised preventive measures against disease
– insisting on chlorination of cooking and drinking water, and introducing
immunisation against typhoid. Old RAMC men recall that, in general, the aid
posts treated two or three cases of sickness for every wound victim. They
were warned that to miss a case of typhoid could put a battalion out of
action for six months, and they had to be extra vigilant.

The wounded were easy to deal with. It was the man with a rise in
temperature and a sore head and a sickness in the bowels that really
worried you. Had he had bad food and was it food poisoning or was it the
beginning of a fever … Sure as fate if you sent one man back in the
morning you'd have had a dozen with the same complaints before the
night came. Then you'd think – are they skiving or is it serious? … By
May and June we could fair sum up the men and separate the sick from
the skivers.

All the training the men had done in Britain and France – learning about the body and health, about broken bones and splints, about how to stop bleeding, how to sterilise instruments, and how to use the saws and cutters required for amputation – did not prepare them for the first shock of drastic surgery:

> The first time I had to hold an arm while it was being cut off, the surgeon, an Englishman called Mr Chamberlain, gave me a couple of tots of brandy. It fair turned you to be left holding some poor soldier's arm in your hands. Later on it took less out of you.

What made the work particularly difficult was that the conditions were cramped and unhygienic. Very often, in emergencies, a medical orderly would have to perform a quick job that a doctor of experience should really have done:

> There was not enough room to swing a cat in them [the first-aid posts]. When you broke a seal on a dressing it was blue-moulded. Bandages were black instead of white. There was no water. The smell of blood would have made you retch. Maybe a man would have lay out for a night and you could have smelt the gangrene before they brought him in. Now and again when you got more experienced you had to try your hand at work a doctor should have been doing. I was in charge of the post one night when they brought in a soldier with the left wrist cut through and the man was bleeding to death. We put on a tourniquet which stemmed the flow a bit but there was only a few strands of flesh holding on the hand. We tried tying off the main blood vessels but it was no use. He was dying and would be dead before reaching the next station unless we did something at once. I decided to cut the hand off. I ran the blade of the scalpel through the flame of a spirit lamp, and cut. We used a sealing iron and got the bleeding stopped. When I thought about it for a week or so afterwards I broke out in a cold sweat. Even when the doctor told me I had saved his life it gave me little comfort. There it is: you just did your best; we all did.

It is not surprising that many doctors and medical orderlies developed stress, and that some 'took to the bottle'. Others, though, developed their own form of spiritual consolation:

131

I once asked this doctor who seemed so hard on the outside how he stuck it ... 'Do you see that star up there?' He pointed to a bright one over our heads. 'It's the nearest to us, others lie millions of times further away. Surely the God that made that can give me the inner security and ability to turn to Him for comfort rather than the bottle. At times when I operate I pray that whatever lies beyond will sustain me just through this operation. I never think of the next. One step is enough. I do not ask to see what is round the corner. Live by that, my man. Live in day-tight compartments, you'll do your work better and live closer to God.' The thing about this was I never saw him at a church parade or anything like that. But somehow he seemed to be on talking terms with God and talked to him the way you and me talk to each other. If he asked God a question he expected God to answer him. One night after he worked all night to try to save a sniper shot through the lung, he said to no one in particular, 'I wanted to give that youngster another chance. The hardest thing in life is to have to take no for an answer.'[71]

FOOD AND DRINK

To keep body and soul together, regular food was essential for the men in the line. The divisional supply column would go daily to the rail head to meet the 'pack train'. The supplies would then be brought up toward the front and divided into four batches: one for each infantry brigade and one for the rest of the divisional units. Rations were brought up to battalion HQ after dusk, very often by mule. In a well-organised battalion (and battalions did vary a lot), the food was prepared as far as possible before it was sent to the men – usually leaving only the heating-up to be done. All the men were supposed to obtain at least one hot meal per day. However, heating was often impractical, and the infamous ration biscuits proved to be the staple diet, along with bully beef. The biscuits were sometimes minced up to form the basic dough for sausage rolls and jam tarts.

> Sometimes you got a tot of rum to take the winter coldness out of your bones. When it was broad daylight the men stood down for breakfast. Tea was usually lukewarm with condensed milk in it, bread and margarine if you were lucky. Now and then we got cheese. A boiled egg was a luxury.

If things was bad it was hard tack and water ... we got one hot meal
nearly every day. It came down in containers like the old blue stone
copper sprayers you used for spraying the potatoes. It was hot when it left
the field kitchen but it was cold by the time it reached us so we heated it
up in the dugout ... The hard tack biscuits were like compressed sawdust
and about as tasty. I've seen me knocking the grubs out of them by
hitting them against the butt of a rifle. We nearly always soaked them in
water to soften them up a bit. Them that had bad teeth used to make the
biscuits with a tin of beef and water into a sort of pie and eat that. We got
brown bread now and again but it went blue and moulded in a day or
two and was not good to eat ... Cigarettes came up every evening with
the rations and a bit of pipe tobacco, also we got a plug of chewing
tobacco or a piece of pigtail.[72]

'McConaghie's rations' – beans, peas and meat heated in a tin to make
a kind of stew – were soon developed, and became common fare on the
Western Front. Hugh Stewart recalled with pleasure the lovely smell of
McConaghie's rations cooking, and although a loaf of bread had to be
divided up amongst four a day, there was sometimes the bonus of a parcel
from home that might contain an apple tart, a tin of pears, a cake or some
chocolate. When Tommy Ervine received chocolate in the winter, he
would sometimes melt fresh snow into water and drop a bit of chocolate
into it, making a tasty hot drink.[73] The local *estaminet* behind the lines would
provide some pleasant alternatives in food and drink. G.H.M. used to enjoy
spending a good part of a winter's day behind the lines 'in a café close to the
stove drinking citron and grenadine'.[74] Tommy Russell enjoyed a delicacy
he described as 'jelly with an egg in the middle', as well as fresh bread –
'dupang', as the men called it – for two centimes.

Of course, any opportunity for acquiring fresh food was to be taken.
When the North Belfast Volunteers were marching to join the 4th Division,
they passed through a region full of apple trees laden with fruit – unripe
but irresistible. Time and again men left the ranks to pick the apples. After
two days of this trouble, there had to be discipline, and officers were ordered
to march at the rear of the column to see more clearly who the culprits
might be.[75]

Standards of cleanliness often deteriorated as the men grew used to army

Stew being served up in the trenches
ROYAL ULSTER RIFLES MUSEUM

life. Food was food, no matter about a little accompanying dirt. G.H.M. sometimes found that his breakfast had been dropped in the mud and picked up again – but the men ate it all the same.[76] Hugh Stewart recalled bacon and eggs being fried on dixie lids behind the lines in the local farmyard; when the food fell on the mucky ground, there was a race between the hens and the men.[77]

The processes of reheating food were primitive and dangerous. Each dugout was allocated candles or paraffin oil for oil lamps; using old biscuit tins or empty shell cases, the men built a candle stove to reheat the food. It was slow but gave the soldiers something to do when they were bored and inactive. Some other means of reheating were unorthodox:

> We used to get the powder from a few bullets and set small stones round it, then put a tin of bully on the stones. When you lit the powder it burnt very quickly but it heated the meat up a bit. Another way we tried was to wind a length of slow-burning fuse round the tin then light the fuse with a cigarette end. If the fuse burnt slowly as it should have then the meat was warmed to a nice eating heat but if it burnt up quickly then the tin exploded, pieces of tin and meat all over the place ...
> If you were right and well back in the support trenches times was not

too bad. You could light a fire well down in the trenches and it could not be seen from the front. That way you got a drop of hot soup or a mug of cocoa made in the condensed milk. We had a tinker with us, very slow at the reading and writing but with a great pair of hands. He made mugs and tea drawers from scraps of tin. He even made a stove. But one night we brought it in to the shelter we had near the picket lines for the mules and horses, and the fumes from the stove nearly killed us. That put an end to the warm hut at night.[78]

The officers' mess provided a much better standard of comfort and cuisine. A hint of the extra luxuries the officers were able to enjoy may be had from the following description by Stewart-Moore:

Willie Ewart remained Battalion Mess Secretary and in that capacity he bought ... butter from Rathkenny creamery on the Ballymena–Cushendall Road, tinned foods of the more luxurious kind, and whisky. Once when he ordered a case of whisky he was sent a case of cherry whisky, which is very like cherry brandy, by mistake. Being a liqueur it lasted us a long time; I would have liked it better had we had liqueur glasses; drunk out of an enamel mug it had a peculiar taste which I can still remember. In 'C' company we had a cook called Pollock who could be relied upon to produce a three-course dinner cooked over a charcoal brazier in his kitchen dugout.[79]

CHRISTMAS IN THE TRENCHES

As winter closed in, the men began to anticipate Christmas. But the month of December also included Lundy Day on the eighteenth – an Orange celebration in which the Ulster Protestants re-enacted the execution of an infamous traitor to their cause. The South Antrim Volunteers went about their celebrations in a businesslike way, preparing two stuffed figures of Lundy – the largest was eleven feet in height, full of straw and with rockets stuck in various places on the traitor's person. He had large wooden feet and wire knees, and his head was filled with gunpowder and topped with an admiral's hat. A torch-lit procession, headed by this figure, wound its way to one end of the village where the South Antrim battalion was based. A band

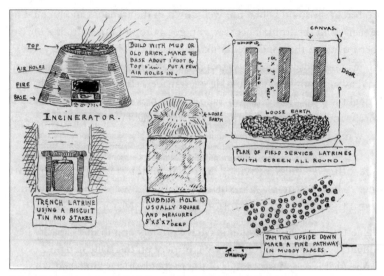

Some of the basics of trench life, from Jim Maultsaid's sketch book
MICHAEL MAULTSAID

played famous Orange airs such as 'No Surrender', and then Lundy was set on fire amidst cheers and yells. Bombs made of jam tins were thrown into a pond, and inevitably broke the windows of nearby houses. Then the procession re-formed and marched to the other end of the village, where the second Lundy was burnt with similar ceremony.[80]

Leading up to Christmas, there were more peaceful forms of recreation. The men sang and played cards, and sometimes, in quieter periods in the line, the performance of a carol would be followed by a German recital coming back across no-man's-land. Hugh Stewart recalled:

> A fella in the German trenches had a cornet and he played 'Silent Night' in the evenings, and soon an eejit near us let rip at him. When it died down we heard a voice in lovely English call over to us – 'What are you shooting for? What are you shooting for?'[81]

Battalion officers provided turkeys, geese and hams for their men as seasonal gifts, and these were supplemented by food sent over from home by such bodies as the Irish Women's Association. Some men bought sucking pigs from local French farmers, and fed them to a good weight before killing them for Christmas meat. Bottles of brandy were purchased from *estaminets*, and luxuries such as dried fruit and candied ginger made a miraculous appearance. Presents from home were opened, and men were delighted to find such useful things as shaving sticks, socks, gloves and scented soap.[82]

How Christmas Day itself was spent depended on where each battalion was stationed. Stewart-Moore, with the North Belfast Volunteers, had a miserable day; as newly appointed Lewis-gun officer, he was shunted from one end of the battalion to the other. Like his men, he was annoyed at having to spend Christmas Day in the line, and when he finally 'came to roost' in D Company, he managed only a slice of pork pie for his main course.[83]

The South Antrim Volunteers had a better time. Arthur Samuels, in his comfortable billet, enjoyed excellent fare; the menu at Madame Vivien's house was: *potage Vivien* followed by *poulet roti au capitaine* and *rosbif*, then plum pudding, *café* and liqueurs, and the accompanying wines included muscatel and Bordeaux. Everyone rose to drink the health of the French president, the king of England, 'Mesdames, Messures Vivien' and 'Les Allies au paix glorieuse'.[84]

The Young Citizen Volunteers, based at Ergnies, had an excellent Christmas dinner, followed by 'several impromptu concerts'. There had been a competition to see whose billets could be the best decorated and the judges awarded the £2 prize to A Company.[85]

But within a matter of hours, it was back to the old routine. The next important event in the calendar was when the division, having been reunited with the Belfast Brigade, was given full responsibility for a section of the line.

INTO THE LINE, FEBRUARY 1916

At noon on 7 February 1916 the 36th took charge of the line from the River Ancre to the Mailly-Maillet–Serre road, with the 107th and 108th Brigades in the front trenches and the 109th in reserve. A field company of engineers was attached to each brigade, and a separate machine-gun company was also formed in each brigade. Further back was the artillery; the 36th's own gunners arrived from their training bases within a few weeks, and stationed themselves with guns hidden in pits or amongst trees or houses; in open positions, they were camouflaged by materials that matched

Soldiers of the Royal Irish Rifles dressed in sheepskin and goatskin jackets during the cold winter of 1915–16. John Martin is second from the left in the back row.
WILL MARTIN

the surrounding fields. The men had dugouts close by, and there were also adjacent pits containing up to four hundred rounds of ammunition per gun.[86]

One group of soldiers particularly envied in the division were those in charge of the well-appointed observation post on the Mesnil Ridge, manned by members of the Cyclist Company, including George Lindsay, who found the job interesting and could remember clearly the one train from Bapaume to Arras that steamed along punctually each day, several miles behind the German lines. The time could also be read each day, with the aid of a telescope, on Bapaume church clock tower; the countryside over there seemed rich and verdant. For its interesting view and good facilities, Mesnil Ridge was hard to beat; in one soldier's words, it was 'quare and homely'.[87]

Another specialised unit was the 'Trench Mortar Battery' – a number of which were established. Stewart-Moore was transferred to the newly formed 107th Battery, and the change necessitated a training course in Amiens. This was a pleasant diversion, as Amiens, although only a short distance from the front, still preserved a reasonably normal lifestyle and had several fine hotels where Stewart-Moore, true to form, managed to dine in style. On arriving back to his trench-mortar responsibilities, he found the discipline in this

A trench in the Ulster Division's Hamel sector after a
bombardment by the enemy
SOMME MUSEUM

much smaller unit appreciably more relaxed than in the infantry. Seven
officers and two or three dozen men were responsible for four mortars.
They practised on a scale model of the German trenches, which had been
dug outside the village of Varennes.[88]

The whole division was now gaining much wider and more intensive
experience of trench warfare, and the possibility of death was ever present.
The first soldier in the 36th to die in action had been Samuel Hill, of the
Mid Antrim Volunteers, who was killed on 22 October 1915.[89] Other
deaths had soon followed. Tommy Ervine had had a friend named Tom –
a good carpenter who 'carried his saw around as much as his rifle' – who was
shot by a sniper and died, much to Tommy's grief. Another friend, named
Hopkins, had a lucky escape: a bullet lodged in the entrenching tool he
carried on his thigh – caught in the leather scabbard, and spent and flattened
like a coin against the blade.[90] Jim Maultsaid was never to forget it when his
friend Willie was killed by a shell. He recalled the horror of seeing his
friend's hand severed and still clasping the handle of the machine gun he had
been holding when he was suddenly blown to pieces.[91]

As the months passed, experience taught the men how to act safely – to
keep their heads down, for instance, to avoid the sniper's bullet. No one

could avoid the unexpected shell that landed precisely where you had been standing, but casualties were still few and far between, and the Ulstermen were occupying a relatively quiet sector.

G.H.M. helped steel himself by inserting inspiring quotations in his diary, seeking perhaps a philosophical calm:

> We, who neither are nor ever will be great men, and who do not much care whether we are great men or no, at least let us strive to be honest men, and to have common sense.

This quotation from Oliver Goldsmith was followed a little later by the famous, if impossible, dictum, 'To know all is to understand all and to understand all is to forgive all.' Gradually, like so many men, G.H.M. learnt to adopt a kind of indifference without which each spell in the trenches would have been unendurable:

> I brought up hot cocoa to 10 platoon at 10 p.m. Fritz had the impertinence to send over some shells when and where I was giving out the cocoa. We took no notice.[92]

Indeed, there was little point in ducking once you heard the whizz of a bullet, as Stewart-Moore explained to one visitor to the front line:

> One evening our Brigade Chaplain, Padre Quinn, turned up as I was about to visit my two machine-gun teams ... as we walked ... every now and again we would hear the crack of a bullet going by and each time we heard it the padre would duck down on the ground. I could not convince him that when he heard the bullet it had gone past and all danger was over. The bullet that gets you is the one you don't hear.

After a severe bombardment – if he came through the din safely and ascertained that no infantry attack was following – there was nothing Stewart-Moore enjoyed more than to head back to the dugout and calm down by eating some good food. After one shelling, he managed to finish a tin of excellent pears with tinned milk (no cream being available), rounded off with a strong cup of coffee.[93]

Even during the worst bombardment, someone would be capable of relieving the tension, as Arthur Samuels found out:

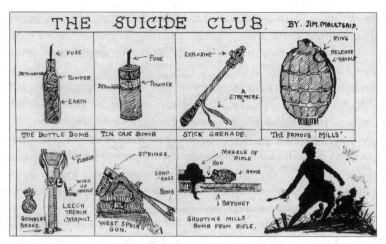

Jim Maultsaid illustrated some of the weapons
available to the Ulster soldier
MICHAEL MAULTSAID

While the shells went over and round us … I was lying flat on my
stomach to avoid some shrapnel that burst near. I … noticed a head
emerging from the earth which had fallen in all around. Suddenly there
was a splutter, the head moved and a very solemn voice said,
'Boys–o–boys, it's about time the referee blew his whistle.'[94]

Some men had better luck than others in avoiding confrontation with
war's horrors. The 240-or-so men of C Company, South Antrim Volunteers,
for instance, did not experience any fatalities until 29 February 1916, when
a young man called Watts was blown to pieces whilst standing outside the
door of his Mesnil billet, smoking a pipe. It was a stray shell.[95]

For those finding the whole experience of war a strain, alcohol was a
temptation – especially for the officer with the resources to consume drink
and possibly to avoid detection. Crozier, the ever-zealous teetotaller, was to
record with glee the consequences of the 'demon drink'. Hackett, his
orderly, got so drunk that he fell asleep in no-man's-land, was taken
prisoner, and spent the rest of his war in Germany. On another occasion,
Crozier went up to inspect the company commanded by that 'portly
schoolmaster', George Gaffikin, and found him drunk and asleep under a

waterproof sheet, with an empty whiskey bottle nearby. He decided to deal with the situation tolerantly but firmly, and next morning – over a welcome hot breakfast at HQ – he extracted a promise of teetotalism from Gaffikin for the duration of the war.

One moonlit night, near Hamel, Crozier found another bibulous officer in his dugout, drunkenly gazing at a picture of his wife and refusing to go out and supervise his men's trench-digging activities. That night, a high explosive shell killed the officer. When they dug the corpse out, little was left but a leg, an arm and a scrap of cardboard with a portion of his wife's photograph on it. 'I send you the enclosed photograph', wrote Crozier to the widow. 'He always thought so much of you and spoke so feelingly of you. This photo was on him when he died.'

For 'cowards', the army had no place. Crozier, as a top officer, was in a position to know about those men for whom the strains of the front were too much. He knew of one sergeant-major – an excellent and experienced soldier – who threw a detonator into a brazier so that it would explode and cause him some minor injuries that would warrant sick leave. Evacuated to hospital with a wounded hand, he was tried by court martial on suspicion of cowardice, and reduced to the rank of sergeant.

The strain was to take its toll, too, in suicide victims. Crozier once came on the corpse of a man in a front-line trench with a fresh bullet wound to the head. The man's rifle lay nearby with an empty cartridge case in the breech. Reluctant to expose the soldier's problems, Crozier gave 'the credit' to a sniper.[96]

The threat of punishment for 'cowardice' was always firmly emphasised to the men, and punishment would take the form of humiliation in front of one's fellows. The brutal laws of war became evident:

> You had the authority to shoot even your chum if he showed the white feather at all. They'd have shot you just for lookin' round! And then there was number one field punishment – they'd have braced you to the wheel of a gun with a rope. They'd even have tied you to a gate – but the French was none too keen on that because they thought we was imitating the crucifix.[97]

In fact, a soldier of the 36th Division was indeed shot for cowardice during the winter of 1915–16. He was a private in the West Belfast

Volunteers, and by admission of Crozier himself, he was 'a refined lad, of good family; an upright, honest lad with his young faith and his ideals … he was merely fragile'. According to the details, which Crozier allows us to glimpse in his books about his war experiences, the young man had been only seventeen when he had joined up, much to his mother's distress. During the worst of the winter weather in 1915–16, he disappeared from a post at the Serre Road section of the front. A fortnight later, he was picked up by the military police, in civilian clothes, at the coast, having divested himself of rifle, ammunition and equipment. It was decided that the desertion was a serious enough offence to warrant an execution – probably, in large measure, *pour encourager les autres*, to stiffen resolve and to instil greater discipline.

The deserter from the 9th Battalion wrote his last letters, prayed with the chaplain, and was then allowed to get very drunk before being taken out and tied to a stake in the back garden of a villa at Mailly-Maillet. Beyond the wall of the garden, on the road outside, the battalion lined up. There was snow on the ground. The victim was bound by ropes, and 'There are hooks on the post; we always do things thoroughly in the Rifles. He is hooked on like dead meat in a butcher's shop'. The firing party, due to nerves, did not manage to kill the victim with the first volley, and a final shot was required to complete the execution. Afterwards, 'we march back to breakfast while the men of a certain company pay the last tribute at the graveside of an unfortunate comrade. This is war.'

Later, the divisional commander wrote to Crozier to commend the battalion on its 'soldierly bearing in the face of great strain'. With the assistance of the chaplain, the deserter's death was reported at home as a 'death in action' so as to spare his relatives. However, news of the execution seeped through, and was not well received in certain circles in Belfast. A little later, one of Crozier's officers, when on leave, was tackled about it, and the incident was described to him in angry terms as 'a very discreditable affair for the battalion and a disgrace to the city'. To many, it seemed to confirm Crozier's reputation as a callous officer; he could easily have used his influence to have had the death sentence rescinded.[98]

Most men hoped that if they had to die, it would be an honourable death. Before a major offensive, those who had not already done so were encouraged to fill in their wills. Usually, for a young man with few possessions, it was simply a matter of indicating that the whole of his property should go to his next of kin. Part of that property would, of course, include such personal effects as were found on the soldier's body or in his haversack or valise – to be sent back home as a tangible reminder of the death in battle of a son, a husband or father.

The first news a family would receive of a soldier's death would usually be an emotionless letter from the War Office, indicating that the Army Council had asked the War Office to inform the relatives of their bereavement. The usual phrase was 'killed in action', unless the soldier had 'died owing to wounds'. After a major incident, men could simply be reported as missing, leaving the relatives to wonder if there was hope in the possibility that the soldier had been taken prisoner.

HOME THOUGHTS

What the relatives did look forward to was a regular note or letter from a loved one in France. The simplest form of communication was the field postcard, but it was very limited. Letters in ordinary envelopes could be sent frequently, but might be censored by officers of the man's own battalion in case they revealed any demoralising or secret details; many men were therefore reluctant to disclose much personal emotion in their letters. A confidential letter was possible inside a 'green envelope'. This would not be censored locally, but could be subject to a spot check at the base. Green envelopes were available only infrequently.

Some men, like Hugh James Adams, never wrote a letter, and made do with the occasional field postcard. The reason for many men's unwillingness to write was a sheer reluctance to engage in the emotionally disturbing effort of composing a letter, but there was also the problem of illiteracy. (This was also a problem for relatives in Ireland, and so the trade of 'letter writer' flourished: for a few pence, you could get a professional writer to put together the letter you wanted for your son, brother or husband.)[99]

Such letters as did arrive home – like this one from a South Antrim Volunteer – often revealed little of what the trenches were actually like:

NOTHING is to be written on this side except the date and signature of the sender. Sentences not required may be erased. If anything else is added the post card will be destroyed.

[Postage must be prepaid on any letter or post card addressed to the sender of this card.]

I am quite well.

~~I have been admitted into hospital~~

{ ~~sick~~ } ~~and am going on well.~~
{ ~~wounded~~ } ~~and hope to be discharged soon.~~

~~I am being sent down to the base.~~

I have received your { ~~letter dated~~ _____
telegram ,, _____
~~parcel~~ ,, _____ }

Letter follows at first opportunity.

I have received no letter from you

{ lately,
{ for a long time.

Signature only } S. W. Forster

Date 20 May 1940

Forms/A2042/7. 51-4997.

1993/3

The field postcard was the option for those who did not wish to write a letter home or lacked the literacy to do so
SOMME MUSEUM

'D' coy 11th Batt R.I.R.
B.E.F.
France

Dear Robbie,

Just a few lines to let you know that I am keeping well and I hope that you are keeping well also. I received your parcel of cigs and I thank you very much for them. Tell Francie Mallon I got his photo and it was very nice. How is all the boys getting on I suppose you have a notion of listing on the Army. We have good sport here we have plenty of football 'A' company beat us 5–1 and we got knocked out of the 66 Francs. Are you still in the Machine Room. How does Hugh Turley like the Irish Guards. I think this is all at present
from your old chum

2223 Bugler C. Lynes

tell all at home I was asking for them

xx Write soon xx[100]

145

Letters that did manage to convey the darker side of trench warfare could only have stimulated anxiety at home, and in writing them, there must have been a conflict between the need to say how bad life could be and the desire to quell relatives' anxieties. C.S.M. Adams, from County Armagh, wrote:

> We are up here in the trenches these last few days. I am writing this letter
> on the side of the trench. No less than five shells have burst beside me
> since I started to write. One may get used to rifle bullets and [one] does,
> but you can never get used to the shells they make such an awful noise …
> [but] the German bullet is not made yet that is to kill me.

He tried to persuade his mother not to waste money on postage sending out cigarettes and food – these goods, although welcome, made Adams feel guilty about the sacrifices his mother must be making:

> I must thank you for what you sent me in your parcel. You are so awful
> good to me. I do not know how I will ever repay you. All in the parcel
> was alright … you must have spent some time in packing it …[101]

Perhaps more moving were attempts, maybe for the first time, to write poetry in order to express love and longing so deep that prose could not convey it, as when Corporal William Hill, from the Shankill area of Belfast, wrote home:

> Dear Sis.

> Just a few lines in reply to your kind and ever welcome letter and glad to
> see by it that you are all well at home … Here is a bit of poetry I made up
> in the trenches to my mother so don't laugh as it is my first attempt –

> With love to all at home
> Willie

> Dear Mother though I am in France
> I often think of thee
> And wonder what you're doing
> So far away from me.

For although the seas divide us
And keep us far apart
There's a good time coming Mother
When we'll meet no more to part …

And when I do get back again
I'll think more of home and thee
For I've learnt the want of a mother's care
When there is anything wrong with me.

I hope my father is keeping well
My brothers and sisters too
So I'll close by sending my love to them
And also the same to you.

So I'll just say Goodbye for the present
And I pray that this war will soon end
Then I'll return to old Ireland
To my one and only true friend.
My mother.[102]

SPIRITUAL MATTERS

Many families of recruits to the Ulster Division would have been specially
concerned that the spiritual as well as the physical needs of the soldiers were
adequately catered for. In the Ulster Protestant tradition, there was a stress
on strong, personal religious commitment, and some men joining the
division would have had experience of lay preaching in the mission halls and
churches that dotted the Ulster landscape. This vigorous religion of the rank
and file supplemented the basic structure of the official chaplaincy, which
was sometimes rather impersonal. Some soldiers, in later years, could not
remember the names of their chaplains though they still knew the names of
their officers. In and around the trenches and rest centres, there were
numerous lay preachers who would take Bible classes and prayer meetings;
often, in the better weather, these would be in the open air.

One of the
Ulster Division's padres
SOMME MUSEUM

I remember one Sunday evening … we were holding an open air service behind the wood … in the middle of the service the birds around us started to sing and the preacher told us to be quiet and listen. All we could hear was the birds singing. After a while he said that the birds had praised their Maker better than he could and he asked us to repeat the Lord's Prayer and we went back to the trenches … What I'm trying to tell you is that you can get close to God anywhere and anytime. Some of us in the 36th lived close to death and God at the same time.

One way in which death 'came close' was when a soldier had to receive news about a friend who had become a casualty while also serving at the front. In such a case, the chaplain had an important role, and as a result, the soldier would have more reason to remember his chaplain individually, as the following story suggests:

> There was one Presbyterian minister. I remember one cold night ... he led me to a quiet corner of the line and gave me a fag and a tot of rum. Then he said, 'I've got bad news for you son; your brother was shot a few hours ago. There's hope he'll live but he may never walk again. I've come to take you back to see him at the station ... I'll pray for him and to spare you the pain I'll write home for ye.' That was the type of man that I call men of God, willing to spare me the pain of writing home that my brother was wounded.

There may have been poor chaplains, but there were also many good chaplains who were always practical and down to earth in identifying with the men; they

> talked to you about God all right but they also talked to you about the cold and the wet, the food and the sickness. They wrote letters for them that could not write and read the replies from home. They did the same thing for them that was blinded or wounded in hospital. Any of the ones I knew carried a packet of cigarettes for they knew that a cigarette was as much comfort to some of the men as a long-winded prayer.[103]

The Scripture Gift Mission provided each man with a pocket hymn and text book and a pocket Gospel, with the instructions on the cover that the soldier carry it in his pocket and read it every day. Among the items included in the pocket hymn book were favourites such as A.M. Toplady's 'Rock of Ages', Isaac Watts' 'When I Survey the Wondrous Cross', and emotional hymns such as 'Nearer My God to Thee' and 'Lead Kindly Light'. They must have been sung in many miserable or fearful moments, and provided solace and strength. Other favourites included 'Abide With Me' and that rousing gospel hymn of many a mission service – bringing thoughts of death and the afterlife to everyone who ever sang it in France – 'When the trumpet of the Lord shall sound and time shall be no more ... And the roll is called up yonder, I'll be there ...'[104]

The prospect of imminent death no doubt encouraged many to respond to the call for 'personal salvation'. The YMCA ran an organisation called the War League for servicemen who decided to 'take the Lord Jesus Christ as their saviour'. On signing a card that indicated that he had committed himself to God, the soldier sent his name and address to a place in England from which he would regularly receive little booklets designed to encourage him in his new-found faith, particularly through daily prayer and Bible reading.[105]

SOME LIGHT RELIEF

To make such a commitment would, of course, prevent a man from visiting a local *estaminet*, according to the strict teetotal rules of the evangelicalism of the day. But such relaxation was welcome to those whose principles allowed it. Throughout the winter and early spring, the bad weather reduced the men's desire to be anywhere out of doors, and many a night was spent in an *estaminet*, gathered round the stove, drinking, chatting and singing. Occasionally also, music-hall-type entertainment in a local barn was provided by groups of men in each battalion who were keen to perform. There was even a 'Divisional Follies' concert troupe, a group comprising of some of the best talents in the 36th and who called themselves the Merry Mauve Melody Makers.[106]

The opportunity for sexual contact with Frenchwomen was limited. Amiens was reputed to be the place where officers could visit prostitutes, but the average soldier in the ranks could not expect much chance of a liaison in a quiet French village – at least, not without incurring the wrath of the woman's family. Crozier, however – never one to miss out on life's variety – discovered that 'free-love in billets' was a possibility for a 'young' officer when he billeted in the Vignacourt area and the landlady's pretty twenty-year-old daughter apparently tried to seduce him by regularly coming to his room with a hot-water bottle late at night, 'clad only in a simple night-dress'. Crozier noted with approval how 'her long hair nestles round her neck and over her shoulders'. She sought to question him in broken English about his life and his exploits at the front. No doubt he supplied her with some fine anecdotes, but whether Crozier yielded to temptation is not recorded.[107]

By and large, the men had to work off surplus energy in the endless but popular round of competitive football matches. In more private hours of relaxation, there were many games of cards and a little reading. Tommy Ervine practised on his mouth organ, and Stewart-Moore enjoyed playing

Sports Day at Varennes – several Ulster soldiers
about to engage in a tug of war
ROYAL ULSTER RIFLES MUSEUM

records on his gramophone, until it disappeared in transit from one billet to another early in 1916. He had fantasised about placing the gramophone on the parapet of a front-line trench and pointing the horn towards no-man's-land to taunt the Germans with *Tannhäuser,* 'Die Lorelei' or some other Teutonic melody.

For officers, there was also the possibility of a horse ride out into the countryside. Stewart-Moore and his friend I.W. Corkey, a medical officer, went for an occasional gallop after a hare, imagining that they were riding with hounds. All this within a few miles of the war zone![108]

In more sophisticated battalions, such as the Young Citizen Volunteers, attempts were made to entertain the men with war-zone journalism. The YCVs' magazine, the *Incinerator,* was supposed to be for everyone in the battalion, but the editorial was officious and verbose, and the *Incinerator* did not often manifest the mordant wit and scepticism of the more famous *Wipers Times,* first published in February 1916 by the 24th Division. The editor of the *Incinerator,* Lieutenant S.H. Monard, said he hoped to have in future magazines regular correspondents from Belfast, Lisburn, Ballynahinch, Donaghadee, Banbridge, Newtownards 'and wherever our readers have interests'. One of the cartoons showed Kaiser Wilhelm saying 'Farewell, a long farewell to all my greatness', a quotation from Shakespeare's *Henry VIII*. Another mock advertisement made fun of the Kaiser and his navy:

GREAT SALE

Owing to our inability to use same, we offer a large number of first class vessels, including dreadnoughts, cruisers, torpedo boats etc ON VIEW in Kiel harbour – Kaiser Billy & Co.

late von Tirpitz Ltd

A later issue of the *Incinerator* contained more jovial adverts, but there was a disturbingly bloodthirsty note in the editorial, designed perhaps to stir up spirits for the approaching offensive:

Our pals have been killed by a nation of murderers and by all that is true we are not going to be satisfied until we have had the lives of a dozen Huns for every comrade of ours who is lying in a lonely churchyard in Flanders. Revenge! Revenge! Let it be our watchword … Let us get through the hideousness of waiting like cattle in a slaughter house – which is what French life means – and then go mad until we have had an eye for an eye and a tooth for a tooth – we will show him a few conjuring tricks with rifle and bayonet … Let us think only of the Day – that Day when pent-up hate, anger and revenge combine to give us herculean strength and unconquerable energy … If a fat, juicy Hun cries 'Mercy' and speaks of his wife and nine children, give him the point – two inches is enough – and finish him.

The editorial continues in this vein, referring to the German soldiers as 'Hate-fiends', but also displaying considerable resentment towards those in 'comfortable armchairs' at home in Britain who talk about the front. The editor ends with a longing cry: 'What price the Shankill Road on peace night?'

The magazine reveals evidence of the soldier's frustration and tension: a 'News in Shallow' column, with a report on the home front, attempts to offer reassurance about attentions being paid to girlfriends left in Belfast:

The Picture Drome, Shankill Road, continues to draw crowded houses. But those of the khaki suit who now squeeze the fickle maiden's hands will be quite out of it when the boys come marching home again.

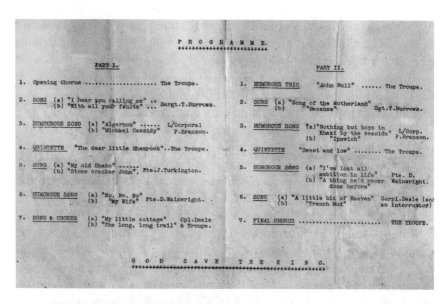

P R O G R A M M E.
+++++++++++++++++++++

PART I.

1. Opening Chorus .... The Troupe.

2. SONG (a) "I hear you calling me" .. Sergt.T.Burrows.
   (b) "With all your faults" ...

3. HUMOUROUS SONG (a) "Algernon" ...... L/Corporal
   (b) "Michael Cassidy" P.Branson.

4. QUINTETTE "The dear little Shamrock"..The Troupe.

5. SONG (a) "My old Shako" ......
   (b) "Stone cracker John". Pte.J.Turkington.

6. HUMOROUS SONG (a) "No, No, No"
   (b) "My Wife" Pte.D.Wainwright.

7. SONG & CHORUS (a) "My little cottage" Cpl.Deale
   (b) "The long, long trail" & Troupe.

PART II.

1. HUMOROUS TRIO "John Bull" ...... The Troupe.

2. SONG (a) "Song of the Motherland"
   (b) "Because" Sgt.T.Burrows.

3. HUMOROUS SONG (a)"Nothing but boys in
   Khaki by the seaside" L/Corp.
   (b) "Ipswich" P.Branson.

4. QUINTETTE "Sweet and low" .... The Troupe.

5. HUMOROUS SONG (a) "I've lost all
   ambition in life" Pte. D.
   (b) "A thing he'd never Wainwright.
   done before"

6. SONG (a) "A little bit of Heaven" Corpl.Deale (and
   (b) "Trench Mud" an interruptor)

7. FINAL CHORUS .... THE TROUPE.

G O D   S A V E   T H E   K I N G.
++

1st PROGRAMME

of

The Ulster Division

Merry.
Mauve.
Melody.
Makers.

Prices of admission
Officers 1 franc
Other Ranks 30 Centimos

A programme for a performance
by the Ulster Division's own
concert troupe
ROYAL ULSTER RIFLES MUSEUM

The *Incinerator* also contained news of social and relaxation activities –
recording D Company's whist drive and the C Company concert where
'Ginger' McMullan won the singing prize and entertainment was provided
by the Local Auxiliary Service Corps Folly Troupe, the 'Jolly Jesters'. There

was news of how the YCVs beat the Tyrone Volunteers 4–1 at football, and of a 'regular field of sport' the following day in which Jim Maultsaid tied for first place in the hundred-yard sprint, and the tug-of-war contest was won by B Company. That evening, Sergeant Cole – who rescued G.H.M. off the Donegal coast – gave a memorable series of Charlie Chaplin impressions to collect first prize in an entertainment competition.[109]

The one type of relaxation that everyone wanted was a visit back home to see family and friends. But leave was not easy to obtain. An officer had a much better chance of it, and Stewart-Moore paid one visit home. Getting there was arduous. He slept a night near the rail head in Acheux on the stage of the 4th Division's improvised theatre-cum-concert hall. He got to Le Havre at dusk the next day, took the night boat to England, and arrived at Waterloo station in the morning. After a day in London with a friend, he caught the sleeper train to Stranraer that night, in the middle of a Zeppelin raid – the train pulling out with all its blinds securely drawn. Snowstorms in the north of England disrupted the signalling system, and so it was nearly four in the afternoon before Stranraer was reached. Stewart-Moore made good use of his ten days' leave, and no doubt needed it after the journey. Wisely, perhaps, he returned to France via Kingstown and Holyhead.[110]

THE ORANGE SPIRIT

Many men were in Orange and Masonic lodges at home, and these parent lodges often had military 'offspring' with a special wartime charter for meetings at the front. At these lodge meetings in France, men encountered old friends, made new ones and caught up with what was happening at home. They talked openly at these meetings without fear of disciplinary proceedings, and so the lodges may have been a valuable vent for feelings stirred up by the miseries of war. Officers and men met on an equal basis, much to the displeasure of some HQ staff, and yet this allowed the officers to know – much more accurately than in many other divisions – just how the men were feeling. When the lodge meetings were held in one of the French villages, the occasion could prove very enjoyable, as one Orangeman recalled:

> You couldn't get a pint of porter, but the wine was cheap and there was always a hunk of French cheese and long loaves of French bread and we

had these after the meeting was over. There was little or nothing to do at times, and it broke up the night for you ... now and then we had officers present and it did your heart good to see them respect the Worshipful Master and maybe him a private. It was just like home at some of those meetings ... you felt the better of them for a week afterwards.

The bonding effects of the Orange and Volunteer spirit are also emphasised in the following comment by a soldier:

I could not turn down an invitation to go and meet again men who stood with me on the quayside that Friday night we brought the guns in ... It is difficult for the English to understand the loyalty we have for each other and the comradeship we enjoy as Orangemen.

In a war where there was a considerable social barrier between officers and ranks – a barrier that would have been detrimental to good leadership – lodge meetings amongst the Ulster Volunteers let the men in the ranks see that their officers were, indeed, fellow human beings. A lodge meeting

showed the other side of the officer's character. He was not a bloody minded fearless man ordering you out to be shot, but a man with a job to do – and he did it, not because he liked it all that much but because he had it to do.

Other anecdotes indicate that some of the Orange spirit spilled out and affected even the men of the artillery – who came, of course, from London:

I remember one meeting we had ... we sung all the old favourite Orange songs, them that goes with a swing. Out comes the pennies and the tin whistles; we really got it going ... As we were leaving we saw about five or six of the RFA men and a few of the officers. They had been standing outside listening to us. Now a few days after this I saw one of the artillery men and he pestered me to give him the words and tunes of some of the songs ... we were digging in some of the French artillery just before the Somme and some of the London men were helping us. Do you know, a couple of gun crews were singing 'The Sash' with all the get-up-and-go you'd hear on the Twelfth night in any Orange Hall.[111]

Another aspect of the Ulster character that intrigued fellow soldiers was the (at least official) passion for order and neatness in billets – a passion displayed also at the division's base depot near Harfleur, which was one of the showplaces behind the lines, with its bright gardens and trim paths lined with whitewashed stones.[112] Accompanying their proud efficiency was a fierce contempt for those units of the New Army whose zeal for good organisation and tidiness was inferior to that of the 36th. The war diarist of the YCVs was particularly angry when moving into the billets at Martinsart Wood:

> No incinerators, no latrines, no arrangements of any kind. I sometimes wonder how other regiments get off with it ... If the soldiers, especially of the New Armies, would bear in mind what they will find in every book of instruction 'REMEMBER OTHER TROOPS MAY OCCUPY THE BILLETS AFTER YOU' or words to that effect. It is the system that is all wrong and one is afraid of offending the other.[113]

However, it would be false to assume either that all battalions of the 36th were model units or that there was a harmonious divisional *esprit de corps* at all times. Clearly, the Young Citizen Volunteers were not pleased at the label of 'Young Chocolate Soldiers' awarded by the country lads from Tyrone, Derry, Donegal and Fermanagh who comprised the rest of the 109th Brigade. John Kennedy Hope, as one of these 'chocolate soldiers', perceived also that there was no love lost between the YCVs and the other four Belfast-based battalions. They complained that the Young Citizens were given soft jobs, such as 'scraping the village streets', while the others were kept busy 'holding the Hun back'.[114]

Some battalions had a greater reputation than others for military prowess and skill. The 9th Fusiliers, the Armagh Volunteers – known as 'Blacker's Boys' after their commanding officer, Lieutenant-Colonel S.W. Blacker – had a reputation in some quarters as being the best battalion in the division.[115] The indiscipline in the Belfast Brigade has already been referred to, and Crozier was particularly scornful of one of its battalions, whose officers 'drank' and whose CO was an ineffectual leader – a contrast to his own battalion.[116]

Despite the importance to the soldier of feeling that he was one of the 'Ulster Volunteers', it should be remembered that the most relevant unit was the battalion. Indeed, for the ordinary private, the platoon (about sixty men) or company (240 NCOs and men) was the social unit to which he belonged.

An infantry division such as the 36th, comprising some eighteen thousand soldiers, was a huge, amorphous group, and although the men were tied together by bonds of political and religious allegiance, the ties of love or hate that connected them with their immediate circle of fellow soldiers, NCOs and officers were those that ultimately mattered.

THE ENEMY

There is little evidence that the average soldier at this stage felt much serious antipathy towards his enemy on the other side of no-man's-land, despite the efforts of propagandists such as the editor of the *Incinerator*. German prisoners were caught occasionally, and while some men reacted aggressively towards them, others did not. Tommy Jordan recalled:

> I felt quite sorry for the Germans when they were wounded. I remember a fellow, called Wilson, grabbed a prisoner but I got him to let go and says to him, 'You ought to be ashamed …' The prisoner says, 'Thank you so very much' and gave me German money.[117]

In fact, there was a great deal of curiosity about the men who lived in such close proximity across a narrow strip of earth. One Sunday morning, Jim Maultsaid was startled to hear a church service in full swing:

> We were astonished to hear the singing of hymns and the playing of concertinas from across no-man's-land – in perfect harmony. Needless to say we did not interrupt them.[118]

Other soldiers were astonished by the excellent command of English that German soldiers frequently possessed – even if what they said was sometimes misinterpreted:

> A German shouted over to us the once, 'Do you know Bachelors Walk?' Well, he meant the one in London, but my mate beside me from Lisburn says across to him, 'I do indeed and I wish I was in the Robin's Nest at this moment!' [The Robin's Nest is a pub in Lisburn.][119]

The war diaries of men like John Kennedy Hope reveal a great deal more detestation of the fellow soldiers with whom he had built a bad relationship than of the supposed enemies he had come out to France to

A postcard from France illustrates the popular image of the 'Hun'
SOMME MUSEUM

If der Royal Irish RIFLES haf gone by, den I kan kom out.

fight, but whom he had rarely, if ever, seen. Many men recognised, perhaps, the shared vulnerability of the front-line soldiers on either side in a crazy war of attrition where bullet and shell reigned supreme, and the individual had so little say in his own fate.

SPRING 1916

In the first week of March, the weather began to improve, just as the division extended its front south of the river to include all of Thiepval Wood.[120]

'The Wood' soon provided the Derry Volunteers with a baptism of fire. Throughout the afternoon of 10 March, there had been unusually heavy fire from the Germans, which had aroused suspicions. Then at midnight came a big, sudden bombardment that lasted until 2.00 a.m. When the shelling

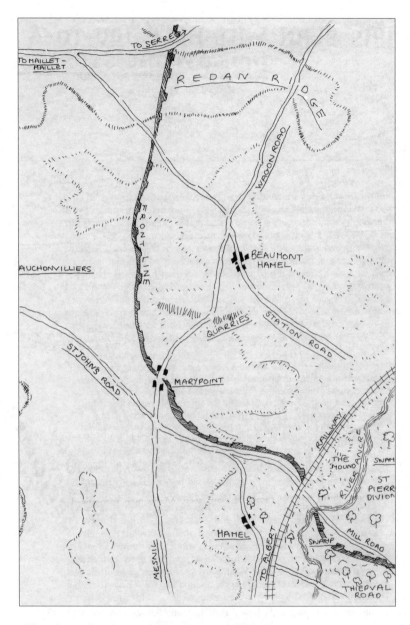

Ulster Somme front line, northern section, spring 1916

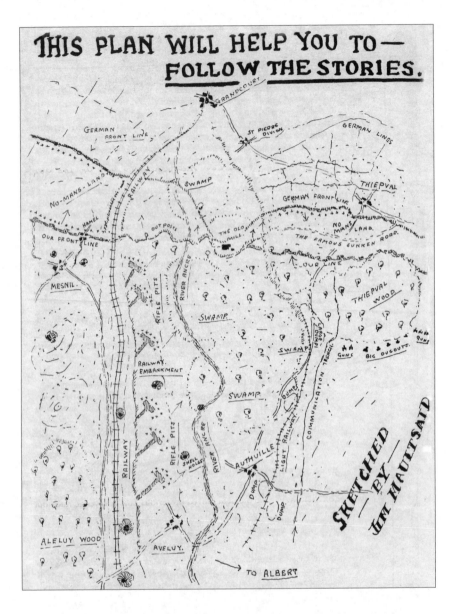

Jim Maultsaid's map of the main part of the Ulster Somme front line, spring 1916

MICHAEL MAULTSAID

died down, it was discovered that the enemy had penetrated trenches manned by the Derry men. Flares had failed to go off, and the telephone lines had been cut at the start of the bombardment, so there had been a delay in getting the 36th's own artillery to open up in defence. The Germans had time to do sufficient damage to the British defences to result in thirty dead and wounded, and a number of prisoners had been taken. But some of the Ulstermen had managed to inflict a toll on the Germans, once they had organised themselves in defence:

> In the hand-to-hand fighting with the Germans in the trench, there was a German caught on the wire and a fellow from Cookstown called Ned Anderson tried to send up a flare. Well it caught the German on the wire. Now whether or not the fellow was alive or dead I don't know but we could smell him burning as the fire blazed up. It fair turned your insides but we had to fight on until the Germans went back … They tried to bomb a dugout we had at a cross-trench but one of our men had the presence of mind to throw across the main trench a couple of rolls of wire and we sniped at them every time they tried to force their way across.

Eventually, when dawn came, the casualties – including a number of German prisoners, wounded or dying – were removed from the scene of destruction.[121] The incident stirred up serious talk of revenge raids, but the immediate business in hand was to repair the trenches. March 12 and 13 were beautiful sunny days, and more were to follow.[122] Some men vowed that they could hear, in the wood, a cuckoo calling.

On 17 March the troops celebrated St Patrick's Day. At Hédauville, where they were resting, the band of the Armagh Volunteers woke the battalion at 6.00 a.m. by playing Irish airs.[123] Stewart-Moore was at Beaussart, and went to a concert a few miles behind the lines – an evening made memorable by a rendering of that beautiful song of the trenches 'There's a Long, Long Trail Awinding Into the Land of My Dreams'.[124] Crozier recorded that on 17 March he and his fellow officers received shamrock from John Redmond, the Irish nationalist leader – meriting a swift and sharp reply. In his letter of thanks, Crozier conveyed the hope that Mr Redmond would, in turn, wear an orange lily in his lapel on the Twelfth of July, to be sent with the best wishes of the men of the 9th Rifles.[125]

Soon, Thiepval Wood was gaining foliage and birds were building nests in its branches. By the end of March, a decision had been made to shorten at the northern end the front held by the 36th.[126] It was now to be a front 'astride the Ancre', with two subsectors known as Thiepval Wood and Hamel. This was to become Ulster territory, and was to remain so long after the 36th had departed, long after the war was over. Now, in the early spring of 1916, Ulstermen named their trenches in the Picardy soil after Belfast streets and place names: Royal Avenue, Great Victoria Street, Sandy Row.[127] With April came further severe bombardments, and on 6 April a number of men were killed and wounded when the YCVs were shelled. Easter Sunday, on 23 April, prompted G.H.M. to enter in his diary, somewhat prematurely, the triumphal verse of a hymn:

> The strife is o'er, the battle done;
> The triumph of the Lord is won;
> O let the songs of praise be sung.
> Hallelujah![128]

Stewart-Moore spent Easter in Varennes, and joined a group of officers standing in the main street to discuss the news that had come through of the Irish republican rising in Dublin.[129] Arthur Samuels, with the South Antrim Volunteers, spent Easter in Martinsart village. On Easter Monday he travelled through Albert, up the famous poplar-lined road to Amiens, to enjoy a meal in a restaurant and a little sightseeing in the ancient capital of Picardy. The ride back at night was unforgettable, with the sky lit up like sheet lightning as he approached the front. The villages on the way were dark, ghostly places with no light to be seen. Then came halts at the different outposts, the constant flashes and rockets in the sky, and, nearer Albert, the sound of guns. The famous leaning golden figure of the Virgin on the church tower at Albert was outlined against the gun flashes. Legend had it that when the Virgin finally fell, the war would end. As Samuels made his way back to his billet, it must have seemed like a journey into the mouth of hell.[130]

But the front line had its less horrific aspects. The two subsectors of the Ulster front were very different in character. Thiepval Wood, despite its beauty, was a dangerous place, but the Hamel front, in the earlier weeks at least, was quiet. The battalion holding this subsector was responsible, among other things, for the defence of the River Ancre's swampy valley. This was filled with small lakes, and occasionally the men got a chance to fish or to take a shot at the wildfowl that still frequented the valley. The trenches ended on either side of the swamps, and a row of posts marked the line.[131] At night, the men could see the river and swamp water glistening. If it rained hard, the men down in the valley sheltered in an old mill or in one of the ruined cottages. To some of the County Antrim men, the Ancre valley was not unlike home: 'like one of the small glens of Antrim. There was a river going through the valley which was like a turf bog in parts and the low hills rose on each side.'[132]

PREPARING FOR THE 'PUSH'

In the spring of 1916 preparations began for an attempted breakthrough on the Western Front. The sustained German assault on Verdun, which had begun in February in the southern, French-held sector, was putting increased pressure on the Allies. There had been ninety thousand French casualties in the first six weeks. The Allied high commands therefore brought forward to early summer the planned date for opening a joint offensive along the Picardy front, where the British- and French-held zones were adjacent. Sir Douglas Haig, the British commander, hoped that the New Army battalions raised by Kitchener would take the prime role in the new campaign. The Ulster Division would thus have an important task in what was soon referred to by the men as the 'Big Push'. Much preparation would be needed to facilitate an all-out assault on the German trenches opposite the Ulster lines. In April and May, two causeways were built over the River Ancre and its marshes to supplement the inadequate wooden footbridges put up by the French, and enable free movement of large numbers of troops up to the front-line trenches. The 122nd Field Company Royal Engineers was entrusted with the construction, and employed large infantry parties to work from dusk to dawn on the task. The causeways were built of sandbags filled with chalk, and because the river was increasingly the target of enemy gunfire, there were casualties among the men carrying them. The Pioneers, fresh from construction of the Candas–Acheux railway, played a crucial role, especially in helping to remove obstructions from the river (including a German field gun), and in deepening and clearing the feeder streams: all this to make the valley less swampy and more accessible. The job was not easy:

Behind the lines, Ulster soldiers swim in the
River Ancre, spring 1916
ROYAL ULSTER RIFLES MUSEUM

Some bright glow-worm, who had no father, was of the opinion that the
Germans would look on the work parties as Pioneers having a well-
deserved rest and let us get on with the work. The first day we lost, I am
sure, a dozen men killed, wounded or drowned. We were expected to
use simple dredging tools and picks and long-handled shovels, and float
the rubbish away in flat bottomed boats. It was like cleaning a drain out
on a farm at home. A party of R.E. from the 4th Division under Capt.
Howard blew up the gun and in the best army tradition destroyed a
footbridge at the same time. After about a week we got more men and
dredging machines pulled by teams of up to four horses. It was rough
going on the horses for they sunk up to their hocks in the soft banks.

Also under construction at this stage were the trenches in the artillery
observation system, and a tramway to facilitate ready removal of wounded
men from Thiepval Wood to the rear of the front. Heaps of stones were set
by the roadside to fill holes left by shelling of the tramline. Dugouts were
also enlarged and deepened, and good strong doors and effective wooden
ceilings were added.[133]

Throughout the month of May, training the infantry of the 36th Division became the crucial task. Attacks on dummy trenches well behind the lines were co-ordinated, and battalions took turns to leave the front for exercises in rapid firing, bayoneting and consolidating newly won ground. Lewis gunners went to work under their respective commanders, and bombing competitions were organised to encourage accurate use of the Mills bombs. The YCVs won their brigade competition, and were awarded their prize by the newly appointed Brigadier-General R.J. Shuter. During May, the blankets the men had used at night were called in, and from then on, the soldiers slept in their greatcoats. The milder weather was appreciated. One note of unease was struck by the war diarist of the YCVs during a spell in the line: after recording the lovely spring, he commented, 'We can get practically no support from our own artillery owing to shortage of shells and what we do get are 50% duds ...' The same complaint was made a few days later on 5 May: 'Duds about 50% – something wrong surely. Record was kept with the following result: Heavies, out of 24 shells, 15 failed to explode; 18 pounders, out of 12, 8 were duds.'[134] Despite a reorganisation of the artillery undertaken during May, this inadequacy was to play a role in rendering the great offensive of 1 July less effective than had been hoped for and proposed.

Raids on the German lines, usually at night, were now given a high priority in an attempt to step up the sense of oncoming battle. The first serious and co-ordinated large-scale raid carried out by the 36th Division was undertaken on the night of 7 May 1916, a night coincidentally chosen by the Germans to raid the 1st Dorsets, part of the 32nd Division, on the right flank of the Ulstermen. The 36th's raiding party was from the 'Tyrones' (the 9th Inniskillings), and consisted of six officers and eighty-four men. They were already out of their trenches and waiting in the deep-cut Thiepval–Hamel road (known as the 'Sunken Road') when the German bombardment began as a prelude to their attack on the Dorsets. The raid went ahead nevertheless, and six German dugouts were bombed and a machine gun destroyed. With one of their men killed and two wounded, the Tyrones withdrew, but a great many more casualties occurred when the raiders became trapped in the Sunken Road on their way back to the trenches. Many had to lie there for a couple of hours, pinned down by German gunfire.

Meanwhile, the Derry Volunteers came to the support of the Dorsets, and held out against German advances;[135] the GOC of the 32nd Division was to express warm appreciation. However, there was a feeling in some quarters

Two Ulster officers planning
their men's role in the
new offensive, early in the
summer of 1916
ROYAL ULSTER RIFLES MUSEUM

that artillery should have been present to cover the enemy machine-gun nests on the rise behind the German lines, which had caused such havoc for the returning Tyrones. One officer laid out the blame as he saw it:

> Errors of judgement made by the officers responsible for liaison between the Artillery and the Infantry was the indirect cause of the death of our fellow soldiers ... initiative is not only necessary in commanding officers but subordinates must accept some degree of responsibility and when deprived of direct orders because of communication difficulties, initiate such action as they think present action demands ...[136]

On 16 May Arthur Samuels was delighted to see that the spell of good weather had made the Thiepval trenches dry and habitable as the South Antrim men took over from the County Down Volunteers for a spell on duty. Samuels could hear at night sounds from the enemy lines that indicated they were busy: picking, shovelling and driving stakes into the ground. What Samuels did not seem to realise was that these sounds might spell doom to the offensive, as the Germans dug deep into reinforced dugouts to await, and hopefully to survive, the supposedly devastating British artillery barrage that would precede infantry attack. At the end of the month, Samuels and his battalion retired to the large training ground known as Clairfaye Trenches, where an exact reproduction of the German trench system opposite the Ulster lines had been created from aerial photographs.[137]

Men were by now becoming aware of the vast scale of the oncoming battle. Soldiers returning from dugouts behind the front told of huge stockpiles of supplies. One driver in the 36th told his comrades he hoped that the lowest boxes in the piles would never reach him, for 'by that time the grubs would have left so many holes in the hard tack that the biscuits would be like nets and about as filling'.[138] Other men talked of the medical supplies being built up, of extra beds in wards, of tents erected to increase hospital capacities.

Such preparations seemed ominous.

4

INTO THE DEVIL'S DWELLING PLACE
THE SOMME, JUNE–JULY 1916

Ulster Division machine-gunners pose proudly with their Lewis gun, prepared for
battle. In reality, the gun was not always reliable under battlefield conditions.
ROYAL ULSTER RIFLES MUSEUM

THE BIG PUSH

For Britain, the prospect of a victory in Picardy had an aura of romance. It was
here that the Black Prince had won the Battle of Crécy, here that Henry V
had led his 'happy band of brothers' to triumph at Agincourt. Now, Picardy
was to see a battle that would dwarf all previous conflicts.

By January 1916 the war was swallowing up such vast numbers of men
that conscription was deemed necessary in Britain. Military service became
compulsory for young single men – though not in Ireland, where the recent
history of discontent would have made it too controversial a measure.

Meanwhile, the Gallipoli campaign had come to a standstill, the British having made no progress, and troops had been diverted from there to the Western Front. There were now thirty-eight British divisions in France, and the joint offensive with the French was to be meticulously planned. However, the planning was speeded up and simplified as the casualties at Verdun mounted and the French pleaded for the British to take an increased share of the burden of war.

The Somme sector of the front was relatively quiet, but it was an area where the Germans held a lot of advantageous high ground. They had also fortified numerous villages that lay along their lines, incorporating strong machine-gun posts and shelters in the cellars of ruined houses. Trenches were deep and well equipped, with fine dugouts. Nonetheless, it was here that Haig planned his infantry breakthrough, which the cavalry – hitherto unsuccessful in the war – was to exploit, setting up a fast-moving thrust towards Germany.

June 29 was the date eventually fixed for opening the campaign. The troops were to go forward at 7.30 a.m. – rather than dawn, which was normally considered the optimum time for infantry attack. The later hour was chosen to allow better artillery observation. Superior artillery was to dominate this battle, in an unprecedented eruption of might and terror. It would smash the German defences several days before 29 June; then the infantry would move over no-man's-land to the German trenches before the enemy could properly assemble. The British soldiers would, in fact, simply walk across in waves and occupy the shell-battered enemy territory. This strategy – which Haig, as the British commander-in-chief, had adopted – had been evolved in large measure by General Sir Henry Rawlinson, who was in charge of the 4th Army, the body of troops to carry the main burden in the forthcoming battle. It involved the use of nearly three million rounds of artillery ammunition. As well as the preliminary artillery assault, the advancing infantry were to be further protected by a 'curtain' of shells that would continue to fall just in front of them as they moved forward through the lines of German trenches. This curtain of shell fire was termed the 'barrage'.

The infantrymen would need all the protection available, as to a German machine gunner they would be easy targets when loaded down with sixty to eighty pounds of equipment, and plodding along in dense formation, each man only five yards from the next. If the unthinkable happened and the Germans could survive the bombardment and make it to the parapet to man their guns, carnage could ensue.

Rawlinson had 520,000 men at his disposal. The outlying regions of the British Isles were well represented in the attack, with twenty-nine battalions from Yorkshire, twenty-two from Lancashire, twenty from Ireland, and seventeen from Tyneside. The majority of these men were volunteers who had joined up in the heady summer and autumn of 1914. There were some battle-hardened veterans, too, including the 29th Division, which had just returned from Gallipoli and had gained for themselves the title, the 'Incomparables'. They would be fighting just to the north of the Ulster Division, which had been given an important job as part of the 4th Army's 10th Corps, attacking astride the River Ancre – an area of ground with which they had become familiar over the previous few months. Opposite the 36th were the Schwabians, from Württemberg – soldiers of the German 26th Reserve Division: these were the enemies who must be killed or taken prisoner.[1]

THE TASK OF THE ULSTER VOLUNTEERS

The overall objectives of the Ulster Division were dominated by, and dependent on, an attempt to take the Schwaben Redoubt, a parallelogram of trenches, dugouts and fortified machine-gun posts lying south of the Ancre on the highest ground overlooking the river. Protected by four lines of German trenches, the redoubt was known to some of the soldiers who looked across at it as the 'Devil's Dwelling', to others as 'Hell's Corner'. Between the Ulster trenches and this stronghold, the ground rose 250 feet in 1,000 yards. An observant artillery officer had counted sixteen rows of wire guarding the front-line trench on one part of the Schwaben Redoubt, and an average of five rows guarding the second line. The dugouts could be up to thirty-feet deep in the chalky earth, and afforded tremendous protection. Having captured the redoubt, the 36th had to press on and reach the fifth and final line of German trenches, beyond which lay open country. They must dominate the land between Beaucourt, to the north of their sector, and Thiepval village to the south (the capture of Thiepval itself was the task of the 32nd Division).

North of the Ancre, the 36th had the objective of crossing a ravine to

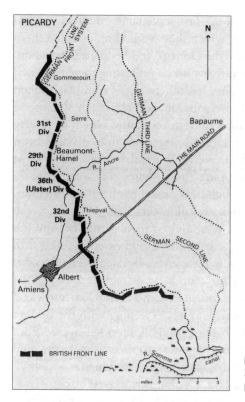

PICARDY

N
↑

Gommecourt

31st
Div

Serre

Bapaume

29th
Div

Beaumont-
Hamel

R. Ancre

36th
(Ulster) Div

32nd
Div

Thiepval

GERMAN FRONT LINE SYSTEM

GERMAN THIRD LINE

THE MAIN ROAD

GERMAN SECOND LINE

Albert

←
Amiens

BRITISH FRONT LINE

R. Somme

canal

miles 0   1   2   3

1 July 1916 – the
position of the
36th Division in the
British front line

the north of Hamel village, and moving through the German-held
Beaucourt trenches to take Beaucourt railway station. This would be the
particular goal of the Armagh Volunteers and the Mid Antrim Volunteers.
They also had to capture a mill situated on the river bank; and a platoon
from the Mid Antrim battalion was to patrol the marshy ground around the
river.

South of the Ancre, the Down and South Antrim Volunteers were to
attack the northern slopes of the Schwaben Redoubt, with the North
Belfast Volunteers in support. Special detachments of men with mortar and
machine-gun reinforcements were deputised to clear the trenches north
towards the river valley and the road between St-Pierre-Division and
Grandcourt. The assault on the southern flank of the Schwaben Redoubt
fell to the four battalions of the 109th Brigade. The Derry and Tyrone

battalions would go over the top in the first wave, and would advance to the fourth line of German trenches, which they would hold. Behind them would come the Young Citizens and the Donegal and Fermanagh battalion. The latter was to have special responsibility for consolidating the vital trench junction known as the 'Crucifix', on the southern slopes of the Schwaben Redoubt; and both the YCVs and the Donegal and Fermanagh Volunteers had to consolidate the first three lines of trenches against which the Derry and Tyrone men had led the attack. These objectives having been accomplished, the troops were to make their assault on the fifth line of German trenches. The three remaining Belfast battalions were to be in charge of this attack, marching through land gained by the other battalions and on to their goal. The East Belfast Volunteers would dominate the northern part of the fifth line, the West Belfast men would occupy the central portion, and the South Belfast battalion would extend southwards.

Artillery, of course, had a key role in the overall strategy. The five-day pre-attack bombardment – aimed at cutting wire and entombing the Schwabians in their dugouts – was to conclude with a redoubled 'hurricane' bombardment just before zero hour, the mortars joining with the heavier artillery. Then there would be the barrage: as the Ulstermen moved from trench to trench, so would the shell fire, in a series of timed 'lifts' that would keep the shells falling just ahead of the advancing infantrymen.

At zero hour, 7.30 a.m. – as the Ulster Volunteers moved off across no-man's-land – the barrage would lift from the first German line to the second; at 7.33 it would move to the third line; at 7.48 it would advance to an area some four hundred yards beyond the third line; then at 7.58 it would move up to the fourth line. At 8.48 the shell fire would shift to the distant fifth line, then there would be a halt to allow the three battalions of the Belfast Brigade to move through and effect the capture of the fifth line. At 10.08 the barrage would finally move to an area three hundred yards beyond the final German line. At each 'lift', the 18-pounder and 4.5 howitzer guns had to 'walk' up the communication trenches to the next main trench line.

The artillery was reinforced by French guns that were to drop tear-gas shells in the Ancre valley.

The mode of infantry attack was much the same as elsewhere on the Somme front. The infantrymen would have moved forward into preparatory positions, packing the front trenches in the Thiepval Wood and

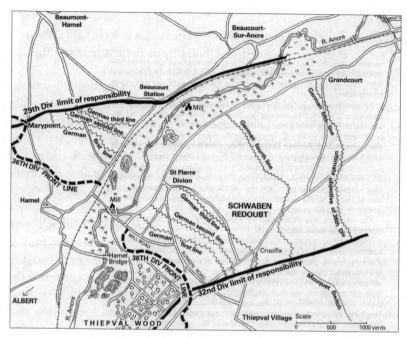

I July 1916 – the objectives of the 36th Division

Hamel subsectors in the hours before zero. At 7.30 they would march across no-man's-land under cover of the barrage; at their head would be officers carrying the polished blackthorn stick of the Irish regiments, and, if they wished, a revolver. (Commanding officers of each battalion were, however, asked to stay out of the assault – a controversial decision.) The battalions varied their formations of attack, but generally went in eight successive waves of men at fifty-yard intervals. With the division would go eighteen Stokes mortars and twenty-four machine guns – a number that seems small in consideration of the formidable objectives being assaulted.

To help inspire the men to the task in hand, and to inject a sense of identity in the labelling of the trench map, important objectives in the German trench system were given the names of Ulster towns – although there was some humorous dispute about the wisdom of attacking a place called 'Derry', as the fact that Londonderry had once *resisted* a besieging army was a crucial element in Ulster Protestant mythology.

PLANS FOR THE WOUNDED

Medical organisation was of great importance, and it was vital to ensure the swift removal of the wounded and dying from the battle zone. But there were only thirty-two stretcher-bearers to each battalion.

To the north of the Ancre, the stretcher cases and the walking wounded would go down a special trench from Hamel village to the Hamel–Albert road, from where they could be evacuated to the dressing stations either at Clairfaye Farm, where walking wounded would be dealt with, or at Forceville, for stretcher cases. The 110th Field Ambulance manned the Clairfaye Farm station, and the 108th Field Ambulance was at Forceville.

South of the Ancre, the walking wounded were to go to a collecting station west of Martinsart, and then by horse-drawn wagon to Clairfaye Farm. Stretcher cases were to be taken on a little tramway through Thiepval Wood, or else by stretcher-bearer from the aid posts at or near the front line to the advanced dressing station at Aveluy Wood, where initial attention could be given. The motors of the Field Ambulance would then pick them up south of Martinsart, and convey them to the Forceville dressing station. Some major surgery could be carried out there, albeit rather crudely. If the patient survived, he would then be hospitalised or receive further surgery behind the lines.

If the gunfire of the heavy artillery had done its job, and the Germans had been physically and morally devastated by it, then the infantry might obtain their objectives with relatively light casualties. The Ulster Volunteers also needed to be sure that the 32nd and 29th Divisions on either side of them were going to capture their objectives; for no matter how well the Ulstermen advanced, if Thiepval village to the south or Beaumont-Hamel to the north remained in German hands, the 36th would be exposed to fire from each flank and, indeed, virtually from the rear. If all were to go as planned, the medical facilities would be adequate, but if things were to go badly wrong, the main dressing stations at Clairfaye Farm and Forceville would become congested with intense suffering on a scale no one dared to think about.[2]

PREPARATIONS

To the ordinary soldiers, the month of June must have seemed a long and tense wait for the curtain to open on a great drama in which they were principal actors. The scale of the play to be enacted gave potency to the atmosphere of expectation. All along the Somme front, a whole generation of young men from across the British Isles stood ready to step from the wings onto the stage of battle. One of the most striking, and ironic, aspects of this time was that as the battle loomed closer, so the beauty of the French countryside increased in power:

> ... the Somme valley was filled with splendour. The mustard seed had spread a yellow carpet in many meadows, so that they were fields of the Cloth of Gold, and clumps of red clover grew like flowers of blood. The hedges about the villages of Picardy were white with elder-flower and drenched with its scent. It was hay-making time ...[3]

As a result of the good weather, health improved. Fewer men reported sick in the 36th Division during the first two weeks of June 1916 than in any other two-week period that year.[4] The final month before the opening of the battle began with great business and efficiency when, on 1 June, the 108th and 109th Brigades were taken from the line for a few days of special training. The 107th Brigade remained in the line whilst the other Ulstermen practised assault strategy on the dummy trench system at Clairfaye Farm.

Monday 5 June

On the night of 5 June, the Mid Antrim Volunteers moved again to the front to undertake a raid on the German lines, north of the Ancre. An artillery barrage was laid down, and the Ulstermen moved up to the wire, broke through and raided the German trench that ran parallel with the main railway line just north of the river. Dugouts were bombed, an officer shot and two tunnels leading towards the British lines were discovered and blown up. The pre-raid shelling had seemed to do a thorough job, and the dangerous assumption was made that under the intense bombardment planned for the few days before battle commenced, the entire German front would be similarly smashed up. But the trench destroyed in this raid was not nearly so well fortified as most of the German line – it lacked deep bunkers and machine-gun nests – and it was not a good example from which to generalise.

Saturday 10 June

Five nights later, the Germans paid a return visit to the British trenches in a sector being held by the North Belfast Volunteers, and after a few moments of hand-to-hand fighting, the raiders were expelled from the trenches. However, it took several days of hard work to repair the battered line.[5]

By this stage, individual men were being allotted specialist tasks in the forthcoming battle. G.H.M. was appointed a 'runner' – he had to carry back news of the fighting to his own lines – and on 10 June a distinguishing red band was sewn on each of his coat sleeves, contributing to his sense of anticipation. Two days later, he wrote in his diary: 'There is excitement in the air we breathe ... the pace of events seems to be quickening now.'[6]

His battalion, the Young Citizens, had now been sent with the rest of their brigade to Aveluy Wood to help the Pioneers with preparation work for the offensive – such arduous tasks as carrying ammunition to new gun positions.[7] Other battalions had to help to construct gun pits and erect shelters for the regiment of French field artillery that had joined the Ulstermen's ranks.[8] But the move came at an unfortunate time for the 109th Brigade. There was wet weather on 12 and 13 June, and the tents provided were flimsy and sometimes ill repaired: of the five officers' tents for the YCVs in Aveluy Wood, only one was fit for use.

Wednesday 14 June

On the following day, the weather improved but many men's clothes were still soaking wet.[9] The work was hard, too. For an entire week, from 13–20 June, G.H.M. was to carry ammunition up towards the front. It was a dangerous task, as a stray German shell could blow a party of men and their explosive load into fragments.[10]

For part of the journey from the rail head to the front, pack mules or horse-drawn wagons were used. The wheels of carts were covered in old rubber tyres, straw ropes or old coats and blankets so as to muffle the noise of the rims on the road. The animals wore special leather or rubber boots, and were muzzled so as not to give a friendly 'neigh' to another, passing horse. The drivers of these wagons worked hard in the short June night to bring up two loads under cover of darkness. The relationship between man and beast was close, and at least one driver with the Ulster Division claimed he kept his horse content by teaching her to chew tobacco as she walked![11]

British artillery on the Western Front. The huge bombardment that preceded the Somme offensive was meant to break the Germans.
ROYAL ULSTER RIFLES MUSEUM

In their occasional rest spells, many of the men took the opportunity to bathe in the Ancre, further downstream from the line. It could be a pleasure interrupted by danger, as Stewart-Moore and his friend Corkey discovered one day, when German shells started to land a few hundred yards away:

This made us hurry into our clothes and we did not feel comfortable until we were fully dressed; illogically we felt that it would be more painful to be wounded without the protection of our clothes.[12]

No such disturbance upset Crozier when he joined four of his young officers on the riverbank and fixed his admiring eyes on the naked bodies before him. His description, with its sexual and racial overtones, reads strangely:

As I arrive they are all standing naked on the improvised spring-board, ready to jump in for a race. How wonderful they look, hard, muscular, fit, strong and supple, yet devoid of all coarseness. They ask me to start them and I comply with their request. As they fix their eyes on me and wait for the word 'go' I realise I am, thanks to circumstances, in the presence not only of boys versed in war, but men already known to women. I think as I watch them ducking each other in the water and

177

playing like young seals I have so often seen up North, 'What a pity they are not married that they might plant their seed.' Mankind has ordained that they shall shortly die. Alas! the weaklings and shirkers escape and breed like rabbits while the strong suffer and are wiped out.

Thoughts like this would not be allowed expression when he was in front of his men. As commanding officer, Crozier felt he could not show emotion. He had to be dispassionate, as for instance when twice in one June night he came upon mangled human remains being transported along 'Elgin Avenue' trench. A shell had annihilated two riflemen, and the torn and severed trunk of one of them was fixed in the branches of a shell-stripped oak above the trench. A soldier passed Crozier carrying a single human arm in his hand.[13]

One Sunday, Stewart-Moore decided to visit his friends in the South Antrim Battalion to see how their preparations were going, and he found their attitudes strangely out of keeping with the grim reality of what was ahead:

> One was responsible for having dumps of Mills Bombs ready to hand, another for small arms ammunition and another for picks and shovels or sandbags. All were worried should they not be ready in time for the day. The barbed wire had not turned up. Would it ever come? It was like the preparations for a bazaar. Each had his own stall and was afraid it would never be ready … It was a warm, sunny day and after lunch Arthur Samuels and I sat on the bank under the trees above the river talking and reading a copy of the *Irish Times* which Arthur had just received from Dublin.[14]

Thursday 15 June

On 15 June the South Antrim Volunteers joined the Armagh men bivouacking in Martinsart Wood. Working parties were sent down to Thiepval Wood to help dig assembly trenches, and a considerable number of men were wounded by German shells in the process.[15] Meanwhile, the war diarist of the YCVs also recorded 'everybody working at high pressure' on the digging of assembly trenches. 'Everyone looking forward to the Great Day', he wrote on 16 June, despite the fact that the YCVs, along with

The famous golden statue of the
Virgin drooping from the ruined church
tower in Albert. When the statue
fell, said the men, the war
would be over.
SOMME MUSEUM

the ten thousand or so other troops sleeping in Aveluy Wood, encountered, each night, enemy machine-gun fire playing through the trees, and high-explosive shells bursting overhead.[16]

Monday 19 June

On 19 June the preliminary attack orders for the YCVs came through, and were read to all the officers.[17] When the West Belfast officers got their orders in mid-June at Forceville, Crozier lectured them all for hours in a big barn, aided by a cloth map twenty-feet square.[18] On Tuesday 20 June Stewart-Moore and his 107th Trench Mortar Battery also arrived in Aveluy Wood. For the officers, there was a Nissen hut (quite a novelty), but as the weather was dry and warm, the men began by sleeping in the open air, until one night a man was wounded by machine-gun fire. Stewart-Moore dug himself a trench to sleep in, and put his camp bed in it. Unfortunately, it looked rather like a grave: an intimation of mortality that chilled him to the bone.[19]

Seven new officers described by the war diarist as 'very fresh' joined the YCVs on Wednesday 21 June. On the following day, final attack orders were given to the battalion, and tools and stores were placed carefully in assembly trenches.[20] The same day, Samuels of the South Antrim battalion gave a last pep talk to his NCOs, and enjoyed a final concert in D Company mess.[21]

Friday 23 June

On Friday a warm day was followed by heavy rain that made things most unpleasant for the men. More than six hundred of the YCVs were extended from the ammunition dump to the front line, carrying ammunition; they worked through until dawn on Saturday, wet to the skin and very hungry. On finishing the job, they marched straight away to Hédauville.[22] On the same day, the South Antrim men paraded at 7.45 p.m. and marched to their trenches at Thiepval Wood.[23] By the end of Friday, the infantry that were to occupy the front-line positions during the bombardment were in place – the Tyrone Volunteers and the South Antrim Volunteers in the Thiepval Wood sector, and the Armagh Volunteers in the Hamel trenches. These troops would have hell to endure under increasingly furious German shelling.[24]

The same shelling would make bad work of the little tramway for the wounded that had been constructed through Thiepval Wood. Tommy Jordan and his fellow Pioneers had made it from eighteen-foot lengths of rail bolted together with small hexagonal nuts that proved difficult to work with. The track needed constant repair.[25]

THE BOMBARDMENT

Saturday 24 June

Then, on Saturday, the British bombardment began. The final, violent prelude to the Big Push was under way.

The din of the bombardment was perhaps the most fearsome man–made noise yet known on earth. In London, at night, the distant thunder of the guns could be heard. Close at hand, in Thiepval Wood and Hamel, it seemed as though all thought must be drowned out in the hypnotic cacophony of shell fire. Cyril Falls saw the big shells burst and send forth huge columns of earth into the air.[26] Another soldier looked up and 'could actually see the shells flying through the air: red bits of steel, red pokers'.[27] George Lindsay – now in the Observation Corps, since the Cyclists Company had been wound up – looked down from Mesnil and swore that, surely, nothing could live in the German trenches.[28] Tommy Jordan's ears became sore, and would later bleed under the constant pressure of nearby explosions.[29] To make things worse, the weather began to deteriorate once again:

> We moved up to the Thiepval Wood and into the slit trenches and for
> the next four or five days it rained. We were always wet, the food cold,
> our feet swelled up, our fingers stiffened. Our guns thundered away day
> and night … we watched the gunners – every time they fired a shot the
> wheels of the gun moved, splashing mud all over them. They were in a
> worse state than we were. You could see where the rain had washed bits
> and pieces of mud off their faces and hands and they were all streaked like
> a zebra.[30]

Sunday 25 June

Sunday was the second day of the bombardment, and against the background of the infernal din, church services were held. What the chaplains who conducted such services must have felt is indicated in the recollections of one of them, George Birmingham – the Ulster-born cleric and writer, acting as chaplain in another division:

> It is my turn to speak, to pray. Surely never to any Minister of God has
> such opportunity been given. But what words can I find? What
> supplication fits the time and place? … I am feeble, helpless, faithless,
> without vision; but at least I can give the benediction. 'The Peace of God'
> – Even war cannot take that from the heart of him who has it.[31]

On the same day, Lieutenant-Colonel Pelly of the East Belfast Volunteers gave his final operational orders to his officers. He could not yet tell them when zero hour would be, but it was clear that half an hour before zero, the brigade would be starting from Aveluy Wood, and move towards the front trenches in Thiepval Wood, the West Belfast battalion leading the way, with the South Belfast men just behind. When the brigade moved out over no-man's-land towards its distant goal, the East Belfast battalion would follow one hundred yards behind the other two. The two rear platoons of each company would be carrying iron 'screw' stakes and barbed wire to consolidate their gains against counter-attack. All in all, the men were going to be hugely loaded down, as the instructions about equipment and ammunition indicate:

> Packs and greatcoats will not be carried but haversacks will be worn on the back.
>
> A waterproof sheet and cardigan inside will be rolled on the back of the belt. The roll to be the length of the bottom of the pack.
>
> Every man of the 2nd and 3rd platoons will carry a pick or shovel.
>
> In the haversack will be carried shaving and washing kit, 1 pair socks, iron rations and rations for 'Z' day.
>
> Every man will carry two bombs, one in each side pocket.
>
> Every man will carry two sandbags tucked into his belt.
>
> Wirecutters will be carried by the leading platoons of each company.
>
> Each man with a wirecutter will have a white tape tied round his left shoulder strap.
>
> 170 rounds S.A.A. per man will be carried.
>
> 5 flags for indicating the position of the most advanced infantry will be carried by each company.

The operational instructions ended with a grim reminder: 'All ranks are to be warned that if taken prisoner they are only bound to give their name and rank and should refuse to answer any questions.'[32]

If the average infantryman was going to be weighed down, the scout, or runner, was not. G.H.M. received his scout's shorts; he would be trimmed down for speed and agility. He felt a sense of personal freedom and anticipation, recording in his diary on Sunday 25: 'I am perfectly fit and feel on top of the world.'[33]

Monday 26 June

Monday 26 June arrived. It was the third day of the bombardment. A raid was planned in which the Down Volunteers would play the lead role, and gas would be used for the first time by the 36th. A heavy German barrage

Thiepval marshes, between the wood and the river
ROYAL ULSTER RIFLES MUSEUM

landed just as the gas was being liberated from cylinders in Thiepval Wood, and a number of Ulstermen were casualties.[34] (Also a casualty on that Monday night was Arthur Samuels, who 'got a touch of shrapnel from a whizzbang', and ended up in a casualty clearing station, thus missing the Big Push.)[35]

The purpose of the Down Volunteers' raid was to take prisoners, and they managed to capture one officer and twelve other ranks. On the return journey to their own trenches, the Down men got caught by heavy machine-gun fire, and had to shelter in the Sunken Road. There was little protection there, and six Ulstermen died and nine were wounded. The raid gave some men the first opportunity to use a bayonet – not a pleasant experience:

When you shoot a man you never see his face and it is as easy as shooting a fox. A few days before we went into the big battle we raided the German lines. It was the first time I had to kill a man at close range and I did it with a fixed bayonet. It was not very light and he was a shadow but as I twisted … the bayonet clear he squealed like a stuck pig. It was not till I was on my way back that I started to shake and I shook like a leaf on a tree for the rest of the night.[36]

Wednesday 28 June

Tuesday had been another wet day, and Wednesday showed no sign of drier weather. The decision was taken to put back the assault by a day or two – until the weather improved. Careful plans would have to be adjusted.[37] Certainly, two days of extra shelling of the Germans could only boost the chances of destroying them, but more loads of high-explosive shells would have to be carried up on wet, slippery ground – a fearsome task. Also, the battalions who had been holding the line had to be relieved by fresh men. As the Down Volunteers moved up through Martinsart to replace the South Antrim men, they encountered disaster. No. 11 Platoon and the HQ staff were marching out of Martinsart when a shell fell right in the midst of the party. Fourteen men were killed on the spot, and almost all the others in the group were wounded, including Major Robert Perceval Maxwell, second-in-command of the battalion. With a total of almost sixty casualties, the confusion in the darkness was grim. A group of the South Antrim men took charge of the clearing-up operations. As dawn broke, Tommy Russell could see the ghastly debris of the tragedy: a huge crater in the road, bloodstains everywhere, and, most horrifically of all, men's internal organs blown up and scattered over the statues on the walls of Martinsart's damaged chapel.[38]

Thursday 29 June

On Thursday 29 June – originally to have been the day of battle – battalions moved back and waited. Men who had endured the spell in the forward trenches were particularly relieved. Thiepval Wood had been 'hit with as many shells as raindrops', and the men were 'soaked with water and caked with mud'. They had had little hot food for days, and they had been denied the use of many of the better shelters, which were now full of supplies.[39] The YCVs moved to Forceville with instructions to wait there until further notice. The men appeared to their war diarist to be in the 'best of spirits'. However, the Germans kept up their counter-bombardment on Thiepval Wood; the trenches were in a terrible state by now, and casualties increased. Nervous rumours came through to the headquarters of the YCVs that the casualty list was long, and that 'clearing of wounded arrangements were not all that might be'. There was a rifle inspection for the Young Citizens at 3.00 p.m.[40] In the evening, some of the men occupied themselves by writing letters home.

An Ulster officer in a trench
in Thiepval Wood
ROYAL ULSTER RIFLES MUSEUM

Many were in serious mood. One soldier wrote to the secretary of his
Orange lodge near Portadown. He had been a teacher before joining up,
and his letter was long and written with a steel-nibbed pen and ink:

Dear Br. Secretary,
There is no doubt that when you receive this note I shall be dead.
There are all the signs that something bigger than has ever taken place
before in this war is about to be launched.
    The more I brood on what may happen the surer I am I shall not
survive it. All of us say, 'It'll be the other fellow who'll be killed'. I feel
that I am one of those other fellows. I am not afraid to die but for every
death there are a number of lives which will never be the same again,
they suffer more than the one who passes on. We have had good times in
the 12th rifles – good times and bad but it is the good times we remember.

… we have got our first hot meal for near a week and tonight we are to sleep in an old stable and it will be our first night's rest since the guns began the barrage.

He ended the letter with two brief aphorisms: 'Life's short span forbids us to enter on high reaching hopes', and 'Man shall not wholly die'.[41]

The same evening, Private Robb, with the Mid Antrim Volunteers, was present at a small and rather unusual burial service. A badly wounded German had been brought in from no-man's-land, but he soon died.

> The rain stopped that day and we were asked to dig a grave for him in the corner of a field where we buried our own dead. There was two men of the 12th Rifles being buried that same day. It still sticks in my mind that a Protestant pastor said the same burial service over the three men. I wondered what in hell we were doing fighting one another. After all we were all men, only the uniform was different. That night there was a glorious sunset. The guns were silent for a while and I heard someone in the reserve trenches start to sing 'Abide with me'. Then slowly all down the line the men took up the hymn. For about fifteen minutes we sang hymns.[42]

The beautiful sunset on the night of Thursday 29 June augured well for the following day. The first hours of Friday proved to be dry, and the weather seemed to be distinctly improved. It was decided by Haig, in HQ, that the British armies would attack at 7.30 on the morning of Saturday 1 July.

Friday 30 June
Morning

A fine day dawned after what had been a very heavy night's bombardment. Men of the Service Corps guarding supply dumps along the river saw the sun come out and the damp ground dry up, with steam rising from the road and from the chalk causeways that had been built a few weeks earlier. By mid-morning, all the battalions had been briefed.[43]

Generals were on their rounds, too. Lieutenant-General Sir T.L.N. Moreland, commander of the 10th Corps, came to the YCVs' headquarters at Forceville and wished everyone luck for the following day. The YCVs had received orders to move off to Thiepval Wood, and the consensus seemed to be that the men ought to be kept 'as fresh as possible'. The battalion war diarist wrote: 'All ranks in the best of spirits and vengeance vowed for great losses.'[44]

By mid-morning, too, the divisional HQ staff had moved to its report centre on the Englebelmer–Martinsart road. A final meeting took place in the humid atmosphere of a shuttered and closely guarded room. When the senior officers had been briefed, they returned to their posts and met their junior officers, who, in turn, briefed the senior NCOs. One element of unease remained – was the bombardment really working? At midday a soldier who had been operating on a firestep near the river for the previous two nights was pulled out and sent to a command post where he was questioned by a colonel. What had he seen during the night and morning? Had there been people moving in the German line? How many? Could he see the wire? Was it cut? Were there many shell holes? Other men were taken from the front line and asked the same questions. Not that it mattered much: the timetable was now quite irrevocable.[45] Meanwhile, the thunder of guns continued.

Afternoon

Among the jobs to be done now was the provision of drinking water:

> I was sent down to the officers' place with a few gallons of drinking water and one of the officers came out to me and asked me if the men had any cigarettes and I tells him not since we went back behind the lines. He says then wait a minute and I'll see what I can do, so out he comes again with a tin box half the size of a biscuit tin and tells me to share them with the lads. We got Woodbines (or Willies as we called them) but these were big, fat ones. We got the tea going as soon as I got back to the hut. Boy, we had a great night's smoking.

Other jobs included the collection of letters and postcards that the men had written home:

> I took these to an office type of place and when I went in I saw an ex-Worshipful Master of one of the Lurgan lodges. He looked tired and had not shaved for a day or two, an odd thing for an officer not to do. As I left the sacks down he looked at me and said that that lot would have to be looked at, censored I think he said, when he got back from the front.

The men of the Medical Corps were also busy:

From the middle of the afternoon to near the time the sun set we checked
the medical supplies in one of the forward dugouts which had been
changed into a first-aid station. I never saw as much morphia at one post
before or after … Everything was checked and rechecked. Blankets,
dressings, spirit lamps, scalpels, the lot. It was hot and stuffy in the dugout,
so we were given a few hours to get our heads cleared. I didn't feel like
eating, but the sergeant stooped over me until I finished a plate of what I
suppose you'd call stew. That was the last food I got except hard biscuits
and water until the next Sunday.

Occasionally, men on the flanks of the 36th's lines had a chance to speak
to the soldiers in other divisions:

One of the English soldiers called me over saying that they had got extra
rations and plenty of cigarettes. The ground was well dried out so we
crawled across. We were well down in the trenches and they had a fire of
wood made from broken-up ammo boxes and had made dixies of tea. We
sat and talked for a while about the next day then we all shook hands,
wished each other the best of luck and we got back to our own lines
again.[46]

Trench mortar batteries also completed their preparations. The bombs
were fused, iron rations were issued, and water bottles were filled. Stewart-
Moore was to remain in reserve with his battery commander, Captain Paddy
Mulley, in Aveluy Wood, and would not be going over the top. At 5.00 p.m.
the chaplain held a service for the men of Stewart-Moore's battery.
Attendance was not compulsory, but all the men were there, though only
one of the officers – a reversal of the usual pattern of attendance at special
services, hitherto dominated by officers.

We were all feeling naturally very serious and solemn; after such a terrific
bombardment there was good hope of a complete break through the
German defences but who could tell what tomorrow would bring forth.[47]

Some Catholics in the 36th got a chance to attend Mass, too:

Late in the afternoon – 30th June – an ambulance came down and I was told to get in. There was about 4 or 5 others in it and we went up behind the 29th's lines. There was a field altar set up and about 10 of us joined the English soldiers in the Mass. The priest was from the West of Ireland and he came over and talked to us.

Evening

Some of the men had been sleeping and resting during the afternoon – now they were wakened and taken down to the field kitchen:

In the early evening we were given a hot meal. In the middle of it a sergeant came down and told us to pack in as much as possible ... I wrote a few lines to my sister ... in the dusk we marched to a store near a church we built (it was really a big hut but we used it for the odd service) and got our battle packs ... it was getting dark.

For some of the machine-gunners, there were last-minute disasters:

We had a Vickers and it was one of the worst I ever handled. It was always jamming even after short bursts. It was getting on for dark when we were asked to fire off a few rounds and it stuck again. Well, the cursing wasn't ordinary. We got butts of candles and stripped it right down. Then we oiled it and put it together again. Fired a few more off and it stuck again. Joking like, somebody said to the sergeant we would be better with rifles. 'To please ye,' says he, 'I'll see what I can do.' Well, in about 15 minutes he came back with about half a dozen rifles ... so we went to battle with rifles.

It was a technical failure like this that could prove costly on the morrow. As the men of the RAMC watched the infantry file up the trenches in the dusk for the final time, their feelings were intense:

There was a doctor and half a dozen of us standing in the door of the Regimental Aid Post ... it was the 9th Skins who were moving up ... somebody shouted 'Look at old Sawbones and his gang of butchers just waiting to get at us'. The doctor turned round and said quiet like 'I trust that not one of you will need my skill.' ... the doctor just stood there waving and saluting until the last man was hid in the trenches ...[48]

The journey of the infantry battalions to their assembly trenches was

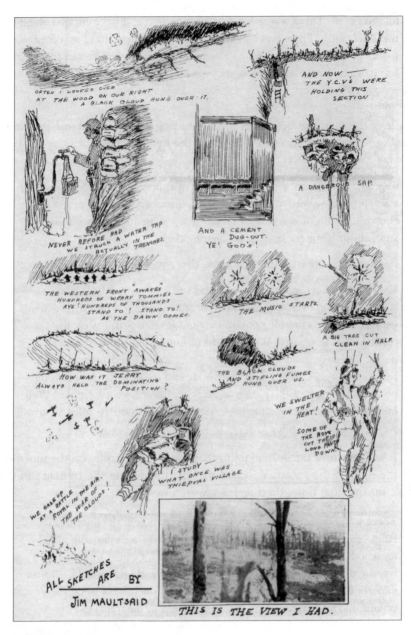

OFTEN I LOOKED OVER
AT THE WOOD ON OUR RIGHT
A BLACK CLOUD HUNG OVER IT.

AND NOW —
THE Y.C.V'S WERE
HOLDING THIS
SECTION

NEVER BEFORE HAD
WE STRUCK A WATER TAP
ACTUALLY IN THE
TRENCHES.

AND A CEMENT
DUG-OUT.
YE! GOD'S!

A DANGEROUS SAP.

THE WESTERN FRONT "AWAKES"
HUNDREDS OF WEARY TOMMIES —
AYE! HUNDREDS OF THOUSANDS
STAND TO! STAND TO!
AS THE DAWN COMES.

THE "MUSIC" STARTS.

A BIG TREE CUT
CLEAN IN HALF.

HOW WAS IT JERRY
ALWAYS HELD THE DOMINATING
POSITION?

THE BLACK CLOUDS
AND STIFLING FUMES
HUNG OVER US.

WE SWELTER
IN THE
HEAT!

SOME OF
THE BOYS
CUT THEIR
LONG PANTS
DOWN.

I STUDY
WHAT ONCE WAS
THIEPVAL VILLAGE.

WE GAZE UP
AT A BATTLE IN THE AIR.
ROYAL
THE WAR OF
THE CLOUDS!

ALL SKETCHES
ARE BY
JIM MAULTSAID

THIS IS THE VIEW I HAD.

MICHAEL MAULTSAID

190

undertaken under a sky in which the first stars were beginning to twinkle. The men marched by cross-country tracks marked with green and red lanterns. The YCVs packed and sent off their rucksacks, and left Forceville at 9.30 p.m. They marched in platoons past the village of Englebelmer, where German shells were dropping; then there was a halt just short of Martinsart, where mounted officers left their horses and proceeded on foot. The battalion marched on through Martinsart and into the sticky mud of Aveluy Wood. Guns crashed and shells whistled overhead. They struck the railway line and proceeded north in single file, led by A Company and Captain Slacke (who had so annoyed J.K. Hope in camp at Finner). As the troops crossed the south causeway over the Ancre, German machine-gun fire sprayed across the marshes and there was one casualty. Then the men entered 'Elgin Avenue' and their assembly trenches, received their entrenching tools, and settled down for the rest of the night.[49]

But to settle down was not easy. There was little space in the trenches, and Jim Maultsaid recorded that the flash of explosives made the wood seem like 'a mass of flame'. He felt a sense of 'confusion and din'. To talk to his nearest chum was impossible. He just tried to wait for dawn, thinking of home and mother. But he couldn't stay still; he kept standing up and sitting down. He wondered what it would be like to lose his limbs or go blind. He kept feeling at his Bible in his breast pocket.[50]

G.H.M. remained calmer, and thought to himself: 'I am happy and confident in my own ability to meet and face whatever comes my way.'[51] But other men grew irritable and openly troubled:

> The only thing I can compare it with is like waiting for someone to die. You know it's coming and you wish to God it was over and done with. You smoked fag after fag, took sips of water, oiled the rifle, did everything over and over again. Even above the shelling you could hear small noises like a man sucking air in between his teeth and this got on your nerves more than the shelling. Now and again a star-shell lit up the night like day. The men, all of them, looked an odd colour and tired and drawn, like people done out. There was one fellow who took off and put on his tin hat until another man shouted at him for Christ's sake to stop it.[52]

Amidst all this, men searched for lucky signs. Captain David John Bell of the Down Volunteers had written home a few hours previously, saying that he was cheered because July was the 'Irishman's month'. What he meant was that in July, Ulster Protestants celebrated the victory of William of Orange at the Battle of the Boyne, a victory seen as the cornerstone of the Protestant heritage in Ireland.[53] The battle was generally celebrated on 12 July, but in the Julian calendar, in use up to 1752, it had been on the first day of the month. It was a good omen. Now, on the first day of July, over 200 years later, Ulster Orangemen and Protestants – 'Carson's Army' – would have a chance to fight another battle beside another river and write another chapter in Irish history. From the Boyne to the Ancre, the thread of history seemed to run clearly. The Volunteers who had brought the guns ashore at Larne, who had stayed firm and true to 'No Home Rule', whose famous watchword was 'No Surrender', would surely give a great account of themselves when zero hour ticked round at last. Or would they? In the shadowy and crowded solitude of the assembly trenches, there must have been little solace in such communal courage. Every man was alone with his fears.

It was now the early hours of Saturday morning – 1 July at last.

Saturday 1 July
1.10 a.m.
The adjutant of the Young Citizens reported to Brigade HQ in 'Paisley Avenue' and was notified of zero hour. Watches were synchronised. Tear-gas shells and goggles were issued. Zero hour was passed on to all the officers in the assembly trenches. The YCVs' war diarist noticed that 'At this time a lull seemed to settle over all the earth as if it were a mutual tightening up for the great struggle shortly to commence.'[54]

3.00 a.m.
The Armagh Volunteers had by now reached their positions north of the Ancre, and awaited the dawn.[55] The lull continued. Meanwhile, south of the river, the adjutant of the Young Citizens heard the call of a water hen and also a bird that he thought was a nightingale.[56]

The Belfast Brigade was further back in Aveluy Wood. Tommy Ervine, of the East Belfast Volunteers, spent the night beside a 'big sandy-haired fellow' with whom he had once boxed on Belfast's Beersbridge Road, and chatted to him until both men managed to fall asleep for a short while.[57]

Colonel Crozier, meanwhile, was quite unable to sleep, and spent much of the time talking to Lieutenant-Colonel N.G. Bernard of the South Belfast Volunteers, resting against a tree trunk, eating sandwiches and drinking tea. Bernard's face looked like parchment in the eerie half-light. He expressed the hope to Crozier that at least this war might settle the 'Irish question'. Each man voiced unease about the battle plans, especially should the village of Thiepval, on the 36th's flank, not fall. They agreed to disobey orders in this eventuality, and to meet and lead their battalions out into no-man's-land themselves, improvising the best route across to the German trenches so as to avoid the bullets that would unquestionably rain down from the machine guns of an untaken Thiepval.

Crozier went over to his saddlebags and tried lying down, but his mind kept going back to the South African war and the final advance to Ladysmith. He got up and wandered amongst his men – 'I talk to some in lowered tones who are looking at the skies in contemplation.'

He found, on the north fringe of Aveluy Wood, a young man called Campbell, writing home. He told Crozier, on being questioned, that he felt doomed. He asked Crozier to take his green envelope and post it for him, if he could.

4.00 a.m.

Dawn started to break through. Crozier heard birds singing, and then the company cooks started to get ready: the West Belfast battalion was to be well prepared for the day ahead – strong sweet tea, rashers, fried bread and jam. Cold tea and lemon was put into the water bottles.[58] Other men were up, bringing fresh water to the reserve trenches in a big tank on a horse-drawn cart: 'We doled out the water the way the milk man used to dole out the milk from the milk bags.'

For others, dawn heralded a less satisfactory breakfast and considerable discussion as to why the attack was to be so late in the morning.

> Dawn came early with a wisp of mist on the marshes below us … As the
> light grew stronger we talked about why we were not ordered out at
> dawn. We knew the ground before us pretty well and even in the half-
> light we could have made our way across without too much trouble. The
> bit of sky above us turned grey then blue. There was a tuft of grass

growing half-way up the trench face and I pulled a couple of blades of grass and sucked them. I was sitting on the remains of an ammunition box. We shared out tins of bully and the biscuits with a drink of water. There was some of us that did not want to eat much, for they were … a bit tight in the belly.[59]

5.00 a.m.

William Montgomery, an officer with Crozier's battalion, ate some home-made bread sent by his family, then put into his lapel a sprig of white heather that he had also been sent, as a token of good luck.[60] Other men deliberately kept themselves calm by an almost ostentatious show of everyday rituals: 'There was a fellow Hobbs from Lurgan and, would you believe it, he was shaving. When he was finished he took out a clean pair of socks and put them on just as if he was back in barracks.'

By now, the command posts were occupied. One post in Hamel village was in a stone-walled cottage with sandbagged windows and its only ventilation through the fireplace. On one wall was a large map of the entire British front and another of the 36th's area of attack. There were numerous telephones, and lighting was by paraffin lamps, some of them suspended from the beams.[61] Near the cottage was a hastily built latrine.

6.00 a.m.

The Germans were now shelling the Ulster lines in a concentrated way, and the Armagh Volunteers were to suffer fifty casualties from shell fire before zero hour.[62] Shells began to fall around the YCVs' headquarters in 'Whitchurch Street'. Candles in the dugout kept going out with the thud and blast of explosions. One victim of the shells was in a machine-gun team to which Hugh Stewart belonged:

We'd been drumming up a cup of tea and Gerry spotted us and sent over a 5.9 and blew the machine-gun up – our Lewis gun was totally beyond repair. I got up after the explosion and I wondered why the ground was all springy underfoot – it was my mate, and he was lying there dead under the rubble and dust. He'd been alive a few minutes ago. Now I was standing on him.

Hugh Stewart was issued with a rifle, and told to go ahead and join the rest of the battalion in the assault. For Hugh, there was scarcely time to grieve over the personal loss; for the 36th Division, another crucial weapon was missing from the armoury.[63]

6.25 a.m.

The final British barrage opened up, soon to be joined by the trench mortars in short bursts of intense fire. This was the 'hurricane' bombardment. To Private Henry Berry of the Young Citizens, it was an awesome experience: 'The air seemed to be filled with a mighty rushing noise and the explosions were like giant doors being slammed.'[64] The YCVs war diarist recorded: 'It is marvellous how anything can live under such a hail of shells',[65] and Stewart-Moore observed: 'As the shells passed over our heads, the air hummed like a swarm of a 100 million hornets.'[66]

Usually, an intense bombardment had gone on each morning from 6.25 to 7.45. That morning, it would lift at 7.30; the hope was that the Germans would be caught all the more unawares when the infantry poured across at them.

6.45 a.m.

The mist of the early morning was beginning to clear. It was warm and the sun shone down on the fury of the bombardment. The sky above was blue with a few flecks of cloud.[67] Some men in the Ulster trenches knelt and prayed; some made out their wills in paybooks. Others stared at photographs of family, or thought of what might be happening at home just at this hour of the morning.[68]

Hugh Stewart had another narrow escape:

A fella called Heron got hit near me and I had to give him a fireman's lift back to the first-aid place. That hand grenade he had on him – I remember it well cutting into my flesh where it was stuck between his body and mine.[69]

The bombardiers were particularly busy, and a tragic incident occurred in one group of Young Citizens. Billy McFadzean and his fellow grenadiers were making final preparations: boxes of grenades were open and bombs were being handed out. Shells were dropping all around. Billy was opening a box – using a knife to cut the cord around it – when the box tumbled off its shelf and two bombs spilt out and shed their pins. An explosion would rip through the trench in a matter of seconds. Billy threw himself on the ground, sheltering the rest of the men from the blast. He was killed instantly, but his comrades were saved from death, and all but one escaped serious injury: one man was eventually to lose a leg as a result of his wounds. Billy's mutilated remains were placed on a stretcher, and as they were being taken away, his fellow soldiers instinctively removed their helmets, despite the ongoing bombardment and the flying shrapnel; many were in tears.

For his sacrifice, Billy would receive the Victoria Cross, the first awarded to a soldier in the Somme campaign.[70]

7.00 a.m.

By now, the traditional issue of rum had been distributed. Many men in the 36th, being teetotallers, did not drink their share, and others got double or even triple the amount. As it was very strong rum, some men awaited zero hour in a considerable degree of intoxication.[71] Some also supplemented the rum with a little illegal alcohol: 'There was a man from Donegal town with us, and God knows where he got it from, but he had a bottle of apple brandy and we all had a tot each'.[72]

Some men had picked wild flowers and placed them in their tunics: yellow charlock, blue cornflowers and crimson poppies. Some had even acquired orange lilies, the symbolic flowers of the Battle of the Boyne celebration.[73] A few men had managed to stow away their Orange sashes, and now they placed them around their shoulders. Some gained solace in a sense of corporate identity, and extemporised an Orange or Masonic lodge meeting in the last minutes.

> Each man there was in full battle kit complete with rifle and gas mask and when the Lodge was called to order a couple of German shells landed …
> but we still went on with the meeting.[74]

By now, laneways had been cut through the 36th's own barbed wire by special groups of wire-cutters. Gaps had also been cut in the parapet within the last hour, to give some platoons easy access to no-man's-land. At 7.00 a.m. an officer in the South Antrim battalion looked up and saw British planes being fired at as they flew over the German lines, but they did not seem to be damaged.[75]

7.10 a.m.

General Nugent's plan, unlike that of most other divisional commanders, was to send his men out into no-man's-land just before zero hour; there they would wait, protected by the curtain of shell fire on the German lines, and that much closer to their objective when the whistle blew. So at 7.10 the first Ulstermen of the day crossed the parapet north of the Ancre – a first wave of Armagh Volunteers who would lie down in long lines and await the cessation of the bombardment. The second wave would follow five minutes later, the third at 7.20, and the final wave at 7.30. Hidden by smoke and by the earth thrown up in the explosions, and especially by smoke shells and tear-gas shells fired into the Ancre valley, they nervously anticipated the crucial moment.[76]

7.15 a.m.

The first troops south of the river began to move out into no-man's-land – the men from Derry, Tyrone, Down and South Antrim. Five minutes later, the second line of battalions began to move into the front trenches that the first wave of troops had vacated. The Young Citizens, for instance, moved up and made brief contact with the Derry battalion as they headed over the top.[77]

7.25 a.m.

In the last moments, the bombardment seemed to reach its horrific crescendo. All along the Somme front, a whole generation of young men awaited battle, tensing themselves for the silence that would herald the start, at long last, of the Big Push.

7.30 a.m.

The gunfire ceased. There were a few moments of stillness before the officers' whistles were blown and the men rose to their feet to commence the walk to the German parapet. One war correspondent, with *The Times*, watched in fascination and later commented: 'When I saw the men emerge through the smoke and form up as if on parade, I could hardly believe my eyes.'[78]

Ambrose Ricardo, commanding his Tyrone battalion, was unable, as a senior officer, to go with his 'dear boys', but he stood at the firestep watching them rise to their feet:

I shall never forget for one minute the extraordinary sight. The Derrys, on our left, were so eager they started a few minutes before the ordered time, and the Tyrones were not going to be left behind, and they got going without delay – no fuss, no shouting, no running; everything orderly, solid and thorough, just like the men themselves. Here and there a boy would wave his hand to me as I shouted 'Good luck' to them through my megaphone, and all had a happy face. Many were carrying loads. Fancy advancing against heavy fire carrying a heavy roll of barbed wire on your shoulders![79]

That view that Ricardo had of his Volunteers turning to wave at him, implausible and over-sentimental as his description seems, is a poignant representation of the fate of the entire division. Ricardo was witnessing the goodbyes of a whole generation, the last few seconds in which communities, villages and families would remain intact.

The Ulster Volunteers waved farewell to the world, strode towards the 'Devil's Dwelling-place', and into the steel muzzles of machine guns.

SOUTH OF THE ANCRE, 7.30 TO 9.00 A.M.

The leading soldiers advanced towards the first German line, their walk turning to a charge as they neared the objective. There were cries of 'No Surrender, boys!' As they reached the German trenches and the first men jumped into them, through the shattered wire, the German machine guns began to open up from Thiepval and from across the river to the north.[80] The enemy were out of their dugouts and shelters, and manning their guns, not just on the Schwaben Redoubt but on the high ground on either side of the Ulster sector. The bombardment had not been as effective as had been promised, and now the heavily burdened infantrymen faced fierce and accurate gunfire.

The South Antrim Volunteers, especially the later waves, were met by a hail of machine-gun bullets. Captain O.B. Webb of D Company fell; other officers were shot; and the battalion was losing those on whom it depended for words of command.[81] Hugh Stewart – a Lewis gunner now without his machine gun since that morning's accident – hurtled for the line. Bullets split his respirator, rendering it useless. Two inches to the left and his chest would have been pierced. On reaching the first German line,

The Charge of the Ulster Division.
This painting by William Conor
was one of a series that
was printed on Christmas cards
to raise medical funds.
SOMME MUSEUM

Hugh caught his boot in the barbed wire, and in a desperate attempt to get
disentangled, he pulled a piece out of it, leaving his big toe sticking out for
the rest of the battle.[82] Albert Bruce, seeing men fall all around him, reached
the Sunken Road, stopped and fell down. Looking up from ground level,
he saw bodies drop so frequently ahead of him that he could not face going
on to what seemed like certain annihilation. He lay there, still as a corpse,
listening to bullets whistling and cries from the wounded.[83]

A new source of destruction became apparent when the German artillery
fire that had been concentrated on the British lines shifted to no-man's-
land. Many men sheltered in shell holes; some were blown to pieces; others
pushed on.

The Down Volunteers – very vulnerable to fire from north of the river
– were devastated. The majority of their officers were casualties before the
battalion had even reached German territory. One soldier in the County

Down battalion looked back and saw the bodies lying on the sun–lit slopes like 'sheaves of corn on the ground'. Another County Down man looked round halfway across no-man's-land and saw his best friend caught in the British wire by his clothing; machine-gun bullets riddled his body as he tried frantically to get free. A seventeen–year-old reached the German lines when suddenly his arm was torn open by a machine-gun bullet. He lay flat, trying to staunch the blood.[84]

The third line had to be reached by 7.48 a.m., so the men who had got to the German trenches immediately began to bomb dugouts and engage in hand-to-hand combat with those Germans they could find.

> We had a young officer not as old as some of us, and as hard-faced,
> crooked a sergeant as ever walked on two feet. As we moved across
> no-man's-land a shell landed on our left. It could have been one of our
> own landing a bit short. Anyway it killed the officer and wounded the
> sergeant and a bit of it hit me on the upper part of my left arm and cut
> me, but not too badly. The old sergeant kept going till we reached the
> German lines. With the first bomb he threw the door off a deep dugout,
> and the next two he flung inside. He must have killed every
> German in it. We left him sitting just below the parapet with a
> grenade in each hand ready for the next live German that came along.
> We did not stay that long in that line but moved on to the next.
> Then to the 3rd line ... It was here that the real fighting started.
> I had never killed a man with a bayonet before and it sent cold shivers up
> and down my spine many's a night afterwards just thinking about it. It
> must have taken our lot about a quarter of an hour to clear a hundred
> yards or so of the trench. I was one of them left to hold the line
> because I had to get my arm bandaged. We found some food the
> Germans had and it was worse than our own rations but we were so
> hungry we ate them.[85]

The bombing of the dugouts was not as efficient as it might have been. Often, the stairways descended in a spiral, so that the explosion of a Mills bomb on the steps did not damage the entire dugout. Survivors were often left, and the Ulstermen, because of the rigorous timetable for advance, could not investigate each bunker thoroughly. Germans could emerge and take Ulstermen from the rear.[86]

Meanwhile, the troops were heading off in the second great wave of the Ulster Division's assault. At 7.30 the YCVs had moved into the positions vacated by the leading Inniskilling battalion. It was a fearsome prospect to see and hear the onslaught that had greeted the Inniskillings. But at 7.40 the Young Citizens climbed over and into the hell of no-man's-land. The battalion war diarist recorded that at 7.45 his worst fears had been realised: 'No sooner were they clear of our own line than the slow tat-tat of the Hun machine guns from Thiepval village and Beaumont-Hamel caught the advance under a deadly crossfire.'[87]

For Jim Maultsaid, stepping into no-man's-land was like meeting 'a wall of flame'. He staggered and gasped with shock. His hair seemed to be scorching. The air was full of hissing, burning metal, and the ground rocked as shells exploded. He was acutely aware of the cries and screams of those caught by explosions or bullets – the sound of those voices would never leave his mind throughout his life. He was also aware of the YCVs' flag – with its distinctive shamrock and Red Hand of Ulster – fluttering somewhere ahead, tied to the barrel of a rifle. On reaching the German lines, Jim's firm friend Wedgewood was killed by a German hand grenade, and another pal, 'Kid' Lewis, was killed trying to organise one of the parties of prisoners that could now be sent back. What was so appalling for the soldiers was that they were watching their friends, relations and neighbours dying beside them, not just other troops. The closely territorial – almost tribal – bonding of the UVF saw to that.[88]

John Kennedy Hope and his friend were carrying consolidating materials – spades and coils of wire – and as they were going over the top, they met an explosion. They flung themselves down. Then they decided to leave spades and wire behind – a 'donkey load', Hope called it. The bullets all around were like a hail storm, but Hope and his friend went forward into the front line. Here, all that he was to remember was confusion and disorder. Hope, half dazed, went off 'on the prowl' on his own. He recalled bumping into Lieutenant R.V. Gracey, who was saying to himself, 'If I could only get a message back to Thiepval ...' The clearest memory by far was to be one that Hope would probably rather have forgotten:

A 9th Inniskilling lying at the top has got a bullet through his steel hat.
He rolls over into the trenches at my feet. He is an awful sight. His brain

Photographs of empty trenches on the Schwaben Redoubt, taken just
after the Ulster Division's capture of the enemy position
SOMME MUSEUM

is oozing out of the side of his head and he is calling for his pal. An
occasional cry of 'Billy Gray, Billy Gray, will you not come to me?' In a
short time all is quiet, he is dead. He's the servant to an officer who is
lying in the trench with a fractured thigh and won't let anyone touch
him, and he is bleeding badly. They die together.[89]

G.H.M. also saw suffering that would make a lasting impression. In the first few minutes, the brother of his comrade Frank McIlvoy was killed not far from him. Sergeant E.R. Powell told Frank to push on – and he did. On reaching the German trenches, Captain J.V. Hyndman sent G.H.M. back to the British lines with a message. He had no time to consider the probability that he would not get back across no-man's-land, but darting from shell hole to shell hole in his light scout's uniform, he made it as swiftly as he could. He found 'Elgin Avenue' 'crowded with walking wounded'. Now – his message successfully delivered to HQ – it was his duty to return again across no-man's-land and find another officer to work for. Amazingly, he made it once again, and joined a mixed company of soldiers in the enemy's third line. He had survived unscathed so far, for the role of the scout allowed his natural cunning to 'function in the art of personal survival. I was isolated and detached, exactly what I liked.'[90]

The battle for the Schwaben Redoubt was at its height, and the Donegal and Fermanagh Volunteers were busy trying to take the Crucifix. These men had seen at close quarter some of the destruction that had greeted the first waves going in at 7.30. Many of them sat in the trenches and joined together in the Lord's Prayer. At 7.40, on the sound of a whistle, they got up and went over. Some were to recall vividly the beauty of the sunshine and the blue sky: 'It was as fair a morning as ever graced God's earth.'

Before long, the shell fire and the machine-gun bullets were pinning men down in shell holes, and it took a long time to get to the German lines: 'A Captain shouted "You're late. What the Hell kept you?" One of the boys said "Sorry sir, but we were delayed coming through Hell."'

Of course, some men never managed to get further than their own parapet, and the stretcher-bearers prepared to gather them and take them back for treatment or, if need be, for burial.

> There was about seven or eight of us right down in the front line with stretchers. The first wave went over the parapet in the regulated Army fashion but the ones that went over late were more canny and did not jump over but sort of rolled over on their sides like. We were soon busy for a burst of machine-gun fire caught a lot of men as they climbed over and some of them fell shot at our feet. The ones we knew were dead we put in a dugout and started carrying the wounded to the posts. Some of

the men were whistling Orange songs and now and again you'd get a few words from 'Dolly's Brae' or 'The Sash'.[91]

Other victims were not so fortunate as to be near help. J.S. Reid of the Donegal and Fermanagh battalion saw figures trying to crawl back the way they had come, or stirring a little, feebly, then lying still, or gathering themselves into a huddle as though to comfort themselves as they were dying.[92] By 8.15 a.m. the war diarist of the YCVs recorded, 'corpses were piling high on the Sunken Road'.

On the Schwaben Redoubt and around the Crucifix, all was confusion. There was barely an officer to be seen amongst the Donegal and Fermanagh men, and NCOs took over the job of command:

This old sergeant took charge of us … the sergeant took us into a dugout where there was less noise and told us … we had to go up a cross-trench to get into the next line. He did not know if there was any Germans in the cross-trench and if there was we would have to fight our way up to clear that trench for the next men coming through.

… We had a man from Roslea with us and he did a bit of poaching and he could move without making a sound, so him and the sergeant set off first. The sergeant could clout a bomb further than any other man I knew. We were to leave in pairs counting twenty between one pair and the next … I had a bayonet in one hand and a revolver in the other. You see I used to shoe horses before I joined up and had powerful strong wrists and it was not a great hardship for me to fire one of them big heavy revolvers. They had a kick like a horse but if you hit a man with a bullet from one of them he gave no more trouble … we all made our way down to the third line … here there was one young officer … and he set about getting us set for a bayonet charge against the trenches in front of us – the Crucifix … we fixed bayonets and charged. There was not many Germans left alive. Few of us got hit on the dash across, maybe we caught the Germans off guard … we cleared the trenches right down to the Mouquet Switch – we settled down to hold the bit we captured. We took no prisoners and we had not to detail any men guard duty. First we gathered up all the bombs, the German ones as well as our own. (This meant going over the dead looking for bombs.) We had a lot of our own men wounded and we took care of these as best we could. Then we collected our dead and put them in two dugouts. We moved the German dead out of our way. It was warm and clammy and we were sweating in the heat. We had little or no water and we were very thirsty ...[93]

Elsewhere on the Schwaben Redoubt, it was a matter of what one survivor was to call 'playing leapfrog with death'. There was bitter hand-to-hand fighting to capture the third line. Then, when the barrage lifted at 8.48, there came an intense struggle for the fourth line – described by one man as 'a Belfast riot on the top of Mount Vesuvius'. The spirit of aggression was maintained by shouting at the Germans. 'We couldn't help taunting them a lot. "Would you like some Irish Rebellion?" we called out to them.'[94]

In a life-or-death situation like this, the German was not seen as a person or an individual with feelings; only a vaguely perceived but highly dangerous object to be destroyed. The vision was of 'a crowd of grey figures', or 'a few swirlings here and there of grey-clad figures with upraised hands yelling "*Kamerad*"'. A German corpse was 'a heap of blood-stained greyishness on the ground'.[95] As for Germans who tried to surrender, there was the suspicion that they were not to be trusted: 'A German I remember pretended to have his arms up to surrender but he threw a bomb as he did so – so we got him.'[96]

Those Germans who had effectively surrendered had to be taken across no-man's-land.

> One man, whose name we shall never know, could be seen walking across
> the open behind about sixty prisoners, some of them apparently wounded,
> holding them together as jealously as a sheepdog holds his flock, urging
> along the laggards, keeping ever behind the last man of his party ...[97]

The only time when mutual suffering was acknowledged was when injured enemies met by chance: 'I crawled into a shell hole and found a wounded German soldier there. I pointed at my wound and he pointed at his legs.'[98] Otherwise, only a vague sense of the human damage done by their weapons occurred to the Ulstermen; the fact of seeing their friends and colleagues mutilated or dying prevented empathy with Germans in similar straits:

> My friend was lying there beside me with his leg off – but conscious –
> there was nothing I could do for him ... I remember a bunch of Jerries

205

stuck in an underground place and we got a trench mortar and fired it down there. We were blown off our feet, so goodness knows what it was like for the Jerries ... and a bunch of Jerries just across from us – we couldn't shoot them, for our rifles was jammed, and they couldn't get us so we threw a couple of Mills bombs over and that was the end of them![99]

SOUTH OF THE ANCRE, 9.00 A.M. TO MIDDAY

Shortly after nine o'clock, the German fourth line had been successfully assaulted, and the Crucifix and the Schwaben Redoubt had, at terrific cost, been captured. Parties cleared trenches north towards the river. Under pressure, the Ulstermen continued to consolidate their position, awaiting the moment, at 10.00 or shortly after, when the Belfast Brigade – which had already crossed no-man's-land – could attempt its assault on the fifth line. However, it appeared highly debatable to the division's commanding officers whether any attack should be launched on the final line. The divisions on the 36th's flanks had made no gains whatsoever, and their reserve battalions were not being committed in an attempt to wrest from the Germans what their first waves had signally failed to obtain. The Ulstermen were driving a very exposed wedge into the German territory and were vulnerable. The Belfast battalions might be heading for destruction if they tried to push further on.

At 8.32 a request had been sent to 10th Corps HQ asking whether the 107th Brigade might be stopped from advancing on the fifth line. The reply given was that new assaults were being planned north and south of the Ulstermen, so the Belfast battalions really ought to go ahead. Three quarters of an hour later, an order was received to withhold the 107th Brigade until the situation on the Ulstermen's flanks had improved. But the Belfast Brigade had already crossed no-man's-land to the Schwaben Redoubt, and the men were waiting for the barrage to lift so as to launch their big assault. Because telephone lines taken forward had been cut by German fire, and runners such as G.H.M. were few, isolated and confused, the attempt to inform the Belfast Brigade was to fail, and their assault on the final line took place after all.[100]

Since 6.30 the Belfast battalions had been assembling behind the leading waves of troops. Crozier could feel his adrenalin flow and, according to his later recollections, 'thanked God' for his chance to fight. He was beginning to feel his 'blood boil', and he remembered some poetry: 'One crowded hour of glorious life is worth an age without a name!' He and Colonel Bernard, of the South Belfast battalion, were both going out into no-man's-land, despite all instructions to the contrary. As zero hour arrived and the leading battalions headed towards the German lines, the Belfast men moved up to occupy their places. On their way, they picked up coils of wire and iron posts. Crozier looked to the right and saw the 32nd Division being annihilated in front of Thiepval village: 'live men rush forward in orderly procession to swell the weight of numbers in the spider's web'.

How could he modify his attack to avoid such butchery? As he considered, the noise of German counter-attacking shell fire increased. Men around him tried to sing as they waited in the trenches. Major Gaffikin said, 'Good luck, sir' to Crozier, and then, 'Tell them I died a teetotaller.' Already the South Belfast Volunteers were being mauled on the right, due to the inadequate cover of a denuded Thiepval Wood. Then, shortly after 8.30, the opportunity came. Crozier found the shell fire easing for a few minutes – this was the moment. He ordered his men to rush forward into no-man's-land in small groups and to occupy the Sunken Road. Then he went out and stood there in full view of everyone, giving orders.[101] To Malcolm McKee, one of his men, he looked like a tiger, and he gave McKee 'a feeling of glee that we were in the battle together'.[102]

Bernard, in league with Crozier, was to follow suit, sending his South Belfast men in small squads to the Sunken Road as the West Belfast battalion vacated it in a second mad dash for the German front line. But Bernard was fatally wounded, and his leaderless battalion became dispirited, cowering in Thiepval Wood. Crozier took charge of the South Belfast men; threatening to shoot them if they disobeyed, he ushered them towards the German lines. Then he retired safely to his HQ in the wood, past wounded men lying out in no-man's-land: 'sun-baked, parched, uncared for, often delirious and at any rate in great pain'. And when he got back to the dugout that served as HQ, he found it, too, full of dead and wounded.[103]

Meanwhile. Major Gaffikin helped rally the waverers of the West Belfast battalion as they approached the German lines. Some men later recalled that he was wearing an 'Orange sash or handkerchief'; others, more lucidly, that

On the back of this photograph is written 'Bertie and friend. Missing at the Somme.'
SOMME MUSEUM

it was probably an orange flash or insignia – for orange was the colour of the 9th Battalion.[104]

The East Belfast men were last to leave for the German lines. Tommy Ervine was in one of the later waves of that battalion, and just ahead of him went the sandy-haired fellow from the Beersbridge Road beside whom he had slept that night. He came falling, stumbling back into the trench beside Tommy. At first, Tommy could not see what was wrong, then the man opened his mouth and blood spurted out in great regular beats. Tommy grabbed and held him, and the blood soaked his tunic. He pushed back the man's helmet and discovered a long, deep split in his forehead, caused by shell fire. Tommy and another soldier dragged the wounded friend to one side and prepared to go over straight away themselves. Tommy, as he ran over no-man's-land, felt a stinging heat on his shoulder but thought nothing of it.

Later, he realised he'd been hit by shrapnel. When he got to the German lines, he joined the other Belfast men in helping to consolidate the gains already made. Germans had come back up trenches from Grandcourt and Thiepval; others emerged from dugouts. Tommy threw his grenades down a dugout as if he was throwing a cricket ball, and shouted: 'Divide that amongst yez!' Still there was confusion all around:

> Somebody shouts 'Go that way', so I did and sure enough somebody got me on the leg, so I made for him – a German and I got him, shot him in the face. Then I tried to walk back and I couldn't. I'd been shot. A big fella called Andy Robb pulled me back … I'd have liked to get in among them Germans with my bayonet because they'd mowed us down like pieces of wood … It was terrible … it was cruel.

Tommy was badly enough injured to be brought in by the stretcher-bearers. His fighting career was over.[105]

At 8.45 a runner had brought a message back that the Belfast Brigade was, despite considerable casualties, implanted on the far side of no-man's-land, itching to help take the fourth line and then await the moment for the rush to the last line.[106]

Crozier had now joined the few men who were in the 36th's own front trenches watching the progress of the battle out on the Schwaben Redoubt:

> There is a shout. Someone seizes a Lewis gun … I see an advancing crowd of field grey. Fire is opened … The enemy fall like grass before the scythe … 'Good heavens,' I shout, 'those men are prisoners surrendering, and some of our own wounded men are escorting them. Cease fire!'

But the chance of killing some enemy soldiers proved too tempting:

> The fire ripples on for a time. The target is too good to lose. 'After all, they are only Germans,' I hear a youngster say.[107]

Meanwhile, even before the barrage had lifted off the fifth line, men of the Belfast Brigade, aided by some from other battalions, were thrusting out across the inhospitable, bullet-raked stretch of land between them and their objective. This would prove a foolish move as some of the artillery fire was landing short, and men were killed by their own shells. But the Ulstermen – trying to learn the lessons of earlier in the day – were determined to get as close as possible to the final trench system before the barrage lifted off it. Few recollections exist of that final struggle for the fifth line. The 36th was the only division on the Somme to break this far into the enemy's trench system. Those who survived the fight for the last line were to be very few: 'In the final rush ... only about half our men made it. Even fewer made it back.'

The men who got there managed to maintain their position for a while, under enormous pressure. They even, it was reputed, contrived to rewire and fortify a section of about a hundred yards of trench. Above all else, they engaged in hand-to-hand struggles in which only the most aggressive soldiers were able to survive.

> There was one soldier I'll never forget ... He made himself a special weapon for fighting in the trenches. It was about half the length of a pick shaft and on one end he screwed in a pear-shaped lump of cast iron, on the other was a leather thong which he kept tied around his waist. He used to parry a bayonet thrust with the rifle and then swing this lump of cast iron upwards. No matter where it hit a man it broke bones. He'd smash a man's wrist or hand, then when the rifle flew from the man's hands he'd shoot him. I fought beside him in the 'D' line that day. He fought like a devil. He must have killed a dozen Germans ... I don't know how long we were in the 'D' line but while we were there we fought every second, there was no rest at all. The blood had got about the tongue of our boots and our socks were soaked with it.[108]

But the fifth line was a vulnerable position for so few British soldiers to try to hold, and they were exposed to both shells and machine-gun fire. By midday the line had been cleared of Ulstermen as the Germans began to surge up the trenches from St-Pierre-Divion.[109] The tide of advance had reached its furthest point, and the German counter-attack was beginning to gather force. Not only that, but because German gunfire dominated no-man's-land, the Ulstermen were in trouble at the rear. By late morning, the 36th Division was virtually besieged in the four lines it had only just taken.

Meanwhile, stretcher-bearers were dealing with the awful carnage of the wounded, dying and dead. Doctors in the makeshift hospitals – appalled and overworked beyond any expectation – struggled to keep going. Anyone who appeared to have no hope of living was inevitably set on one side to die.

Private Thomas Marcus, an Ulster Division boy soldier. He was just sixteen years old when he died at the Somme.
SOMME MUSEUM

The doctor says to me, 'Bring no more in here.' One big fellow I seen from Donegal had the steel helmet on OK but a piece of shrapnel the width o' two fingers was right through into his skull. He said to me, 'D'you think will I die with this?' And I said, 'No you'll not die,' but I knew he hadn't an earthly. Well the doctor chased us … that fellow was bound to drop … he kept talking about his grandmother too … a big stout fellow he was.

Other victims of bullet or shrapnel were not so lucky as to have companionship in the hour of death. They lay out in the heat of midday in the lonely din of no-man's-land, and experienced the last agonising hours with no comfort:

There was fellas crawlin' back that couldn't walk … One fella lay down, put down his rifle, covered himself with his groundsheet and when we came across him he was dead. No one to touch them! I used to think it was terrible to see young lives – the blood of life oozing out of them. Nobody there to lift their head – not one – nobody there to care – that was it![110]

At the 108th Field Ambulance's station at Forceville, a runner had arrived shortly after 8.30 with a message that there were three or four hundred dead or wounded lying in no-man's-land, most of them in the Sunken Road area. The orderlies at the Forceville station simply did not believe him, and thought there had been a mistake in the message. One doctor got on the field telephone to the command post nearby and queried the number of casualties, but confirmation was given. Immediately, some orderlies, with a few of the walking wounded for extra help, went to the front of Thiepval Wood and set up another aid post in a dugout there, taking dressings, splints, stretchers and bandages with them. A motorbike messenger was sent back to the nearest large medical depot to ask for more morphia. Meanwhile, the new first-aid station set to work, with six stretcher parties operating in no-man's-land saving as many lives as they could.

In the advanced dressing station in Aveluy Wood, the work was gruelling and distressing. Little could be done for those with bad mutilations. Most of the men were thirsty, and orderlies tried to provide clean water to drink or, still better, a mug of hot sweet tea:

> The doctor tried to look over each patient as soon as he arrived … the dead was left to one side. The ones there was no hope for was put in a tent and morphia and cigarettes was all that was used in there. It was a terrible thing to light a cigarette for a soldier and see him die before he finished it. All we did was re-dress a wound if he needed it and if somebody needed a bit of tidying up we did that as well. The only operations that was done regular like was taking off an arm or a leg or stitching up wounds. All the big operations was done at the main dressing station or the hospitals proper.

In the command posts, meanwhile, the atmosphere grew grimmer. In Hamel village, the air inside the sandbagged cottage grew stickier and more unpleasant in the July heat. Men went outside regularly for a smoke to relieve

The corpse of a German soldier lies in the debris and rubble
ROYAL ULSTER RIFLES MUSEUM

the tension. By mid-morning 'you could have cut the air with a knife'. Frayed nerves began to show in bad-tempered commands and complaints. Cups of tea and coffee were drunk incessantly as men came and went, speaking in a hush and walking on the stone-flagged floor without making a clatter. Everyone felt cut off from the battle, but they knew, despite all the confusion of reports coming in, that there had been great loss of life.[111]

During the morning, the men of the 49th Division's 146th Brigade – the official reinforcements in the Ulster sector – moved up to the south-east corner of Thiepval Wood to take up a reserve position. Across no-man's-land on the Schwaben Redoubt, William Montgomery, an officer of the West Belfast battalion, was receiving good news – that Lieutenant Sanderson with a party of men and machine guns had been in action in the southern portion of the fourth line and seemed to be dominating that part of the German trenches. In fact, the party had reconnoitred the Mouquet Switch, which led south to the rear of Thiepval village, and had found it empty of German soldiers. Sadly, there was insufficient strength in the Ulster camp to exploit this promising situation.[112]

In an attempt to strengthen the officers' ranks on the Schwaben Redoubt, Major Peacocke, second-in-command of the Fermanagh Volunteers, went across no-man's-land with a brief to take charge of the Derry and Fermanagh men. By midday a very firm bid was being made to consolidate a significant section of the third line. Mixed Rifles and Inniskillings, under Majors Gaffikin and Peacocke, were struggling to hold on to the gains of the morning, but even as they did so, German flanking parties were moving into the old German front line and attacking the Ulstermen from the rear.[113] In an attempt to get men and supplies to the Schwaben Redoubt, two companies of Pioneers tried desperately to dig a shallow communication trench across no-man's-land.[114] But machine-gun fire rained down from Thiepval, and before long the Pioneers had to give up on this enterprise.

So, at midday the Ulster Division, south of the river, was besieged, but still had a firm grip of the German trenches. What would the commanders do? Would they press the attack again on each flank of the Ulstermen? Could the 36th be reinforced by the 146th Brigade? Could the artillery not be concentrated on Thiepval village, wiping out, if possible, the German machine-gunners? Surely the advances that the Ulstermen had made ought to be exploited? Two thirds of the Somme battlefield had seen complete failure, and some fifty thousand British soldiers had become casualties by noon. What hard-won gains the 36th had made deserved to be followed up, not let slip.

But for men like Hugh Stewart, exhaustion and numbness were already beginning to develop. Hugh sat in a trench and thought vaguely about how lucky he'd been. He could have been dead by now, and, indeed, if a gas attack came he would be helpless as his respirator was riddled with holes. He looked at his fellow soldiers and none of them could recognise one another. Due to a thick covering of cordite and lidite from the explosions, their faces had turned as yellow as that of jaundice victims. The heavy dust and earth everywhere were putting some men's guns completely out of action. It came to Hugh's mind that they'd end up fighting with bayonets, and maybe they would be down to fighting with stones if it kept going on. Hugh tried to speak but had lost his voice. His throat was dry and parched; his eyes watered; his tongue was swollen and seemed to fill his mouth. But one macabre sight stuck in his mind – sitting not far away, another soldier pulled out his Orange flute and managed to play a few bars of a tune, as if in defiance of the hell in which he found himself trapped.[115]

North of the river, the front-line troops had made for the German trenches. The first waves encountered the ravine – seventy yards wide, fifteen to twenty feet high in places, and steep. Despite instructions to walk, they broke into a gallop. Arriving at the first German line, they found the wire fairly well cut and their path to the parapet easy. There was little opposition. They were in the front trenches. One group of men made it right through the third line and headed for Beaucourt station.

But the second wave was just beginning to be caught by machine-gun fire, as Germans who had come up from their dugouts began to man their posts. In particular, gun-fire came from Beaumont-Hamel, with its elevated position. As the third and fourth waves clambered up the ravine, the fire intensified and men fell to the ground, bleeding and in agony.[116]

Those German machine guns could never be forgotten. To some, it seemed that 'the bullets literally came like water from an immense hose with a perforated top'.[117] Others recalled how 'you could see the bullets in the air and it looked like a fine shower of hail, you know the way hail looks as it's thinning out and the sun behind it'.[118]

The Mid Antrim Volunteers, arriving at the German lines, encountered 'great rolls of wire with barbs as long as a man's thumb'.[119] They found that the artillery shells had not done a wholly effective job in their area. The gaps in the wire were few and far between, so the men clustered there, and on them the German machine guns were quickly trained. Clearly, the dugouts had not been severely damaged by the barrage. Bullets spat. The clusters of Ulstermen were prime targets. On three occasions, the Mid Antrim men tried to get into the German trenches. Only a group of five to ten men managed it; scores were casualties. Men scurried for whatever scanty cover the slopes of the ravine offered. Severely injured and dying soldiers lay all around. The orders had been not to assist wounded colleagues but to leave them to be picked up by supporting platoons and stretcher-bearers.[120]

While some advance parties of the Armagh Volunteers and a few Mid Antrim men pushed on towards Beaucourt station, in considerable isolation, German infantry filtered in from the flanks. These Ulstermen were soon fired on from three sides – from Germans guarding the station, from the Germans re-entering the lines to their rear, and from the enemy positions

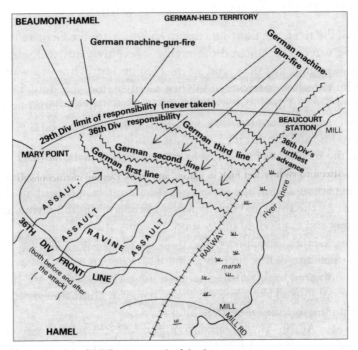

The attack of the 36th Division, north of the Ancre

to the north at Beaumont-Hamel. The 29th Division had made no progress against the Germans in that sector, so they were able to turn south and fire down on the Ulstermen.

Divisional HQ was informed that the enemy had regained his front line. A substantial part of both attacking battalions was dead or wounded, most of the rest trapped.[121] The remainder of the morning would merely involve salvage operations and the minimisation of damage. The British artillery could hardly land shells on the German front lines again for fear of hitting many of their own men, who, at least in theory if not in practice, ought to be there.

German artillery was pounding the Ulstermen's own forward trenches, preventing reserve troops of the Fusiliers and Rifles from assisting in the battle. Another problem was the serious failure – due to lack of ammunition or to damage inflicted by German shell fire – of the Ulster machine guns that had gone forward, as Gunner Ryan, of Tandragee, found out:

The officers of the ill-fated 9th Royal Irish Fusiliers. Ten of the twenty-eight men pictured here would die before the war ended.
ROYAL IRISH FUSILIERS MUSEUM

There were two Lewis guns going over with the 9th Fusiliers – we got held up by the wire … the other gun crew got set up in a good spot behind a natural rise in the ground and we got our gun going from a shell hole. More ammunition had to be carried out to us as the men moved forward but we only got about a third of the supplies we should have had. Suddenly we realised there was no more men going past us, we were on our own. The crew of the other gun was either killed or wounded, and a big man called Hill from near Lurgan crawled to the pit and collected the good bullets, for the other Lewis gun was wrecked and no good to us. The German soldiers got back into their own trenches again and we started to fire short bursts at them … we helped to cover the retreat of the Fusiliers and the Rifles. We ran out of ammunition completely. Gunner Hill and myself managed to trail the gun and two wounded back to our own lines. There was a big gap in our wire and we covered this with the Lewis. By dinner-time we had collected all the spare Lewis-gun bullets and was ready for the Germans we thought would attack us.

Those who made it into the German trenches came back, retreating one by one, or else paid the price as the enemy attacked them:

There was a wee runt of a man from Ballymena, even when standing on a
box he could hardly see over the parapet, but a powerful hard wee
man ... I saw him lying dead with his bayonet stuck into a big German
officer twice his size. The German still held in his hand the pistol
he shot Jimmie with.

The men trapped near the station had to decide whether to surrender or
to try to jettison heavier equipment and head back, if they could, to their lines:

We got to within 100 yards of the station and shot a German sentry. We
got into what must have been at one time a German trench and waited
for the rest to catch up with us but they never came. We could see
nothing but Germans all around us. When we were in the old German
trench ... a sergeant asked us if we wanted to surrender. 'No surrender'
was the shout. 'No surrender, no Home Rule. For God and Ulster.' The
sergeant went over to a young officer and talked for a while. The officer
waved a hand at us and shouted but we could not hear him. We had to
leave him where he was because he was badly wounded and we could not
take him with us ... we were ordered back. While we were going
forward we did not feel the tiredness or the weight of the packs but going
back even the rifle seemed a ton. We dumped all the heavy stuff and
made our way over the railway lines to the top of the bank of the river ...
The Fusiliers and Rifles caught in or near the ditch put down a covering
fire which helped some of us caught behind the German lines to make it
back to the riverbank and back to our own front lines. We then put down
covering fire and helped the men in the ditch get back as well. I heard
afterwards that only a quarter of us got back alive. I led a party of walking
wounded back to Hamel where everything was astir. The ones that was
not too badly cut stayed at the aid post to give whatever help they could.

For the wounded, lying in agony in the blaze of the sun in no-man's-
land, the arrival of stretcher-bearers or retreating comrades was a heavenly
sight. But the journey back to the home trenches could be excruciating:

When there is only one bearer the only way to get a wounded man out is
to carry him on your back or to trail him along on a stretcher or a piece
of stuff like a blanket or a strip of canvas, or even a cape or greatcoat. It
must have been painful for the wounded man but it was better than

leaving him to die in the open. Some of the men not too badly shot brought in their worse-off comrades. Often they carried them on their backs or on a makeshift stretcher made from bits of trench-facing [wooden boards] or stretchers made from a few jackets. You did this by turning the sleeves of the jacket inside out down the inside of the jacket, buttoned it up and put a couple of poles down the sleeves. I've seen rifles used instead of poles.

Throughout the rest of the morning, stragglers and the slightly and seriously wounded arrived back in little groups. Sometimes, lone individuals arrived.

The attack north of the Ancre cannot be seen as other than a military failure.[122] The sheer waste of that July morning is apparent from a look at the fate of one battalion. The Armagh Volunteers had been decimated. Nearly two years of hard work and training in the army – and for many, several months of previous training in the UVF – had come to nothing due to a complete inadequacy in military strategy. The bombardment had failed to cut wire and destroy dugouts, and it was quite inflexible for targeting in emergency situations. The ravine had been far too difficult to negotiate. The Germans had been very swift to their guns, and their machine-gun superiority had been visible and effective. The German occupation of the high ground was invaluable, and the rigid wave formation of attack was quite inappropriate. Above all, it had been a nonsense to expect less than a massacre if the division flanking the Ulstermen to the north did not wipe out the Beaumont-Hamel machine guns. There were no emergency procedures for such an eventuality.

The statistics speak for themselves. Blacker's Boys – the Armagh, Monaghan and Cavan Volunteers – like any infantry battalion had a fighting strength of roughly eight hundred men. Approximately six hundred, with fifteen officers, went over the parapet at zero hour, according to the war diarist, who used the not inappropriate word 'annihilated' in describing what happened to his men.[123] According to the figures given by Martin Middlebrook,[124] the 9th Fusiliers lost a minimum of 518 from the ranks and 14 officers in its assault on the German lines – this included the dead, wounded and missing. By the end of the day, 532 of Blacker's Boys were victims. A mere handful of those who had gone over the top at zero hour were left unscathed. In the space of a few hours, a fine battalion had been destroyed in a monumental waste of military resources and human potential.

Lieutenant Geoffrey Cather of the 9th Royal Irish Fusiliers. He gave repeated assistance to the wounded in no-man's-land in full view of the enemy, was killed by a machine-gun bullet, and subsequently awarded the Victoria Cross.
ROYAL IRISH FUSILIERS MUSEUM

MIDDAY TO NIGHTFALL: GRADUAL RETREAT

At about one o'clock in the afternoon, it became apparent that the enemy was gathering south of the Ancre for a large counter-attack. Before long, it could be seen that German reinforcements were arriving by train into Grandcourt – fresh, fit men of the 8th Bavarian Reserve.[125] Meanwhile, the southern flank of the Schwaben Redoubt was under strain. By 2.45 Montgomery and his men – holding on to the third line – were aware of Germans advancing steadily up the communication trenches from the fourth line. Some men in the Belfast battalions began to turn and run for it, and many were stopped by their own officers at the point of a revolver.[126]

Tommy Russell, lying wounded somewhere on the Schwaben Redoubt, looked down towards Grandcourt and saw hundreds of German helmets glinting in the sun. He was parched, and one man sheltering near him was so thirsty that he tried to drink some of his own urine.[127] Still battle raged nearby. At 3.45 a fierce fight developed around a trench on the southern slope of the redoubt; Ulstermen were sandbagged in at one end of it and Germans at the other. What Montgomery was later to call 'a very pretty fight' continued until the Germans forced through about an hour later. By this stage, Montgomery had received a message that Lieutenant Sanderson – who had reconnoitred the Mouquet Switch earlier in the day – was dead, shot in the fourth line.

But Montgomery's spirits revived when he was informed that strong reinforcements were due to reach him at 6.00 p.m. – there was reason to hold on hard and fight to the death. His troops were particularly handicapped by lack of water and ammunition for their machine guns. The guns could now be fired only in short bursts, and soon rifle cartridges were being used for the machine guns – but the reinforcing soldiers would bring plenty of ammunition.[128]

However, because of a serious misunderstanding about the deployment of the 146th Brigade, the promised reinforcements did not arrive until too late. At 4.00 p.m. the 36th's divisional command had been informed that the 146th was at their disposal, and this resulted in the message to Montgomery. But two battalions of the 146th had already been committed to the attack on Thiepval village, and by the time sufficient numbers of the Yorkshiremen had been requisitioned and sent forward towards the Schwaben Redoubt, it was well after 7.00 and too late to make an impact. The Germans by this time had made even more inroads on their third line, and had taken back the greatest part of the fourth line.[129] Those reinforcements who survived the journey across no-man's-land – the bulk of eight companies of Yorkshiremen – joined the Ulstermen in the front German trenches. Many of them looked grim-faced and terrified by the ordeal they had become part of. The machine guns in Thiepval continued to kill, and were unmolested by British artillery because it was wrongly supposed that a British company had managed to penetrate the village.[130]

Meanwhile, behind the Ulster lines, the wounded kept moving towards the dressing stations. Carts full of exhausted, bandaged men made their way slowly over the pot-holed Hamel–Albert road, each jolt an agony. Some men held on to the tailboard of a cart, and hopped along on one leg.[131]

Also behind the lines, German prisoners were being taken across the

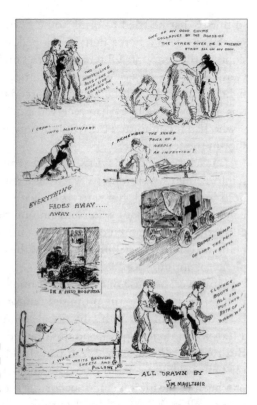

Jim Maultsaid's pictorial
account of his injury and
removal to hospital
MICHAEL MAULTSAID

Ancre, many of them being made to wade across the narrow bridge and
receiving abuse from Ulster soldiers who had been deputised to look after
them. Some Germans who were clinging to the bridge while trying to cross
were knocked on the heads and hands by their captors. As a battalion of
the supporting Yorkshiremen crossed the bridge towards the front line, even
the wounded German prisoners had to wade through the water, and their
desperate cries sent shivers up the spines of some of the Yorkshiremen.[132]

The battle was now taking place on ground strewn with corpses from earlier
in the day, and a fierce German counter-attack was gaining real headway:

In one part of the B line, the trenches near the river, there was a carpet of
dead and dying Ulstermen and Germans. Blood lay like a layer of mud
and, do you know, you couldn't tell one blood from the other … in

another part ... a party of the Skins left the B line and hid in shell holes within bombing distance – the distance a man could throw a Mills bomb. The Germans re-entered their own trench. The sound of the first hand-grenade exploding was the signal to start bombing the two or three hundred yards of the trench where the German soldiers were collecting ... after the last grenade had been thrown there was a bayonet charge. There was not one German soldier left alive ... they collected all the grenades, ammunition, even rifles, water and food the Germans were carrying – a bloody messy job.

Still the Germans kept counter-attacking – fiercely, courageously, trying to regain the Schwaben Redoubt. In the final battle over the third line came a chance to employ the 'Bangalore Tube' (a kind of flamethrower used to burn wire) for an unorthodox and deadly purpose:

A squad of German soldiers went from the trench to the dugout ... these soldiers of ours ... managed to get the tubes burning and pushed them into the dugout where the Germans were. We were a right distance away but we could smell the burning flesh as the Germans inside the dugout were burnt to death.[133]

Whilst this desperate battle was taking place, Major Gaffikin fell – hit by grenade shrapnel while standing on the parapet using a rifle in support of a bomb party. He was evacuated by some men of his own company, but died later that night.[134] As the stretcher-bearers crossed no-man's-land, they would have seen the Sunken Road now full of blood and bodies – earning its new nickname, the 'Bloody Road'.[135]

Gradually, the unevenness of the contest became apparent – fresh German reinforcements pushed exhausted Ulstermen back into the first two lines. Many men had been fighting for well over twelve hours, and had reached a point when morale could sustain them no longer. As nightfall approached, some did try to settle into the German front line and hold it overnight: 'No Surrender' would be the watchword once again. But other men had had enough, and started to turn their backs on the enemy and make for the home trenches. Montgomery noticed a serious breaking of the ranks between 9.30 and 9.45 – headed in particular by a Stokes-mortar battery. On seeing over 150 men making across the open for Thiepval Wood, he ran after them,

Wounded soldiers lie awaiting transport to medical care behind the lines. Note the attempt to shield many of them from the heat and glare of the sun.
ROYAL ULSTER RIFLES MUSEUM

shouting. Major Peacocke followed him, and between them they tried to rally their troops. Montgomery managed to persuade some forty men to stay in the first line for a while, firing their rifles, but twenty minutes later, they also broke and headed for home in the gathering gloom. Despondently, Montgomery followed them, recrossing his front line at 10.30 and reporting to the 9th Rifles' HQ. Meanwhile, out in the darkness, the German soldiers filled up the trenches he and his men had fought for.

What Montgomery did not record for posterity was that he actually fired shots into a group of the soldiers who were on the run.[136] He did not know to which unit they belonged, but hoped (in vain) that he could stem the tide. Montgomery told Crozier of the incident, but Crozier had already seen a lot of falling back and had observed one young officer, possibly Montgomery himself, firing at one of his own retreating soldiers, who fell to the ground. To Crozier, this was a quite acceptable act of war.[137] He had told his men he would shoot anyone who turned back on the day of battle, for 'The moral appeal is generally stronger than the armed threat ... if there is time. But there seldom is time'.[138] However, there was soon no point in complaining at the little groups of weary and disorientated men who were trickling back under cover of darkness.

Among the survivors was John Kennedy Hope. Lost and alone in the German front line, he remembered looking up into the sky and observing 'that clearness associated with a July night'. He had met Major Peacocke on his travels, and then, trying to escape up out of a trench some yards further on, he got caught in barbed wire and had to struggle to release himself. Then, trying to negotiate his way across no-man's-land, he saw a flare go up and flopped to the ground. When darkness resumed, he continued on his way. Before long, he heard voices – he had come across a British party in a large crater, and he joined them for a while. Eventually, he decided to join a small group who were prepared to head towards the British lines. They reached the Ulster front line just at the head of 'Elgin Avenue', and dropped into the trench without even a challenge from a sentry. He drank some water and then lay huddled in the wood, unable to relax for fear of a German shell landing on top of him.[139] The enemy was still bombing the wood quite heavily. It was, as the YCVs war diarist recorded, 'a night of tumult'.[140]

But some parties of men remained in the German front line throughout the night:

> … we collected all the ammunition we could from our own dead, a
> terrible task, but it was necessary, for we knew we would need every
> bullet we could get. In the big trench we set up sentries and some of us
> tried to get some rest. It was hard for we kept seeing the bits and pieces of
> the dead bodies and the terrible bleeding of the wounded, and the smell
> of sweat and the hunger kept us from sleeping. Funny thing was we found
> ourselves taking orders from other privates and giving them ourselves …
> It brought a lump to our throats when we thought of all the friends that
> was dead or wounded.[141]

Those who had been stranded in inaccessible positions, or lay wounded north or south of the river, would soon become prisoners of war, or if their wounds were too severe, they died in some lonely hour of that short July night. Tommy Russell was one of the luckier ones. All he remembered was a German giving him a drink out of an unfamiliarly shaped glass bottle, and then he was stretchered away to a brief hospitalisation and, eventually, a longer stay in a POW camp. For the rest of the war, Tommy would remain a prisoner.[142]

Albert Bruce, who had 'played possum' in the Sunken Road when the South Antrim Volunteers first went over the top, now found himself, at nightfall, helping to sort out the corpses in Thiepval Wood. He had to take off the identity disc that was draped round the neck of each corpse. Albert had just stacked forty corpses in a dugout, from which they would be taken for burial, when he heard moans coming from the pile of broken bodies. Immediately, he tried to extract the one still-living body from the rest. When he had done so, he realised the man was calling out faintly that he was still alive. Albert sent for a stretcher, and they placed the still-conscious soldier on it. To everyone's amazement, one of the soldiers standing nearby came across and looked long and hard at the pale face on the stretcher. It was his brother.

In a few moments, the stretcher-bearers were heading back across the wood towards medical help. In a cruel twist of fate, the stretcher party and their precious load did not reach safety. Albert never saw any of them again, and his comrade never again came across his injured brother. Albert presumed that a shell must have landed on them. One miraculous escape from death had not been enough to save one man. Albert was to see the brother of the dead man several times after the war, and every time he used to ask Albert, 'Whatever happened to that brother of mine? Whatever happened to that brother of mine?'[143]

Back in the casualty clearing stations and the advanced dressing stations, behind the lines, doctors and their assistants were literally falling off their feet with exhaustion. They stared in horror at the wounds made by the German machine guns, 'so big you could put your fist into them'. And yet they worked on, taking only a few minutes' break each, to have a bite to eat. Throughout the night, there were amputations to be done, many of them quickly and crudely improvised, as in the following case of a crippled finger:

> The doctor gave the man a shot of morphia to knock him out, pulled out the blade of a penknife, cleaned it by pushing it through the flame of a spirit lamp and set the blade across the knuckle and simply hit the back of the blade with a hammer and cut off the finger that way … you see we were pushed for time … and the doctor by doing the amputation that way saved a few minutes and got to the next case that bit quicker.

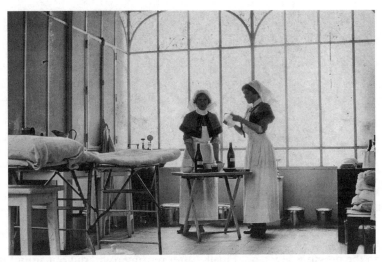

Two nurses prepare to treat a patient. The medical care was, by current standards, very limited, and many men died who would have been saved by modern methods.
SOMME MUSEUM

In command posts, such as the one at Hamel, despondency alternated with desperation as the full day's calamity came home to those in charge. Eventually, some tried to get a little sleep on the hard, wooden chairs, or curled up in greatcoats on the stone floor. There were lorries parked on the village street, and some men slept in these.[144]

Stewart-Moore, meanwhile, spent the night in a dugout in Thiepval Wood. Throughout the day, he and Paddy Mulley had had little to do, whilst the battle raged so close to hand. They had come across a deserter making his way out of the wood, and Stewart-Moore tried to reason with him, but the man was determined that he could not go back into the inferno he had just left. Stewart-Moore knew he ought to have arrested him, but 'he was probably the more powerful of the two so reluctantly I let him go and said nothing'.

Stewart-Moore had also come across some German prisoners being escorted back, and had encountered some tear-gas shells that 'smelt like a mixture of pineapples and bananas'. Donning his goggles, he went on. For most of the day, the wood seemed deserted compared with what it had been

Night scene on the Somme front, 1 July 1916
ROYAL ULSTER RIFLES MUSEUM

like in the previous few days. Finally, after retiring to his dugout at nightfall, Stewart-Moore was wakened at midnight by an infantry officer who plunged into the dugout in a state of utter exhaustion. 'We have been fighting all day', the officer cried out, 'and we have got nowhere'.[145]

His words were an apt postscript to the day's activities. At midnight the sole remnant of the day's conquests was a scattering of troops in the enemy's front line; all else was lost. Although at 11.30 p.m. word had come through that men of the 148th Brigade would be placed at the disposal of the 36th in an attempt to retake the Schwaben Redoubt, it seemed futile to consider such an operation by night with troops who did not know the terrain. Equally, it would be foolish in the extreme to attempt an attack by daylight unless Thiepval was first taken. Later in the night, the proposed operation was cancelled.[146]

SUNDAY 2 JULY

At seven o'clock on Sunday morning, as the ground mist dispersed in the warmth of the sun, observers in Mesnil could see the Ulstermen and their assistants from the 146th Brigade in small groups in the German trenches. Major-General Nugent ordered that an attempt be made to support them, sending forward supplies of ammunition and water along with more machine guns.[147] The task would be made more difficult by the fact that the enemy had brought up a high-velocity gun on the Grandcourt–Beaucourt railway overnight, and it was firing southwards into the Ancre valley and beyond.[148]

The men of the Pioneer Battalion were particularly busy during the morning, gathering supplies and crawling along the shattered trenches to vantage points in the front line. Some men found the task of bringing up ammunition from the dump a frightening one:

> I was given a box of bombs and told to put them in a pack for my back. It was a hard thing to ask a man to carry a box of bombs this way for if a pin worked itself loose then the whole lot went up and me with it. That was bad enough. I was given a couple of pouches of clips, a rifle and a can of water for a Vickers. Back at the front they pointed us at the infantry in the German lines, told us they needed us over there and we were to make our way over. One of the officers told us to try and not get ourselves shot.[149]

Up to four hundred men were to be rounded up and made to undertake the journey across no-man's-land at about 2.00 p.m. Many were reserve troops who were holding the Ulster line, others were from the 148th Brigade. Two guns of the 107th Machine Gun Company went with them, and the entire group was led by Major P.J. Woods of the West Belfast Volunteers.[150] Meanwhile, more wounded and dead were being brought in. Often, the stretcher-bearers would be in tears at recognising some friend or relative.[151]

John Kennedy Hope, hearing that another attempt was going to be made to retake the redoubt, was terrified. He had just lit a fire, made tea and enjoyed a tin of pilchards in the rear part of Thiepval Wood. Surely he would not have to return to the horror of the Schwaben Redoubt? Fortunately for him, Hope was not drafted into Major Woods' party.[152] Indeed, by 2.00 p.m. most of the remaining YCVs had made their way back to Martinsart Wood in single file, via the causeway. The party of men was only 120 strong, with just two of the officers who had gone over the parapet on the previous morning.[153]

Meanwhile, Major Woods and his men set out for their objective, only to meet the same horrific gunfire as on the previous day. Each man carried far more supplies than in the previous advance, and was grossly weighed down. When a man fell, killed or wounded, his comrade lifted as much as he could of the other man's load, and so some of the fitter soldiers arrived at the German lines with twice the weight of supplies they had started with. A third of the party, however, never got there.

Thus strengthened, the British troops in the German trenches proceeded to hold their own against enemy counter-attacks, but never really managed to advance further into German territory. Later, two small parties of Pioneers went across with bombs and ammunition from Thiepval Wood. It was a question of holding on now, until the 49th Division finally and fully relieved the Ulstermen some time that night. The 36th had contributed all that they ever effectively would to the Somme campaign, and they were played out.

Casualties who had fallen on the previous day were still being brought in – occasionally, and incredibly, some were still alive. The tramway had been hit in several places, but the engineers always got it working again. Mechanics also worked hard to keep the engines of the motor ambulances ticking over.[154] In the medical stations, everyone's help was appreciated. Montgomery of the West Belfast battalion had made his way there, and he stripped and dressed many of the wounded. He was asked by the matron to move all the worst cases from the stretchers to the beds, and to place the less seriously wounded back on the stretchers. He held one of his best friends for an hour while surgeons put probes into his back without anaesthetic to test if he was paralysed. And there was water to be carried to the hundreds of stretcher cases lying out in the hot sun waiting for attention. As he put it in a letter home, Montgomery 'learnt a lot of life and death' on that day.[155]

To Tommy Ervine – regaining consciousness and clarity as one of the wounded – it appeared that he was receiving more fuss than he deserved. Although he had two wounds – one in the shoulder and one in the leg – much of the blood on his clothes was not his. It belonged to the comrade who had fallen back into his arms, mortally wounded, early the previous morning. This, plus the chalky mud of the Picardy soil, combined to make him look a mess. Tommy could clearly hear a French voice repeat over and over again, '*pauvre garçon – pauvre garçon*'. Soon, he was taken by train to hospital where they operated on his leg.[156]

Finally, in the hours of darkness, the 49th Division relieved the 36th of responsibility for the front line. The last remnants of the Ulster advance were sent back across no-man's-land to the wood, utterly worn out. Battalions endeavoured to re-form and then head back to rest areas in Martinsart, where they could throw themselves down and try to sleep, despite the thunder of continued bombardment.[157]

3–12 JULY

On Monday 3 July came the task of assessing the losses. Stewart-Moore in his Trench Mortar Battery discovered that his friend Barry Brown was missing. They sorted out his kit and, with great grief, sent it down the line, not knowing if he was dead or alive. The other three surviving officers were in no mood to talk, and Stewart-Moore asked no questions about the battle.[158]

In Crozier's West Belfast battalion, only seventy of those who had attacked were left. He looked at them and thought: 'The fighters seldom come out best [but] they keep their souls intact'. He found that he still had in his possession the letter that young Campbell had asked him to take on the night of 30 June. He resolved to post it. And there were, of course, occasional 'shirkers' to be dealt with. A young officer who had fled the scene of battle was found asleep in Martinsart and had to be court-martialled. But Crozier felt it likely that no court would ever find him guilty, 'for all the men who were with him are dead and cannot give their evidence'.[159]

The Young Citizens also attempted to take a roll of survivors. John Kennedy Hope sat and looked at the remnants who turned up in Martinsart in the course of the day. Each looked down-hearted until the rest of the men already there gave them a great cheer, a cheer to celebrate survival, to let them know that they were the lucky ones who had returned from the 'Devil's Dwelling' unscathed. Hope brooded on the tragedy of it all: 'The company is but a shadow … gone to the place where there is no chin-wagging, no kit inspection, no dirty rifles, no unshaven chins.'[160]

G.H.M. echoed the feelings of many survivors as he thought to himself that he had at least kept his conscience clear. He had come through the battle and had risked everything for king and country, as he was supposed to do. It was some consolation alongside the grief for friends that were missing, some forever. Field postcards were handed out, and G.H.M. posted

OFFICIAL PHOTOGRAPH.
CROWN COPYRIGHT RESERVED.
52. ARMY CHAPLAIN TENDING BRITISH GRAVES.

An army chaplain tends freshly filled graves

one to his father. A letter from home arrived for him, too – from the Revd Hayes. If all was chaos at the front, life was clearly still smooth and efficient behind the line.[161]

Montgomery was one of those officers who wept openly on looking at the men he had left after the battle. He wrote home to his father:

> Mother would have cried and quite possibly you also when I called the
> remnant of my coy. to attention ... Not a few of the men cried
> and I cried. A hell of an hysterical exhibition it was. It is a very small
> coy. now. I took 115 other ranks and 4 officers (incl myself) into action.
> I am the only officer and only 34 other ranks are with me now
> out of the 115.[162]

In the County Down Volunteers, David John Bell called the roll. Name after name was read out and nobody answered. It seemed that only about one man in ten among the 13th Rifles had been left on his feet.[163]

To each of the battalions, a 'special order of the day' was addressed by Major-General Nugent:

> There is nothing in the operations carried out by the Ulster Division on

the First of July that will not be a source of pride to all Ulstermen. The Division has been highly tried and has emerged from the ordeal with untainted honour, having fulfilled in particular the great expectations formed of it ... The General Officer Commanding the Division deeply regrets the heavy losses of officers and men. He is proud beyond description ... of the magnificent example of sublime courage and discipline which the Ulster Division has given to the Army ...[164]

But no words of commendation or regret, especially words so formal, could soften the impact of what happened. Major-General Nugent met each of his brigades in turn. On 4 July at Hédauville, the 109th Brigade assembled in a football pitch and was addressed by Nugent. After he had spoken, Brigadier-General R.J. Shuter, commander of the 109th, also addressed the assembled men, and then each battalion received an 'appreciation' from its commanding officer. At noon the rain began to fall heavily, deepening the gloom.

Later that day, small parties returned to Thiepval Wood to make an attempt to find wounded men who might have been lying out in no-man's-land all the while. At 9.00 p.m. a group of YCVs left their battalion to search in the Sunken Road area. Incredibly, on the following day they arrived in with twelve men who were still alive.[165]

On 5 July, also, the 36th Division made its way back to the vicinity of Rubempré and its neighbouring villages – all except the artillery, the Pioneers and the Engineers, who remained in battle for some days to come. The Pioneers attempted another communication trench across no-man's-land – work that left the men exhausted.[166]

On 10 July the main part of the division moved back from the Rubempré area to Bernaville, and then prepared to leave the province of Picardy by train for Flanders. Montgomery – fortified by a bottle of wine – sat down and wrote home, his letter degenerating at times into nervous merriment and even a degree of bombast:

Dear Father and Mother,
I feel it is more than time that I wrote and told you something of the war.
'The wee war' as your dear sweet wee grandson called it.

... I am still funking writing to Mr Gaffikin about his son George. He got his death wound when fighting desperately side by side with me in the wildest hand grenade and machine gun fight man could live or die in ...

... I have satisfied the Great Curiosity as to one's personal behaviour in action ... It is quite evident mother cannot get rid of her wandering boy that easily. I got two gold bars vertical on my right arm. Both scabs are now gone. The scratches are healed and I can no longer find the bruise on my head to exhibit to admiring friends in A.S.C ... I am said to have absolutely no nerves. I have seen and done since 30th June some truly awful things and they never even fizzed on me and I have had absolutely no reaction. I saw over a hundred of our men blown to fragments by a very big shell about 200 yards from where I was lying. I never even stopped smoking ... Excitement or exhaustion – finest sensation in life.

... [I have had a] good bottle of white wine – good company ... More tomorrow, it is turned midnight and I think I will sleep now. Will you please tell Emmie I would like her to send me two light linen mesh suits of underclothes. And I would just love you to send me a good small one of those Acetylene lamps ... I could do with the luxury of a good real Thermos flask. If this push goes on, as I hope and think it will, we will find ourselves open fighting in the late summer.

... Tell Uncle Willie I am a hell of a better soldier than a fire assessor. Please tell Bertha I ate her lovely bread last thing before going into action and wore her white heather. It certainly did bring me luck. C'est un souvenir le plus bon. Everyone is in the wildest possible form – joie de vivre – I think with a very special significance.[167]

On Tuesday 11 July the 36th Division left Picardy. They had experienced over five thousand casualties, and were a very different body of men from the one that had arrived in France all those months before. They would never be the same again.[168]

The YCVs entrained from Conteville at noon, and arrived at Berguette by 7.15 p.m. to begin the long march to Blaringhem, where they were going into farmhouse billets overnight, before marching up to yet another front.[169] The Twelfth of July was, of course, a special day of celebration for Ulster Protestants. Some of the men who were marching into Blaringhem

How Jim Maultsaid, recovering from his wound, relived his battle

MICHAEL MAULTSAID

saw small orange flowers growing by the roadside, and they were given permission to break ranks and put the blooms in their hats, jacket pockets or the barrels of their rifles. The bands marched ahead of the soldiers through the Flemish village, playing 'King William's March'.[170]

THE NEWS REACHES HOME

On Saturday 1 July the north of Ireland had gone about its business, oblivious of the battle raging in France. On Monday morning the *Belfast News Letter* reported that the 'long awaited Franco-British offensive' had begun. Then, on Thursday 6 July, the paper published Major-General Nugent's special order to the 36th Division delivered before the battle. The following day, news was released that the Ulster Volunteers had played a crucial role in the opening of the offensive, and had 'won a name that equals any in history'. A correspondent who had seen the beginning of the division's attack wrote a description of what he had observed, indicating that there had been great heroism but also considerable loss of life. There was also the first list of dead and wounded from the battle. The news of what the Ulster Division had been through was only just beginning to emerge.

Small buff-coloured envelopes began to arrive at the doors of homes throughout the province, and continued to do so for many days. The Mabins of the Shankill area of Belfast had two boys in the army, and the postman had two little envelopes for Mrs Mabin. He could not face the prospect of delivering both letters at once, and delivered only one in the first visit, holding back the second in case the full impact of knowing that she had two sons missing, believed killed, should prove too much for the mother.[171] The prospect of receiving such a letter was a nightmare, as one woman recalled:

> I was giving the two boys in the yard their dinner when the wee buff-coloured envelope arrived ... A few days before I had a card saying he was well but this was sent off before the fighting started. My heart was in my mouth when I went to the door. All I could do was pray. It just said on the paper inside that my man was wounded. It was nearly a month later when I got a long letter wrote for him by a nurse telling me that he had lost the parts of his hands from the middle fingers to the heels of his hands.

This kind of news was dreaded by all who had relatives in the division, but it also affected the whole community. Every time a postman or delivery boy arrived at a house that had a son in the Volunteers, people gathered at the door to see if there was bad news. But no neighbourly comfort could soothe the grief.

> I worked on a Saturday afternoon and night in a shop in Hill Street …
> When my dad came down to us and told my cousin and myself he
> wanted us in the house. When we got there he showed us a piece of
> paper saying that Edward, my brother, had died of wounds in France.
> Now my dad was a gentle man and he was crying and saying 'How'll I
> tell your mother? How'll I tell your mother?'

Often, it was the local clergyman who had the job of informing the family if news of a casualty had come through before the relatives had received a letter:

> My mother and I was lapping a field of hay beyond Bleary school … My
> mother saw the minister up at the house and she called him down to
> where we were working. She just looked steady at him without blinking
> and said, 'Is it Ted [her brother] or Willie [my father]?' He said, 'I'm sorry
> to say it's Willie.' She walked along the head-rig back to the house, her
> back as straight as that of a girl of nineteen. The minister helped me to
> finish the field and gave me a hand to get the cows milked. It was not
> until I got the cleaning up done that it hit me I'd never have my father
> around the place again. It broke my mother's heart but I never saw her
> crying except that first night.

> I was coming home from the mill [in Gilford] and we had been working
> late and it was gathering down dark. The mill-pond was full and there
> was a mist like steam rising from it. I was going down past the manager's
> house when his wife called me in … I took off my hat and held it in both
> hands. She led me into this big room full of easy chairs and lit with oil
> lamps and this thing hanging from the ceiling with candles in it. My
> mother was sitting down in a chair and crying. I didn't know what to do
> or where to look but I saw the Church of Ireland minister there and there
> were three or four other people I knew from round about. The minister

had on one of them long frock coats ... and he had a piece of paper in his hands. I was told to sit down and I sat on the very edge of the chair. Then the minister prayed for a while and started to read from the paper in his hands ... Well the minister read out about half a dozen names and then he read out my father's. It dawned on me that this was a list of the wounded. There was nothing we could do but wait and pray.

As well as individual notification to a casualty's family, the list of wounded, killed and missing appeared in the newspapers. Because not everyone could afford a copy, the newsagent often placed the casualty page in his window. Again, not everyone could read, and now and then, people standing near the window would ask others to tell them who was on the list. Sometimes, a name would be listed in the paper before those at home knew, and the shock would be worse for a family who found out in this way:

After we got our tea we used to go up to the middle of the town to see what was happening ... Every night we looked down the casualties to see who was there. One night I saw my two uncles, one from my father's side, the other from my mother's, one was killed the other missing ... I ran away down the street crying my eyes out to tell them at home what had happened.[172]

The newspapers were now full of long lists of the victims. By Monday 10 July the *Belfast Evening Telegraph* had also started to print letters from wounded men recovering in hospital in England. Often, these gave a very inadequate account of the horrors of the battle. One lance corporal wrote from a hospital bed in Cheltenham that 'the boys were in great form going over'; they had made up a song to sing as they waited, called 'Over the Top We've Got to Go'; and when they got across no–man's–land, 'We could not shoot the Fritz quickly enough.'[173] But the obituary columns told a simple, tragic story:

Rifleman J. Clarke – died of wounds received in action on 1st July 1916.
Deeply regretted by his wife and four little children.

Rifleman John Hodgen, killed in action on 2nd July.
Deeply regretted by his loving mother, sisters and brothers.[174]

The letters written by officers and chaplains to the relatives of the dead also told just how severely the Ulster Volunteers had suffered. On Tuesday 11 July the *Belfast Evening Telegraph* published a letter from Colonel Ricardo to the Hewitt family, whose son, William A. Hewitt, of the Tyrone Volunteers, had just died:

> Your little lad Willie led his platoon over our parapet and the last I saw of him was his happy smile as I wished him luck ... I feel quite stunned and heartbroken. Your Willie was one of the nicest minded boys I ever knew.

Two other sons of the Hewitt family had already died in the war, one of them killed in a machine-gun company in the 36th Division only a few days previously.

Some of the most poignant items to appear in the newspaper columns were the little advertisements in which relatives appealed for news of missing men. As the days went by, the anxiety of the families increased:

> No news has been received regarding L'ce Corporal Walter Ferguson (14596) YCVs since before the Big Push and his relatives, who reside at 2 Collingwood Road, Belfast, are very anxious concerning him and would be grateful for any information. In civil life he was a bookbinder ...[175]

Occasionally, in a moment of great joy, a family would discover that their dearly loved relative was 'back from the dead':

> Following the official report received by Mrs Geo. Nesbitt, Richhill, on Tuesday stating that her son Pte Abner Nesbitt (RIF) had been killed in action on July 1st a wire has been received from a private hospital at Trowbridge Wilts, notifying his parents that Pte Nesbitt is lying wounded there.[176]

The newspapers in July were also full of tributes from political figures, referring to the Ulster Volunteers' sacrifice and stressing its significance as an exhibition of loyalty to king and country. Walter Long MP wrote a public letter to the Lord Mayor of Belfast stating that Ulster people had once again been 'foremost in defence of those liberties and rights which have been the heritage of all British citizens'.[177] Reports of the addresses at memorial services and special commemorations all over the province expressed the conviction that the sacrifice of 1 July would tie Ulster all the more closely to Britain: 'Ulster Protestants took their stand where their fathers stood ... [in] costly self-sacrifice to our Empire.'[178]

In all this attempt to find consolation and meaning in the slaughter, there was an inevitable glossing over of the devastation of bereavement, and an ignorance of the ghastliness of war that pitted men against machine guns and heavy artillery. The *Banbridge Chronicle* spoke of the

> ... young and vigorous manhood, who advanced so gaily to the attack on that first of July morning, to add fresh lustre to the glorious past and uphold the high traditions of their race and, who now, their duty done, rest from their labours on the battlefields of France.[179]

Such writing was long on the nobility of sacrifice but short on the agony, indignity and needlessness of so many deaths. Those who had seen the carnage and then read the newspapers could sense the untruth: Colonel Blacker of the Armagh Volunteers, for instance, writing to a friend on 14 July, noted that there had been 'a lot of extravagant stuff written and published in the press, which is a great pity. The Division behaved magnificently and the point does not want labouring. I am still dazed at the blow.'[180]

But it would take a long time before the full reality of the Somme became part of the consciousness of the people who had lost loved ones there. Meanwhile, there were the verses of the poets who, never having seen gas, barbed wire or high-explosive shells, imagined an idealised kind of warfare, a latter-day Charge of the Light Brigade:

> Nought can stay them, nought can stop,
> A thirst for blood to the last, last drop,
> Charging along on the topmost top
> Of the waves of fire that bore them.
> On with a thirst that nought can quell
> Through a hurricane shower of shot and shell
> To fight or fall as their fathers fell
> In the doughty days before them.
> Merrily every mother's son
> Laughing as though they fought for fun
> With a song and a cheer they charged the Hun

Marring his Maker's image.
Chaffing, as though each shell might be
The whistle call of a referee
And the bloodiest tustle in history
Only a football scrimmage.[181]

This jolly, heroic version of what had been taking place in Picardy was inaccurate and insensitive. The pain of those who were bereaved may have been alleviated by such verse, but it is unlikely. The glib, ignorant celebration of the battle that it conveyed seems now like a blasphemy. Silence and thought were the proper response, not the bluster of poetic pomposity. A more fitting reaction came on 12 July when, instead of the usual Orange parades, there was simply a five-minute silence held all across Ulster at noon; blinds in buildings were drawn down, people stood still in the street, traffic stopped and flags drooped at half-mast in the pouring rain.[182] Numerous other memorial services took place in the province that month.

An important thread of anger and betrayal also ran under the surface in some quarters. Not everyone accepted the scale of slaughter with composure, especially in areas where there was virtually no home untouched by sadness. One Orangeman in Lurgan wrote to a friend:

There is hardly a house in Hill Street in which at least one member of the family has not been killed or wounded. It is terrible, terrible hard news to bear with equanimity, for however just and right a cause it may be, the death of so many young men leaves our land that much the poorer.

The Orange Order was, of course, particularly distraught. Most of the division were either members or had Orange associations, and the Volunteer movement had been nurtured in the Orange Order.

On the 14th night we arranged a meeting in the school house and we had members from all the local lodges present ... each lodge represented at the meeting then stood and gave out the names of their members killed, wounded or missing in fighting in France ... there was over 150 names in all ... We sang 'Shall we gather at the river' and the women made tea and cakes for us all.[183]

Sir George Richardson, commanding the still-existent UVF, issued an

LINES WRITTEN ON JAMES TATE,

WHO FELL IN HEROIC CHARGE OF THE ULSTER DIVISION, ON JULY THE FIRST, 1916.

When war's dread challenge first was heard
  Throughout our Island home,
Our boys responded to the call,
  And hastened o'er the foam :

To fight for King and Country,
  A brave and noble band,
To crush out German cruelty
  From out our peaceful land.

And one among those gallant lads—
  Only a boy was he—
Left parents, all he held most dear,
  To cross the bright blue sea.

Only a boy ; but O ! so brave,
  His young heart knew no fear,
On that fatal July morning,
  Though he knew that death was near.

He nobly did his duty,
  'Mid the storm of shot and shell ;
In a hero's grave, " Somewhere in France,"
  Sleeps him we loved so well.

He little thought when he left home
  That he would ne'er return ;
But now he lies in that far-off land,
  And we are left to mourn.

God knows best, and He alone
  Can take away the pain
From the hearts he loved so dearly,
  Though he'll ne'er see them again.

Some day we shall meet him,
  In that happy home above,
When war's dread sound is heard no more,
  Where all is peace and love.
          LIZZIE SMYTH, Ballyminstra.

Writing to Mrs. Tate, under date 3rd October, 1916, the late Sergeant James Tate's platoon officer says :—

I have great pleasure in saying that your son was in my platoon for sixteen months. He was very much liked by his comrades. He was always anxious to do his duty, and was a most capable Sergeant. He was a first-class musketry instructor and a good shot. In the trenches he was exceptionally cool and seemed indifferent to danger. On the First of July he had his section over the parapet and was keen and eager in the attack. I was always glad to have him with me.

I can understand your feelings and sympathise with you, but pride in his sacrifice must be your consolation. With kindest regards.—Yours sincerely,
          G. T. C. ARMSTRONG.

James Tate, a farmer's son from near Killinchy in County Down. His family was one of many that would be expected to console themselves with pride in a patriotic sacrifice.
SOMME MUSEUM

order of the day shortly after the battle, in which he gave his heartfelt sympathy on behalf of the officers and men of the UVF to the relatives of those who had fallen. Sir Edward Carson issued a much-publicised message to the Ulster people in which he expressed sorrow at the loss of 'so many men who were to us personal friends and comrades'.[184] There may have been a certain guilt attached to his sorrow – it was he who finally gave the word and provided the opportunity for the UVF to enlist.

But the most touching expressions of condolence were the personal ones, for the deepest tragedy of 1 July was experienced personally, not at a political or social level – and grief and sympathy knew no political or religious boundaries:

Postcard to Mrs M. Johnston, Bluestone, Portadown

Dear Friend Mary
I saw in the newspaper that your brother has died of wounds in France. I am sorry that one so dear to you is dead and I want you to know how I feel about it. I said a prayer and lit a candle for him at Mass on Sunday. You may think it will do him no good but it eased the burden I have in my heart for you. May God protect you and all your family.

Love
Lizzie[185]

THE VERDICT

And so the statisticians were left to tally up the grim totals. In terms of loss of life, Saturday 1 July was the most expensive day of the war: twenty-one thousand British soldiers had died or been mortally wounded. Over thirty-five thousand had been injured, and more than six hundred were prisoners. Of all the divisions taking part, the Ulster Division ranks fourth in the table of losses. Middlebrook notes 5,104 casualties, of which at least 2,000 probably died.[186] When this figure is added to the casualty list for 2–3 July and the casualties in the regular Irish battalions and Scottish regiments where Ulstermen also served, it may be assumed that the total of Ulster losses was much greater.

Trying to ascertain the cause of the carnage, one comes across the same factors that made the offensive so costly along the entire front. Serious overestimation of the success of the bombardment was coupled with inflexibility in infantry strategy when the failure of the shelling became apparent, and this inflexibility owes much to the disastrous state of communications between troops and commanding officers. The failure of the divisions on either side of the Ulstermen to take their objectives spelt doom for the 36th, as they ended up receiving the machine-gun bullets that the generals had calculated would be spread across three British divisions. With greater flexibility, perhaps the Ulstermen could have taken Thiepval from the rear – along the deserted Mouquet Switch that Lieutenant Sanderson reconnoitred – but the assault troops were officer-less and disorganised by this stage, and a sufficiently formidable party might not have been gathered up to attempt the onslaught on the village. The inflexibility of the barrage also held up the momentum of the infantry attack. The Belfast Brigade had to wait in the German fourth line for perhaps an hour before they could proceed to the attack on the last line. With better communication and readiness to alter strategy, the barrage could have lifted from the last line earlier, allowing the Belfast battalions to make a quicker and more unexpected attack on this crucial German defensive system. Had a breakthrough then been rapidly exploited by supporting troops, a large hole could have been torn in the enemy's defences before reserves could be brought up by rail to Grandcourt. The war diary of the West Belfast Volunteers states: 'If it had not been for the barrage we could have taken the "D" line sitting … the delay however was fatal.'[187]

It is disturbing to reflect that no support whatsoever was given to the 36th during the daytime of 1 July. Extra troops, when they did arrive, were too little and too late. The Ulster Volunteers had penetrated deeper than any other major unit, but by the end of the day they were merely hanging on desperately to the first line. The secret of their costly but notable achievement has been traditionally explained in terms of the Ulstermen's natural fire and aggression raised to fever pitch by the political heat of the Volunteer years and the *esprit de corps* of the 36th. But against a hail of shells and bullets, even the most motivated troops are ineffectual. In reality, there was surely only one military factor that allowed the 36th to penetrate the German trenches in considerable numbers. If Middlebrook is right to suggest that the British lost the battle by a matter of seconds (the interval between the lifting of the barrage and the arrival of the first wave at the German parapet, where machine guns were already opening up on their targets), then it becomes clear that the Ulster HQ decision to send the men out into no-man's-land before the barrage lifted was a crucial factor.[188] The Ulstermen were able to get there sooner and in greater numbers – and the fact that they broke into a run would also have helped. It is interesting that the other division, the 18th – which sent men into no-man's-land before zero hour – was also relatively successful.

The Ulster Volunteers ended their participation in the Somme campaign with a fine reputation. Not only had they broken through and taken more than five hundred prisoners in the first two days of the campaign, they had gained four VCs for outstanding individual heroism: Captain Eric Bell, of the Tyrone Volunteers, had led his Trench Mortar Battery with especial courage and effect, losing his life in the process; Lieutenant G. Cather, of the Armagh Volunteers, was awarded a posthumous VC for his efforts in bringing in the wounded from no-man's-land; Private R. Quigg went out seven times in search of his platoon officer, Harry Macnaghten, and each time brought back a casualty; finally, there was Billy MacFadzean who had thrown himself on spilt grenades in the last hours before zero, in order to save his comrades.[189]

But of what use was a fine reputation? In terms of a contribution to winning the war, the Ulster Division had done virtually nothing. The ground they had won had been lost again, and not until October was the Schwaben Redoubt retaken and consolidated. By mid-November, when the Somme campaign ended, Grandcourt had still not been taken. The 'Battle of the Somme' as a whole had cost more than 400,000 British casualties and had gained roughly six miles. In mid-November the British troops had still not taken Bapaume, and the war had two more years to run.

Many ordinary Volunteers recognised bitterly that they were expected to make sacrifices that, in due course, would be received ungratefully. The story of Tommy Jordan is instructive. Tommy worked on with the Pioneers at the Somme for several days, and when he left the line, tired and unkempt, he was suffering from what doctors had dismissed as 'the artilleryman's complaint' – damaged and bleeding eardrums. He was summoned to appear before his new company commander, and the first words he heard as he entered were, 'How dare you? Look at those boots! How dare you come in before me dressed like that?'

Tommy lost his temper: 'Don't you know that I've been in a battle, sir? I haven't had these bloody boots off for weeks!' The officer choked with rage and ordered Tommy out of his sight. A few days later, he 'lost a stripe' for his insolence, and received a caution about his behaviour towards superiors. For weeks of exhausting soldiering, in which he had seen friends killed and mutilated, and had suffered irreparable damage to his health, Tommy was rewarded with demotion. He realised that he was not a hero; he was simply expendable.[190]

'YOU DON'T FORGET'
THE AFTERMATH

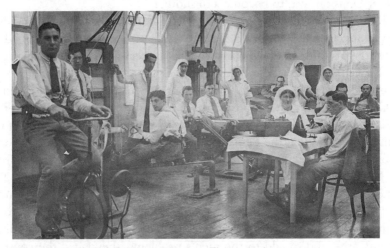

Patients and medical staff in an exercise room. The war took its
physical and mental toll on thousands of Ulster servicemen.
SOMME MUSEUM

FROM THE SOMME TO THE ARMISTICE

An immediate result of the Somme offensive was a drop in enlistment to the
36th Division. But recruitment had already been falling off before the extent
of the Somme casualties became known. On 31 May 1916 Major-General
Nugent, the divisional commander, had written a letter to Edward Carson
in which he expressed alarm about the rumour that the 36th was to be
broken up due to lack of reserves (in other words, due to recent poor
recruitment to the ranks).[1] Possibly a key factor in slowing down recruitment in recent months had been the Easter Rising in Dublin, which had

raised the old bogey of nationalist insurgency and convinced many Protestants that Ulster needed all her unionist young men at home to 'hold the fort'. But a decline in recruitment had taken place all over Britain as the war had gone on, and whereas conscription swelled ranks in the mainland regiments, it was not applied in Ireland. Immediately after the Somme, the reserve battalions of the Ulster Division were able to fill the gaps, but soon the process had to begin of introducing Scots, English, Welsh and, indeed, Catholic Irish. The Volunteer spirit was whittled away and the term 'Ulster Division' was to become a misnomer.[2]

But there were men who stayed with the 36th and who fought and died on various battlefronts during the two years of warfare that remained. A few survivors of the men who had packed the recruiting rooms of Ulster in 1914 stayed until the whole ghastly carnage stopped on 11 November 1918.

On 13 July 1916 most of the 36th was sent to the training area west of St-Omer for training and reorganisation; they were joined five days later by the artillery, which had still been helping to cover the 49th Division at the Somme front. When the drafts of new men from home had begun to be absorbed into the ranks, the division went back to 'holding the line' – from the Neuve Eglise–Warneton road to the Wulverghem–Messines road. The trenches in this part of the Western Front contrasted with those in Picardy: they were shallow – due to the high water table in the soil – and had to be fortified with clay-filled sandbags. There was constant flooding in this dirty, gloomy area, and to add to the men's problems, they faced the constant threat of mining and tunnelling. However, throughout the autumn of 1916 the 36th had a reasonably quiet time; the attention of the Germans was very much focused on the defence of the Somme, further south. For comfort and recreation, one of the famous London Transport buses that did duty on the front took the men back from the pick-up point nicknamed 'Hyde Park Corner' just outside 'Plugstreet' (Ploegsteert) village, to Bailleul with its shops and eating houses.

In the early spring of 1917 there was a rapid increase in the pace of life as a build-up of troops began for the 2nd Army's attempt to capture the Messines–Wytschaete Ridge. On 31 May 1917 the preliminary bombardment opened at the start of yet another effort to break the deadlock.

The Battle of Messines was to prove a success, judged by First World War standards. Careful preparation was done on a model of the ridge constructed behind the lines, and provision of food, water, ammunition and stores was well organised. A thoughtful study of aerial photographs of the enemy under bombardment ensured that no one would throw troops against undamaged and resilient trenches. The military strategy was better than at the Somme in many ways, not least in the evolution of the platoon as a little army in miniature, complete with Lewis-gun section and grenadiers able to operate with greater tactical flexibility. The facilities for the wounded were also better than at the Somme: shorter distances and better roads meant casualties had a better chance of treatment and survival. In the Messines attack, the 36th was to fight alongside the Irish Catholics of the 16th Division, which had been formed primarily from the National Volunteers.

On 7 June at 3.10 a.m. the troops moved forward, making good progress and exploiting the tactical advantage created by huge mines exploding at zero hour. When the 36th was eventually retired from the line on the night of 9 June, 61 officers and 1,058 other ranks were casualties in the division, and losses probably three times as great had been inflicted on the enemy.

Four days later, the 36th moved to the area between Mont Noir and Bailleul, where rest was allowed before the men took over a section of the line between Blauwepoortbeek and Rose Wood, a newly won position that the Germans were anxious to make difficult to hold. In the air, Baron von Richthofen and his squadron of red scout planes provided entertainment as they attacked barrage balloons, but sometimes they made the soldiers in the line scurry for cover as they flew low along the trenches, guns blazing.

On 7 July the division, minus the artillery, Engineers and Pioneers, moved back to St-Omer, where in the summer sunshine the men enjoyed twelve days of rest; especially memorable was a gymkhana on 23 July. The 36th was now in the 19th Corps, a part of the 5th Army, and the division was moved up at the end of July, by bus and lorry, to Poperinge, where, on the last day of the month, the dreadful Third Battle of Ypres began. The Ypres Salient was an area of persistent and bloody conflict throughout the war. Haig hoped that in the summer of 1917 the success of Messines would be followed by the acquisition of the Passchendaele Ridge and advances deep into Belgium towards the German-held Channel ports. In the part of the Ypres campaign known as the Battle of Langemarck, the 36th was to back up the 5th Division, and would once again operate alongside the

Digging out the wounded after an explosion at an aid post near the front line in Flanders. Scenes such as this continued to be a feature of the Ulster Division's war.
ROYAL ULSTER RIFLES MUSEUM

16th Division. The infamous rain and mud of that dreadful August created a total impasse. The quagmire of shell-churned earth swallowed up men who had survived the bullets of Thiepval, and pillboxes and strong wire helped keep the German line immovable. The 36th was not alone in failure. From 2–18 August 144 of its officers and 3,441 men were to become casualties in the Ypres Salient, but the losses of the 36th Division were but a fraction of the total that the British army suffered in the Third Battle of Ypres – perhaps 300,000 or more men were lost for the most trivial of gains.

The 36th was soon on its way south again, where it was to be joined by the 1st Royal Irish Fusiliers, a regular battalion whose numbers were needed in a division that was now deplorably under strength. Increasingly, the 36th was being filled with conscripts from mainland Britain – a different kind of soldier entirely from the UVF recruits of 1914–16. On 27 August the 1st Fusiliers was incorporated into the 107th (the 'Belfast Brigade'), where the 8th and 9th Rifles – the old East and West Belfast Volunteers – were amalgamated. Also, the North Irish Horse had been dismounted, and the three hundred or so men who thus became available were incorporated into the 9th Royal Irish Fusiliers. The 7th Royal Irish Rifles, from the 16th Division, was amalgamated with the 2nd (regular) Rifles, and the new blend was sent to the 36th's 108th Brigade, in which the 11th and 13th Rifles – the old South Antrim and Down Volunteers – were also amalgamated.

Memories of the Somme were stirred when the 36th detrained at Bapaume and Miraumont, towns that had been in German hands when the Ulstermen had occupied the trenches on either side of the Ancre more than a year before. The area was now devastated, and less hospitable than the Picardy the Volunteers had known in pre-Somme days. On 29–30 August the 36th relieved the 9th Division, confronting the redoubtable Hindenburg line of trenches, strong and recently constructed, beyond which lay the beautiful town of Cambrai. On 30 September the Pioneers and artillery rejoined the division from the Salient, where the Pioneers had been erecting camouflage over the notorious Menin Road.

In October 1917 preparations were under way for a new offensive in which the 36th had to capture trenches between the Bapaume–Cambrai road and the Canal du Nord. In the Battle of Cambrai, tanks were to be extensively used in the initial 'surprise' infantry attack. It was hoped that the cavalry would then advance to isolate Cambrai and seize the adjacent river crossings. This would be followed up by clearing the enemy from the entire Cambrai area.

On the morning of 20 November the 36th went forward as part of the 4th Corps in General J. Byng's 3rd Army. The first day brought success, but this was not exploited and the advance petered out. The weather was worsening, and by 26 November snow was falling. Three days later, the division was entrained to an area east of Arras, where the men hoped they would be granted some time out of the line. But a German counter-attack and breakthrough meant that the 36th was thrown back into the thick of things, to face the Germans near the Couillet valley and hold the line on 'Welsh Ridge'. Exhausted and miserable, the men were relieved by 14 December, and retired from the line to spend a comparatively pleasant Christmas resting and wondering, no doubt, whether 1918 would prove to be the final year of this seemingly interminable war.

In January 1918 the division took over the line again in the Somme sector, relieving the French from Sphinx Wood to the St-Quentin–Roisel railway; it was at this stage a fairly placid front. Further reorganisation of the division now took place. The British army as a whole was being restructured, with smaller brigades, of three battalions each, being the new format. More regular battalions were added to the 36th – the 1st and 2nd Inniskillings and 1st Royal Irish Rifles – and the existing battalion structure was squeezed still further. The division was now organised as follows:

107TH INFANTRY BRIGADE
    1st Battalion Royal Irish Rifles
    2nd Battalion Royal Irish Rifles
    3rd Battalion Royal Irish Rifles

108TH INFANTRY BRIGADE
    12th Battalion Royal Irish Rifles
    1st Battalion Royal Irish Fusiliers
    9th Battalion Royal Irish Fusiliers

109TH INFANTRY BRIGADE
    1st Battalion Royal Inniskilling Fusiliers
    2nd Battalion Royal Inniskilling Fusiliers
    9th Battalion Royal Inniskilling Fusiliers

The Pioneers were also slimmed down to only three companies, but the division was strengthened by the inclusion of another machine-gun company.

A German assault was expected any day; the enemy were reaping the fruits of withdrawal from the Russian front, and a make-or-break encounter with the Allies was anticipated. After a prolonged troop build-up, a bombardment heralded a great German infantry advance on 21 March 1918. By 23 March the enemy had broken through, and a couple of days of fighting in open countryside followed. The experience of this great German push was a devastating one for the 36th: the demoralising effect of retreat was compounded by the large-scale loss of troops captured by the swiftly advancing German armies. The 36th, amidst confusion and improvisation, was put at the disposal of the French command, and this created considerable communication difficulties. At the village of Erches, a particularly brave defence was put up, and the division helped to stem the German advance whilst French reinforcements moved in to help consolidate the position. Before long, the tide began to turn.

The last few days of March and the early days of April were spent briefly in the relaxing security of the Normandy coast, where the tattered remains

Scenes of devastation in Flanders. Horse and mules, used for
transport, were also victims of the conflict.
ROYAL ULSTER RIFLES MUSEUM

of the division were sent to be reorganised. Between 21 March and the end
of the month, the 36th had suffered 7,252 casualties, the majority of whom
were POWs. The 108th Brigade had been reduced to three hundred men.

Drafts from England filled up the ranks with young and inexperienced
recruits as the division moved north to the Ypres Salient once again. There,
the 108th Brigade was to participate in the latest battle to be fought in the
Messines/Kemmel area. In May Major-General Nugent was replaced by
Major-General Clifford Coffin, and one of the last links with the Ulster
Volunteer days was thereby severed. There was a break for rest again in
early June; then, at the end of the month the division re-entered the line on
the northern outskirts of the town of Bailleul.

At this stage, the tide of war was swinging irreversibly back in favour of
the Allies. Counter-offensives had started to push the Germans not only out
of the land won in the March advance but back beyond battlefields whose
stubborn stretches of mud had halted the Allies for most of the war. On 22
August the 36th Division began to participate in this advance toward
ultimate victory. Bailleul was taken, and the troops made for the small town
of Neuve Eglise. Throughout the next few weeks, the hope of victory grew
greater.

By the end of September, the 36th had been allocated to Lieutenant-General C.W. Jacob's 2nd Corps, which advanced and took control of landmarks whose names had spelt dread for years – the Menin Road, Zonnebeke, Vlamertinghe; the 36th had an especially difficult task to take the obstinate 'Hill 41'. But by 16 October the division was at the gates of Courtrai, facing a demoralised Germany army that was a shadow of its former self. But the 36th was also wounded and war-weary. Since the opening of this final offensive, the division had suffered more than three thousand casualties, although many were only slightly wounded. On 27 October the 108th and 109th Brigades were relieved from the front line; they would play no further part in the war. The 107th Brigade was expecting a further spell of duty, but the end was now truly in sight. On October 29 the Austrians pulled out of the conflict, and on November 11 the Germans ceased to fight. On the famous 'eleventh hour of the eleventh day', the Armistice was signed and Europe at last knew peace. The Great War was over.

But the men of the 36th Division were not to return home immediately. They spent winter astride the France–Belgium border, and although the Pioneers engaged in some railway construction, the main occupations for most infantrymen were educational and recreational. Men were being prepared for a return to the home life that would at first seem strange to them. The British Prime Minister, Lloyd George, guaranteed 'a land fit for heroes to live in', but the reality was likely to be something else – for one thing, the men would have to find jobs. And in Ireland there were to be further civil troubles. From January to early summer, demobilisation took place. By July 1919 the 36th Division – which had started nearly five years previously as a vehicle for the energies and enthusiasm of the Ulster Volunteer Force – was written off the register and ceased to exist. It had been a home for many thousands of young men, this strangely temporary body where they made friendships as deep as any human relationship could be, and where they learnt the depths of misery, pain and boredom that only war could teach. For thousands, its formalities and etiquette, its in-jokes and banter, had comprised the final society in which they had lived.[3]

The men who had survived the Somme offensive with the Ulster Volunteers each had a different experience of the final two years of the war. And for each, the war left indelible changes – changes they would never have anticipated when the call to battle had come in 1914.

Tommy Ervine spent time recuperating from his wounds in an Essex hospital. While he was there, a Zeppelin was brought down nearby and some of the nurses who went out to look at it brought him back a piece of metal from the wreck. While he was getting better, Tommy spent time making table mats with a Royal Irish Rifles design in the middle. After a spell in Ireland, Tommy went back to France but was not fit to return to the infantry. He joined the Royal Flying Corps instead, putting his mechanic's skills to work in the recovery squad that brought in downed planes and tried to fix them up again or to utilise the parts in other planes. He seemed set to become a leading aircraftsman, but because his education in reading and writing had left him feeling inadequate about his literacy, Tommy did not feel able to take the promotion. He explained to his senior officer that he would probably not be able to cope with the paperwork. So he completed his war in the ranks of the RFC.

One of his most vivid memories was to be of a German POW with whom he became friendly. He called Tommy 'Paddy', and Tommy called him 'Old Fritz'. He gave the German some broken saw blades – quite illegally – so that he could make toys out of pieces of wood that Tommy also procured for him: 'Fritz' made a beautiful series of little figures playing football and swinging clubs, all working off a small windmill. Tommy had no German with which to converse, but Fritz knew some English. 'A friendly ould soul' was Tommy's final verdict on him.[4]

Albert Bruce, of Lambeg, continued to serve in the 36th Division until 1918. He saw British tanks go in at Cambrai, and remembered his friends and himself chalking their names on the sides of these novel weapons of war. He recalled, too, coming down through the Somme area a year after Thiepval and seeing a mass grave for several hundred men of the Irish Rifles. And he had a vivid memory of seeing Harry Lauder sing on stage just after his son had been killed at the front: the famous singer broke down in the middle of a song, overcome with emotion. He tried one more time to carry on, but failed and had to leave the stage.

Identification-Card
for reception of money or parcels.

My address:

Altdamm, Germany

Prisoner of war Nr. *38090*

Weir, William   Sergeant

October. 1918.

Hundreds of Ulster Division soldiers were prisoners of war, many exisiting in dreadful conditions and undergoing forced labour
SOMME MUSEUM

In 1918 Albert was captured in the Messines area and was sent to Germany as a POW, to be kept in various camps and where he met a range of nationalities – Russians, Portuguese and French. Albert worked, finally, in the shipyards in Hamburg as a plater's mate, and discovered that his plater knew more about Belfast than he did, as he had worked on the *Titanic* in the Harland and Wolff shipyard before the war. Albert knew that the war was coming to an end – the navy was mutinying in Hamburg. 'No more war for you, Tommy', the sailors would say. Then the friendly plater was killed trying to get work during unrest in the Hamburg shipyards.

Albert returned to Ireland with a high opinion of the Germans:

They all wanted us to think better of Germany than I got a chance to …
they were civilised and modern … Once, when unloading iron ore, they
showed me just how keen they were on energy saving – they made us use
both arms to shovel instead of just our usual right arm. We had to train to
use the left one. It meant the right arm got a chance to rest.[5]

Tommy Russell, from Newcastle, also ended up as a POW after being captured at the Somme. One of his most lasting memories of two years in captivity was the bad food, enlivened now and again by Red Cross rations – bread and eggs from Holland and Switzerland – and by some rock sugar shared with him by a Russian POW. Occasionally, a woman in the canteen would pour some illicit vodka through the bars into tins that the men held out.

Most of the sentries in the camp were civilians, and often, by the time the war was coming to an end, the job was done by boys. Tommy remembered them saying over and over again, 'We didn't want war.' There was such a shortage of bandages in the camp by 1918 that some dressings were put in the sun to dry, then placed back over wounds. Tommy was glad to hear of the Armistice.[6]

Tommy Jordan, of the Pioneers, spent the rest of the war with his battalion. He saw many of his colleagues die, experienced some minor injuries of his own, and helped build countless cookhouses, billets and miles of railway line. One of his amusing memories was of a place called Locre, where Tommy was part of an advance party looking for billets. They went to a convent where Tommy's friend summoned up his best French and said, very politely, '*Bonjour, madame*', to which the nun at the door replied, 'And what are you blethering about?' She was an Irishwoman from County Kilkenny.

As a carpenter, Tommy had the job of making wooden crosses for the victims of the latest accurate shell or bullet. He would take out the khaki handkerchief from the dead-man's pocket, place one of the man's identity discs in it with papers and paybook, wrap it up and gave it to his officer. The other little disc was nailed to the cross that would mark yet another soldier's grave.

Towards the Germans, though, he never managed to feel much antagonism. He felt particularly sorry for them when they were wounded.[7]

Also in the Pioneers was Hugh James Adams from Crossgar, County Down. From 1916 through to the Armistice, all that Hugh James was to remember was one long decline into degradation. He recalled soldiers gaining a ghastly amusement out of tugging at the limbs of corpses on the battlefields to see if the flesh had decomposed. Where food was short, men might cook and eat pieces of mules that had been killed. Boots were always taken from dead bodies, as they might be a more comfortable fit than one's own. By 1918, although still only in his early twenties, Hugh James was called the 'Old Man' because almost all his comrades were fresh recruits while he had been one of the original Volunteers. He had several injuries, but came back each time to the front line.

In the final months of the war, the suffering he saw continued unabated, and two memories were particularly haunting. One was of a young boy called Sam who got hit in the spine and pleaded with his captain to put him out of his misery. The captain lifted his revolver but then burst into tears and could not do it. Sam was sent down the line, doomed either to die or else to live in a wheelchair for the rest of his days. The other memory was of the retreat in March 1918 during which Hugh James saw a young lad sitting on the ground crying. He had been injured in the back and could not walk, but he was fully conscious. There seemed to be nothing Hugh James could do for him, and he left him there to his tears and pain, picturing all the while a German soldier 'finishing the job' for the injured lad by sticking his bayonet in him.[8]

Hugh Stewart, from Lisburn, survived the Battle of the Somme, but later in July, in Flanders, was wounded. His first conscious memory after the incident was of being hoisted up on a stretcher at the Calais dock and landed into the hold of a capacious boat full of 'glorious, white beds'. In response to Hugh's question, a nurse replied, 'You're heading back to Blighty, son.' Hugh had a prolonged convalescence, and then went to Salisbury Plain to retrain, but he never had to return to the war. At Salisbury, he had the distinction of being the bugler in the cathedral when a service was being held to celebrate the Armistice.[9]

George Lindsay, from County Derry – who had been one of the original members of the Cyclist Company – continued to serve in the Observation Corps throughout the war. He came through alive but had a few 'near scrapes', particularly when a shell demolished a tree above a dugout he was occupying at Messines in 1917. He had had an excellent view of the mines being exploded on the first day of that battle. In the following year, only two out of eight in a party in which Lindsay was marching managed to survive the March retreat. When the remnants of the division went down the coast to reassemble, George enjoyed daily meetings with an eight-year-old French boy; each would teach the other a little of their language. The one embarrassing thing was that George got hopelessly drunk on the day that the little boy brought him home to meet his mother.

When he returned to the front, George suffered a wound in his ankle, and was sent back to England for the duration of the war. By the time the Armistice came, he was utterly disillusioned with the army and the fighting:

The average soldier's opinion of the General Staff was not fit for hearing … in the company of ladies, at least … You were in it and couldn't get out of it. I think most intelligent men saw the folly of the whole thing – we were sent out there to fight against people that we'd no grudge against and who couldn't help being in the same position as ourselves. I think before the war was over we were all pacifists. Most of us were all disillusioned. Oh, that feeling of resentment! And our cynicism! Sometimes chapel bells would start to ring as we marched through a village and we'd say, 'Huh, another French victory.'

But as with a number of other men, some of George Lindsay's worst memories were not just of the front but of the experience of leave. The problem was that relatives of men who had died in one's platoon or company might well want to talk about the death and to find out, if they could, something about the circumstances.

I came to tell Mac's mother of his death in 1917. She lived in Carrickfergus. Mac was only seventeen and my friend. She'd quite a family round her when I visited – four or five maybe. 'Well Mrs Macauley, I said, you'll not be left alone.' 'But,' she said, 'my Robbie was the flower of the flock.' That's the way it seemed to be. All the best chaps seemed to be taken.

The distress of such a visit as this was made all the worse by the fact that the men often had to conceal the true facts of a grisly or prolonged death in the interests of the relative's feelings.[10]

John Leslie Stewart-Moore, of Ballydivity, was, like George Lindsay, one of those who had been well back from the action in July 1916. However, once he arrived in the Messines area, he met with ill luck. He was walking along a front-line trench one day when a shell landed nearby and a piece of shrapnel damaged the back of his neck. After a spell in hospital, he was shortly back on duty, but then received bad news from home. A letter came from Ballydivity in mid-September saying that his brother Harry had been killed on the Salonica front. Another brother, Charlie, had arrived in France by the end of that month, posted to a battalion of the Leinster Regiment near Kemmel Hill.

On 3 October 1916, a year after he had arrived in France, Stewart-Moore got a 'Blighty one'. He arrived at a Bailleul casualty clearing station with injuries caused by a mortar bomb, and was immediately operated on, having his right arm amputated at the elbow. After a week, he went by train to a hospital in Boulogne. Eventually, he arrived in London, and with his one good hand waved to his waiting relatives at the platform of Charing Cross station. Stewart-Moore recuperated in London and returned to Ballydivity for Christmas. He was but one of countless men who would have to adapt to the harsh post-war world with a serious physical disability. But mental and emotional disturbance also had to be faced. Stewart-Moore's friend, James Seymour, had had a serious nervous breakdown some time before he met him again in London in 1917. The strain of the war had broken his mind, and he had been discharged from the army as 'unfit'. Now he was attempting to do an office job, and make his way back to health.[11]

The Armistice found G.H.M. in Bangor Hospital in County Down. In August 1917 he had had his arm shattered by shell fire, and during the following year had suffered from intermittent ill health that had necessitated occasional hospitalisation. He was demobilised shortly after 11 November, and had to face the world without the curiously consoling security of the army:

> If I brought nothing into the Army, they make certain I carry nothing
> out. They take away my uniform which has been my pride and joy; the
> dress of our unique community, honoured and respected since ancient
> times. I am now like Wolsey, left to the mercy of a rude stream that must
> forever hide me. Disguised as a gentleman in my own civilian clothes I
> must fight my battles alone. Like a sheep without a shepherd, I have lost
> the shelter of the fold.[12]

For F. Percy Crozier, the liaison with the 36th Division had ended when he became a brigadier with the 119th Infantry Brigade in the winter of 1916, but not before he had indulged his old obsessions with alcohol and sexuality yet again. He delighted in ransacking the kit of two of his officers who turned up late for a train journey; he discovered 'some ladies' underwear … an envelope full of astonishing postcards and … a pot of Vaseline'. Whilst near Bailleul, he expelled a prostitute whom he discovered spreading VD among his men – 'an infected girl who hops from camp to camp and ditch to dyke like the true butterfly she is'. Also a source of great glee to Crozier was the occasion on which he passed information to a senior officer that two other battalion commanders were secret alcoholics. As a result, they were demoted – or, as Crozier triumphantly put it, 'A change of scenery is arranged for the two tipplers.'[13]

VICTIMS

Armistice Day could only bring the sadness of memory and longing to many families whose sons were now a long time dead: to the parents of Captain Arthur Samuels, killed at Messines in September 1916;[14] to the parents of Billy McFadzean and all the other young men who had died at the Somme. There was a very fresh grief, too, for those who had been bereaved in the final weeks and months of the war. Rifleman David Storey, of Randalstown, died on 30 September 1918, and the news that he was definitely 'killed in action' reached his relatives only in the final week in October. It prompted his mother to write a poem.[15]

> As dawn crept o'er the trenches
> You fell midst shot and shell.
> Our only grief we were not there
> To bid a last farewell
> Somewhere abroad a volley sings
> A bugle sounds farewell.
>
> Sleep on, dear David,
> In a foreign land,
> In a grave we may never see.
> But as long as life and
> Memory last,
> We will remember thee.

For some mothers, the final appalling twist in the story of their son's life was not revealed until the war was over. My great-uncle, John Martin of Crossgar, who had served in the Pioneers throughout the conflict, kept in

Officers and nurses at a UVF hospital. Note the man seated on the right, who is nursing an amputated lower arm.
SOMME MUSEUM

touch with the parents and relatives who had done everything in their power to prevent his enlistment. He had returned on leave and had been greeted as a quiet hero, tall and good-looking in his uniform. Although his written English was always poor, he wrote letters rather than relying on the field postcards. In January 1917 he had written to his brother-in-law, Tommy Rea, to thank him for a recent parcel, and he expressed the hope that the conflict would soon be over: 'You wont have long to wate till the war is over by the look of things it is near an end if he dosent give in before the summer he will get a bad sluttering I am afraid.'

On 21 March 1918 John went missing during the German advance. However, in May a postcard from him arrived from a German POW camp to say that he was alive and well, and that no one should worry about him. When the Armistice came, his family expected to see him return home from Germany, and Mrs Martin kept a constant watch for the men disembarking from the trains in Crossgar railway station. But John did not come off the train, and his whereabouts could not be traced. Then, one Sunday night, when Mr Martin was alone in the house, a man from Killyleagh called. He said that he had been in the same POW camp as John and that they had both been drafted up near the front to work in a German army canteen. On

16 June 1918 an air raid had taken place and French planes had dropped bombs on the cook house where John had been working. His comrade assured the family that John had been killed instantly. Mr Martin sent a message for his wife to come home. She returned from her daughter's house in Killyleagh Street to receive the news. The sense of loss, hopelessness and waste was deep, and Mrs Martin was inconsolable.

In the early weeks of 1919 the Infantry Record Office confirmed the death and sent 'their Majesties' sympathy' to the family. (A measure of the impact of that death is the fact that, over sixty years later, when my grandmother, John Martin's sister, was an elderly and dying woman, she did not recall more recent bereavements but increasingly thought of her long-dead brother and cried for him as if he had died only yesterday.)[16]

REMEMBERING THE DEAD

The process of commemorating the sacrifice of the Ulstermen who had fought with the 36th Division had begun before the war was over.

On Sunday 1 July 1917 in Newtownbreda Presbyterian Church, on the outskirts of Belfast, an afternoon service was held to pay respects to the memory of Billy McFadzean in what had been his home church. A tablet was unveiled on which were the words: 'Greater love hath no man than this, that a man lay down his life for his friends.' The last post was played, the congregation sang 'O God, Our Help In Ages Past', and the choir performed a beautiful anthem, a setting by Woodward of Tennyson's poem, 'Crossing the Bar', which includes these lines:

> Twilight and evening bell,
> And after that the dark!
> And may there be no sadness of farewell,
> When I embark;
>
> For tho' from out our bourne of Time and Place
> The flood may bear me far,
> I hope to see my pilot face to face
> When I have crost the bar.

Billy's father had already received his son's Victoria Cross from the king at

An embroidered handkerchief from the war zone. Mementoes such as this were often all that remained of a vanished loved one – besides the medals, and a scroll and plaque expressing the king's gratitude.
SOMME MUSEUM

Buckingham Palace in February – having been granted a third-class return ticket from Cregagh to London.[17]

In the years that followed, many other plaques were to be unveiled in churches throughout Ulster, and monuments were erected in villages particularly hard hit by the loss. The war-memorial statue of a Great War soldier in uniform became a feature of town squares and prominent road junctions, and along with the names of all the other victims of the war, those of the 36th Division are still to be found inscribed in weatherbeaten stone. Memorial services were held each 1 July, as well as the annual Armistice commemoration on 11 November. In the Garden of Remembrance outside Belfast's City Hall, and in other places in the province, veterans gathered to pay homage to fallen comrades and to lay wreaths of poppies on the anniversary of the first day of the Somme.

On 11 November 1929 a cenotaph was unveiled in the grounds of the City Hall and Field Marshall Allenby laid the first wreath. Scores of different social, religious, sporting and political groups were represented at the ceremony (including the Italian fascist party and the Ulster Women's Unit of the British Fascist Party).[18]

Initially, the shock of the Somme was too fresh for respect and grief to be linked to the more disquieting process of querying the reasons for the sacrifice. What was a source of disquietude throughout the 1920s, however, was the fact that many veterans of the Ulster Division had had to return to a life of poverty and unemployment in the depressed economy of the post-war era. In some quarters, the erection of costly memorials to the dead of the Great War seemed a waste of money that could have been spent in more practical ways in alleviating the distress of those ex-soldiers who could not find work.[19]

But by the 1930s it had become possible to question the whole value of war itself; pacifism had become a respectable philosophy, and the work of writers such as Wilfred Owen, Siegfried Sassoon and Robert Graves had exposed the sordid and inglorious realities of the Western Front. By the twentieth anniversary of the Somme, the homage to the men who had died was mingled with a preparedness to criticise the military strategy of the leaders and, indeed, the attitude of the ordinary soldiers. The *Belfast News Letter* of Wednesday 1 July 1936 devoted an article to the Ulster Division's contribution to the Somme, and explored the possibility that 'The charge of the Division was too headlong and an error in tactics. There was some evidence of inexperience in the mass and sometimes of too great an individual enthusiasm … they had not acquired the skill in manoeuvre and the cunning in expedients'.

The same newspaper was full of articles and reports that indicated the looming threat of fascism, but its readers could not guess that in a little over three years' time, Britain and Germany would be at war once again and a fresh generation of young men would have their names carved onto Ulster's war memorials.

In the period after the Second World War, the 1 July services would see a gradual thinning of the ranks of Somme veterans who gathered at the

The Archbishop of Armagh leads a group around the trenches of the
Schwaben Redoubt in 1921, after the ceremony to dedicate
the Ulster Tower at Thiepval.
ROYAL ULSTER RIFLES MUSEUM

cenotaph. But in 1966 there were still 1,200 old men able to parade in front
of the Queen at a fiftieth anniversary ceremony in Belfast's Balmoral
Showgrounds – the scene so many years previously of Ulster Volunteer
demonstrations in which many of the veterans would have taken part.[20] The
local newspapers contained numerous interviews with men who had fought
at the Somme, and at last, fifty years after the event, some of the real
bitterness of the ordinary soldier came to light. Veteran Malcolm McKee's
article in the *Belfast Telegraph* of 30 June 1966 was headed 'In chains for
execution' – a title unthinkable thirty years previously. The sense of waste
and unquenched, angry grief spilt out:

> I can think of nothing but what might have been – and of the golden
> friends I had … what I want to convey is that my men were my personal
> friends – hence my fury at how they were almost obliterated through
> gross stupidity … we were locked in chains for execution.

McKee went on to savage those who mythologised the battle:

What nonsense is stuck onto the story … Certainly Major Gaffikin waved an orange handkerchief, but orange was the colour of our battalion … If he had said (and if anybody could have heard him) 'Come on, boys, this is the First of July!' – how many would have known the Boyne was fought on the first of July ? I don't know why they plaster such incidents on our battle. Nothing was further from my mind than the Boyne on the Somme.

The irreparable personal loss was the only thing that ultimately mattered:

When the Belfast brigade left Bramshott for France, the bands played 'The Girl I Left Behind Me' … and ilka lad had got his lass. After 1st July there were many broken hearts. Those girleens, if nobody else, remembered the massed dead on the banks of the Ancre.

By 1986, and the much heralded seventieth anniversary of the Somme, there was but a handful of veterans to march to the Belfast cenotaph.

Trips to the Somme to see the field of battle and remember the fallen had also been a feature of the post-war years, and numerous Ulster veterans had made the trip. But in 1986 only three survivors travelled to France. One of these was Tommy Ervine of the old East Belfast Volunteers. The others were Dick Calvert and Sam Neill. These three were the remnants of the several thousands who packed the assembly trenches of Thiepval that July morning, seventy years earlier. They joined the group of seventy veterans and five thousand other visitors who attended the commemoration service at the Thiepval Memorial to the Missing of the Somme Campaign.[21]

Of all the monuments to the Ulster Volunteers, the most striking is to be found at Thiepval on the site of the Ulstermen's battle. Known as the Ulster Tower, it is modelled on the famous Helen's Tower that stands in Clandeboye estate and overlooked the Ulster Volunteers who trained there in 1914 and 1915. Raised by public subscription, the tower at Thiepval was erected in 1921 and unveiled on 19 November that year. On the avenue leading up to it are forty-two trees, and in a memorial chamber inside is a tablet bearing an adaptation of the lines by Tennyson that are inscribed on the original Helen's Tower, erected by the Marquis of Dufferin as a tribute to his mother:

Helen's Tower here I stand,
Dominant over sea and land:
Son's love built me, and I hold
Ulster's love in letter'd gold …

The adaptation consisted of the substitution of 'Ulster's love' for 'Mother's love': as with all public war memorials, the agonising personal bereavements commemorated are swallowed up in the colder dignity of corporate grief.

The tower was unveiled by Lord Carson; the Ulster Volunteers had been, after all, 'his' army.[22]

Each of the three Irish regiments that contributed battalions to the 36th Division has sought to record, at their regimental museums in Enniskillen, Armagh and Belfast, the Ulster participation in the Battle of the Somme. The Royal Ulster Rifles (formerly the Royal Irish Rifles), the Royal Inniskilling and the Royal Irish Fusiliers have since been disbanded and their place in the British army taken by the Royal Irish Rangers, but the traditions and history of each regiment have been carefully preserved. The Royal Ulster Rifles Regimental Museum in Belfast has a particularly rich storehouse of artefacts, uniforms, regalia, weaponry and documents.

PRIVATE GRIEFS

The process of keeping alive the memory and significance of the Somme dead was maintained not only publicly but privately by the families of the victims. Part of this process sometimes involved a search for a grave – impelled by a deep need to know some physical location as the last resting place of the dead soldier. In 1920 the parents of Billy McFadzean were still trying desperately to find some particular gravestone in the military cemeteries of the Somme where their famous son might have been laid to rest.[23]

The Mabin family, from the Shankill, exemplify how clearly the memory was kept alive. Two of the Mabin boys had died at the Somme, although they had only been reported as 'missing, believed killed', and their mother refused to shift from their Crosby Street home, giving as her reason that perhaps the boys might still return and she would want them to be able to find their home when they walked up the Shankill Road again. Mrs Mabin showed few outward signs of intense grief, but she kept a bundle of the boys' letters and frequently pored over them. When the anniversary of the battle came around, or at Christmas time, Mrs Mabin became particularly sad; Christmas Eve had been both her own birthday and that of one of her boys.

Every year since 1917, and long after Mrs Mabin's death, the relatives, like many loyalists, have put out their Union Jack on 1 July. During the blitz on Belfast in 1941, when a bomb destroyed the Crosby Street home, a neighbour sent a few young lads up onto the roof of the deserted house with a flag so that the 'First of July' tradition would remain unbroken. Each July the family also places a memorial to the two dead boys in the local newspaper, a tradition now stretching back through seven decades.

In the 1980s the Mabins still feel a sense of pride in the fact that both men 'did their duty'. Billy Mabin, of Shankill Parade, nephew of the soldiers (who himself fought in the Second World War, in Burma), explained:

> If your country's worth living in, it's worth fighting for … you can't fight a war without losing lives. Although no one wants killing, sometimes it has to be. To keep your country free sometimes you have to fight and die. It was a great honour for us.

On the wall of the Mabins' living-room is a little embroidered postcard sent back from the front at Christmas by one of the brothers. Amidst floral decorations and interwoven French and British flags is the caption 'RIGHT IS MIGHT'.[24] Such convictions have enabled the Mabins and many other families to make some sense of their loss down through the years.

CRAIGAVON

Part of the story of the Ulster Volunteers and their legacy has been the UVF Hospital. In 1914 the headquarters council of the Volunteer Force offered its entire medical facilities to the War Office, and in 1915 a main UVF hospital was opened by Lord Carson in a building adjoining Queen's University, with smaller branch hospitals being established elsewhere in the province during the course of the war. While hostilities continued, many wounded and disabled servicemen were treated by these hospitals. After the Armistice, the hospitals continued to function, mainly providing care for ex-service patients sent there for treatment by the Ministry of War Pensions.

Another hospital opened at Galwally in 1926, closed some four years later, but reopened in 1940, and continued to function until 1969, caring for the needs not only of many First World War veterans, but also of victims of the Second World War and other conflicts in which Ulstermen had found themselves engaged as members of the armed services. The UVF branch hospital set up at Craig's estate of Craigavon during the First World War was still open in the 1980s, and in the summer of 1987 some forty-five patients were in its care, including several veterans of the First World War. The UVF hospitals have, in total, cared for over twenty-eight thousand participating soldiers from that war – a tremendous record of service in the alleviation of suffering and disability.[25]

Among the survivors of the 36th Division who were to be found at Craigavon in 1986 was George McBride, a former YCV and a Shankill Road man by birth. George fought at the Somme, Cambrai, Messines, Ypres and St-Quentin, and spent the last few months of his war as a POW, working in a quarry in the Black Forest. When he returned to Belfast, he found a city where thousands of men were unemployed – 'a town filled with pawnshops, pubs, politicians and preachers'. He joined the Labour Party and met Elizabeth Carney, who had been James Connolly's secretary and had taken part in the Easter Rising. They married in 1926. Thus did one former UVF man's politics turn full circle.

George McBride never lost a sense of guilt about the Germans he may have killed: 'It's an awful thing to kill a man ... I was a Lewis gunner ... and the ones that I did kill, maybe they had wives. Perhaps there's still such a wife somewhere who's still mourning for her husband'. He also felt a strong sense of the continuity between the Great War and the Cold War of the 1980s: 'Even with all the weapons we have now, we can only do on a bigger scale what we did in the last ones.'[26]

DISABILITY

In 1983 one other old veteran of the 36th Division died. John Leslie Stewart-Moore, aged ninety, had had a full and active life, despite the injuries he had received in October 1916 that had necessitated the amputation of his right arm at the elbow.

On returning to Britain, Stewart-Moore had had to learn to write with his left hand, and within a few months had made the necessary trips to Queen Mary's Hospital, Roehampton, to be fitted for an artificial arm:

> I stayed in Dover House which has been set aside for limbless officers ...
> I shared a room with another fellow who had also lost his right hand;
> he had become very clever with his left hand and could even tie a
> bow-tie – something that I had never been able to do even with two
> hands ... before long I had discovered the existence of left-handed
> nail scissors ... When the hospital surgeon looked at my stump he said
> that I had a bulbous nerve which must be removed before I could be
> fitted with an artificial arm ... I went to Dublin and called on Dr Sir
> James Craig who arranged for me to have the operation ... When my
> stump had healed again ... I went over once more to the limb fitting
> centre at Roehampton ... a plaster cast of my stump was made and sent
> off to Kansas City, USA, where the Carnes arms were made. After two
> months I was again summoned to Roehampton ... after I had been fitted
> with the harness I put it on; it had ... fingers which could be opened
> and closed by shrugging one's shoulder. It was rather heavy at first
> so that I could only wear it for two or three hours at a time but gradually
> I got used to it.[27]

The war was to inflict a serious handicap, too, on Tommy Jordan of the Pioneers. The damage done to his hearing by the shell fire to which he had been exposed seemed to have subsided, but in 1941, when the Germans were blitzing Belfast, the noise of the exploding bombs reactivated his old problems. After this, Tommy was incapable of doing a day's paid work, due to his deafness, and when I met him in July 1984 he had not worked for over forty years. Much of his time was devoted to the cultivation of his garden, but Tommy never had a waking moment in those forty years when he did not suffer from a violent rushing noise in his head – 'like a dynamo' – that prevented him from hearing what other people were saying.[28]

OLD SOLDIERS

For Hugh Stewart, of the South Antrim Volunteers, there was no disability to contend with, yet there were the haunting memories of the past to relive. When I met him in May 1984 Hugh was eighty-eight years of age, and his wife had died just two years before. The previous two years had been lonely ones, and memories of the war had flooded back. 'I'm alone all the day', he said, '... the terrible carnage is best forgotten ... but it's hard'. Yet Hugh's life had been an active one, even in the final years:

> I sing, and when I sang in the choir I loved best of all the 'Lament of the Irish Emigrant' ... and when I was in hospital with my back in traction I learnt Grey's 'Elegy' off by heart – that was quite recently now. I can console myself thinking of the poems I've learnt – 'The Village Blacksmith' and Wordworth's 'Daffodils' which seemed so true just this past spring when I looked out on the sea of daffodils in my garden. You are nearer God's heart in a garden than any place on earth. Just think – all that lovely apple blossom – where does all that beauty come from?
>
> But how awful war is. The things people do to other human beings. I remember Whittier's lines – 'Brother man, fold to thy heart thy brother.'

One of Hugh's most poignant memories was of returning to the battlefields of France for the fiftieth anniversary of the Somme.

> When we went back there in 1966 it was touching how the Frenchwomen put their arms around us and we all wept together. We got the plane back from Orly to London and my friend and I were chatting at the front of the plane. 'I wouldn't care if this plane went down now,' said he. And do you know, I felt the same! I didn't mind now if I died. We'd accomplished it all. We'd seen the hallowed ground where there were so many of our friends still lying. They were nineteen and we had grown old. Age had taken its toll on us but they remained nineteen for ever.

Hugh has put the Union Jack out on the flagpole in his front garden every year on 1 July since he returned to Lisburn.[29]

In 1984 I interviewed another South Antrim man, Albert Bruce, who had spent the final months of the war as a POW in Hamburg:

> You hear some old soldiers talk about love of King and country but if you want me to let you know, most men did it because of the monotony of life and because it was a chance to 'be in the crowd'. Many's the time when I'm in bed, these things will come back to me, and I can't get to sleep. Just when I don't want them. You don't forget.[30]

Hugh James Adams at his
hundredth birthday party
HANNAH MOFFAT

Albert was involved in a road accident near his home shortly after this; following a prolonged spell in hospital, he died in 1987.

Another testimony of resilience was to be Tommy Ervine. On one occasion when I met him, he complained of sore knees, caused by the fact that he had walked a couple of miles down the Cregagh Road to watch the Belfast Marathon go by.

'Sometimes I find tears in my eyes', he told me. 'I wouldn't recommend longevity. My wife died eight years ago. You forget things. You lose your faculties'.

Tommy played his mouth organ for me and challenged me to a game of darts on a board hung up on his kitchen door. In 1986 he made the trip back to France for the seventieth anniversary of the Somme. The legacy of seventy years ago was apparent in Tommy's revelation that every time he tried to remember the face of 'Old Fritz', the POW with whom he had become so friendly, he could only see the bleeding face of the German soldier he had shot dead on the Somme.[31]

Hugh James Adams was another long-term survivor. Of one thing he was certain: that he would never have gone to war in 1914 had he known how bad it would be.

> If anyone asked me 'Would you be prepared to come through the war?'
> I'd say 'No I'd rather die.' I'd rather die a thousand times. It would be
> absolutely impossible. I still hear the guns, sure, and the other night I
> woke up and I could hear the guns firin'! If you ask me now, I'll tell you:
> I wouldn't put me dog in the British Army![32]

For some old soldiers, a sudden reappearance of some triggering smell or sound would swiftly reawaken all the old memories:

> My father could never stand the smell of blood and as he got older he got
> worse about it. In the end, if we were killing a few pigs he went down
> to my sister's place for the day. The sight of so many of his friends
> killed or wounded on that day left a sorrow in his heart that stayed with
> him till he died. Now and again he would get up in the middle of the
> night when he could not sleep and light a candle and go down and
> make himself a drop of punch.[33]

And so, seventy years later, the shell fire of the Western Front continued in the minds of those who could never forget. For many, the words of G.H.M. rang true: 'I never cease to wonder how I survived. A guardian angel must have been watching over me.'[34]

For some, the same guardian angel that had protected them in France flew away when they returned to Ireland. Major – later Lieutenant-Colonel – Peacocke, who had rallied the Volunteers on the Schwaben Redoubt on the afternoon of 1 July, was assassinated at his home near Cork in June 1921, when the Irish Troubles were at a height.[35] And Ambrose Ricardo, patron and leader of the Tyrone Volunteers, met misfortune in the summer of 1923. He had recently had a reservoir built to augment the water supply of Sion Mills. One afternoon he took a walk to the reservoir to see how full it was. When he did not turn up for tea, his wife went to see what had become of him. She found his dog, Corporal, sitting on the bank and his hat floating on the water. She rushed to the spot where the dog sat looking into the reservoir, and there she could see her husband's body in the water. The reason for his death remained a mystery, although it was believed he had been attending a specialist for heart trouble, and a heart attack may have made him collapse, unconscious, into the water. Ambrose Ricardo, Brigadier-General, had survived the war but not the peace.[36]

Another officer who had survived the Great War with the Ulster Division met a much later, but equally tragic fate. Sir Norman Stronge, who had joined the Derry Volunteer battalion of the division in September 1914 and had participated in the Battle of the Somme, was killed with his son by the IRA, and his home, Tynan Abbey, destroyed by fire on 21 January 1981, two days before his eighty-seventh birthday.[37]

For the infamous Crozier, the post-war years brought a certain status as an author. He had plenty to write about: after the Armistice, he went to help organise the Lithuanian army against the Bolsheviks, then returned to command the British 'Auxiliary' forces in Ireland, eventually resigning because he disapproved of the authorised reprisals he was being ordered to carry out. Later, Crozier was converted to a variety of political viewpoints, flirting with Irish nationalism despite his unionist and British army background, and leaning towards a kind of pacifism only after having embraced fascism for a while – what he called the 'Mussolini touch' and 'the hand of a superman'.

He scaled the heights of egotism with his ill-written and eccentric books of personal reminiscences and pontifications, and he gave English literary history one of its most tasteless book titles: *The Men I Killed*. F. Percy Crozier died in 1937.[38]

Other men were certain only of one lesson about human conduct to be taken from the war in which they had been involved: that military conflict, whether in the past, present or future, involves the destruction of ordinary, precious lives in the name of patriotism. One such man was George Lindsay, who spent his last few years in Carrickfergus. From the window of his house, he could look towards Belfast Lough, with its ships sailing to and from the harbour. His comments sum up what he had learnt from his experiences:

> Christian teaching: fifth chapter of Matthew. Perfection … If one could live up to it! Next to impossible to do so. Very few people could realise

that they are good enough to do so ... I have the feeling that mankind is going to wipe himself off the face of the earth, really – going to leave no trace of life on this planet at all ...[39]

This is, perhaps, the most bitter blow for any old soldier. His war did not 'end wars', but, rather, it gave the infantryman a foretaste of the vulnerability that all humanity now experiences in the face of its own weaponry. The Ulster Volunteer on the road to the Somme had his foot on the first step of the precipitous path our century is treading between human survival and self-destruction. His voice is a testimony and a warning.

OUT OF THE SILENCE

The question arises as to why it should take so long for the honest witnesses of the Somme to be listened to by subsequent generations. A kind of self-censorship, it is true, tends to exist long after many wars are over – before people are ready to hear about the absurdities, obscenities and immoralities of a conflict for which so much was sacrificed. But in the case of the Ulster Division, the period of inhibition before a proper confrontation with the realities of the Great War seems to have been an especially long one, reflecting, surely, the reluctance of some Ulster people to confront with honesty their own place in history and, in particular, to question the true nature of their link with Britain.

In future, Ulster Protestants may learn to value the actual and individual testimonies of the ordinary participants in history rather than simplistic and supremacist versions of their collective past which pass, for many, as real history. If they do so, they may come to realise that the truth about social and personal realities may be found in the diverse viewpoints of ordinary people and not in the expostulations of public figures. A strident espousal of glory, traditions, sacrifices and absolutes is entirely different in tone from the mundane but authentic voice of the ordinary human being whom circumstances thrust into the crucible of violence. One kind of voice drowns out the other, so Ulster Protestants must make a careful choice about which voice they prefer to listen to, and which kind of history to treasure. It is a choice that every people has to make, with all the consequences that follow. The men we have met on the pages of this book have acted as our guides through one stretch of the dark past. Their voices fade back into the silence from which they came.

> History may be servitude,
> History may be freedom …
> We cannot revive old factions
> We cannot restore old policies
> Or follow an antique drum.
> These men, and those who opposed them
> And those whom they opposed
> Accept the constitution of silence
> And are folded in a single party.
>
> 'Little Gidding'
> T.S. Eliot

The Somme battlefield three years after the war ended. The faint outline of the newly erected Ulster Tower is just visible on the horizon.
ROYAL ULSTER RIFLES MUSEUM

CLIMBING OUT OF THE TRENCHES
ULSTER, IRELAND AND THE GREAT WAR, 1987–2008

The Lord Mayor of Belfast, Tom Hartley, with other Sinn Féin party members, lays a wreath at Belfast City Hall on 1 July 2008
PACEMAKER PRESS INTERNATIONAL

REVISIONISM

Twenty-one years have passed since the first publication of *The Road to the Somme*. The old men whom I interviewed have long since died. The Great War is now receding beyond the horizon of living memory, as far away as Waterloo once seemed to the young men growing up in Edwardian Ulster, who joined the 36th Ulster Division and fought on the Western Front.

However, First World War scholarship in Britain and Ireland has increased during the past two decades, and the 'further reading' section of this edition lists some of the best recent Irish publications. One interesting, if predictable, trend has been revisionism. Some writers now assert that the conflict was not the debacle that folk memory has made it out to be. The historian Gary Sheffield points out that the British Expeditionary Force was transformed in four years from an army dominated by raw recruits to an efficient force that overcame the mighty German infantry. He notes the importance of the Somme within that process:

> The Somme taught the BEF how to fight, while it degraded the quality of the German Army. By the end of 1916 the two armies were much more evenly matched than had been the case 6 months earlier. Moreover, while British morale remained high, German morale suffered ... Captain von Hentig, of the Guard Reserve Division, described the Somme in a famous phrase as 'the muddy graveyard of the German Army' ... the Somme should not be dismissed simply as a bloody disaster ...[1]

If Sheffield is right in this assessment and in his suggestion that Germany was a dangerous foe who needed to be beaten, then perhaps it is not so appropriate for descendants of the soldiers of 1916 to look back on their forebears who died at the Somme as victims of a futile slaughter. In Sheffield's eyes, the terrible casualties of 1916 were the grim price that had to be paid to begin bleeding dry the military prowess of an autocratic regime hell-bent on conquest.

Sheffield's arguments are controversial and at times persuasive. However, they do nothing to wipe away the horror and heartbreak so eloquently described by the veterans whom I met, and who saw their pals wiped out on a bright July morning by German machine guns that a British artillery barrage was meant to have completely smashed.

Among other scholarly developments has been a proper recognition that the Somme offensive lasted for months and involved a great deal more military action than its infamous beginning in early July. This 'opening out' of the narrative has had the fortunate effect of allowing the exploits of the 16th Division to obtain a greater historical profile. This division – established as a 'home' for the men of John Redmond's Irish National Volunteers – experienced over four thousand casualties between 1–10 September 1916.[2] Their deaths make the commemorative meaning of the 36th Division's Somme sacrifice more complex than some Ulster people have cared to realise. This will be explored later in the chapter.

MUSEUMS AND TOURS

Back in the mid-1980s anyone who wanted to find out more about the Ulster Division had work on their hands. In London, the National Archive (formerly the Public Record Office), the Imperial War Museum, the National Army Museum and the British Library all contained sources for the dedicated researcher. In Northern Ireland, hours might be spent in the Public Record Office or in regimental museums in Armagh, Belfast and Enniskillen. Courteous staff members in the three regimental venues always assisted researchers with good cheer. However, in those days, any venue connected to the British army was considered a 'legitimate target' by the IRA, so these museums were low key and did not advertise their presence. Many of the handwritten war journals and photos from the First World War were carefully stowed away, but they were sketchily catalogued and, to all intents and purposes, gathering dust.

Meanwhile, in France – where the soldiers' graves were kept in pristine order by the Commonwealth War Graves Commission – the commemorative Ulster Tower at Thiepval was a rarely visited and somewhat forbidding venue. I recall arriving there with two friends on a sunlit July evening in 1988, and having to summon by telephone the caretaker who held the key to the tower so that we could enter the building, climb the stairway, and observe the eerily peaceful panorama of the former battlefield. According to the caretaker, a trickle of visitors might be expected in the summer months, but throughout the rest of the year the Tower usually stayed locked up. An acquaintance of mine visiting the Somme in the same year witnessed a service being held at the Thiepval Tower on 1 July, and reckoned that there were no more than forty or fifty people present.[3]

In 2008 it is a very different story. In Northern Ireland, regimental museums exist more openly, in a less threatening civic atmosphere, with more accessible and comprehensively catalogued archives, and a fine range of special exhibitions. A Somme Association has also been in existence since 1990, promoting both public and private remembrance of the First World War. It grew out of the Farset Somme project in west Belfast, whose intent was to assist community development through cultural education. A network of 'Friends of the Somme' is connected to the association, and enables its members, both in Northern Ireland and further afield, to keep in

Ceremony at the Ulster Tower, 1 July 2006
SOMME MUSEUM

touch with exhibitions, battlefield tours and lectures. The most significant achievement of the association is the Somme Museum near Newtownards in County Down, first opened in 1994. This venue includes a range of displays, an impressive set of 'mock' trenches, a multimedia recreation of the battle, a 'hands-on' activity area, and a computer database that can be used to trace relatives who died in the conflict, as well as a café and souvenir shop. The museum also contains a remarkable collection of photos and letters from the First World War, and – increasingly – from other conflicts.

Significantly, the centre aims to embrace the memory of all those Irish soldiers who fought in the war, and to be meaningful for 'both communities' in Northern Ireland. In recent times – while many other 'heritage' venues have struggled to attract custom – the Somme Museum has had up to twenty-five thousand visitors annually, including over six thousand young people who are studying the war as part of the history curriculum, many of whom go on to make a school visit to the Western Front. Catholic schools are particularly well represented in visits to the centre.

The Somme Association has also taken steps to turn the Thiepval area into a more significant place of pilgrimage for Irish visitors. The Tower now contains a visitors' centre, and is staffed by knowledgeable resident caretakers from Northern Ireland who are keeping the site in good order and offering conducted tours. To supplement this, the association has recently bought the nearby Thiepval Wood, aided by money from Northern Ireland's Department of Culture, Arts and Leisure, and is making it into a meaningful tourist venue. This is a highly atmospheric site, where the trenches in which so many men of the Ulster Division prepared for their 'Big Push' are still visible today. The wood is only accessible along specified pathways, as unexploded ordnance is still thought to lurk beneath the ground in several places.[4]

Meanwhile, the numbers arriving at Thiepval have grown larger each year, in part because it has become cheaper and easier to travel from Northern Ireland to France, but also due to the rapid growth of Ulster interest in the war, which the association, among others, has done much to foster. My acquaintance, who saw just a handful of people at that commemorative service two decades ago, was part of the much larger group that gathered there in 2006 – a crowd local police estimated as averaging 2,500 on each of the three days of the commemoration. Throughout 2006, no fewer than 125,000 visits to the Tower were recorded.[5]

A MARKER OF ULSTER PROTESTANT IDENTITY

There was no doubt in my mind in 1987 that the First World War had legendary status in Orange culture. I felt it was my job as an historian to query the unlikely story – prevalent in some quarters – that the soldiers of the Ulster Division, as a totally unionist unit, had all 'gone over the top' at the Somme wearing Orange sashes and shouting Orange slogans. Nonetheless, I also knew from my researches that many of these troops had indeed been in the Loyal Orders, and that lodge structures existed in the division. I knew that Orange brethren still cherished the memory of forebears who had perished in the trenches, and often named their lodges and painted their banners to display allegiance to that memory. One of the most famous of these banners in Orange circles was the portrayal of nine men from the Waringstown area in County Armagh who perished in the conflict. This banner has been recently and lovingly restored.[6]

Since 1987 I have discovered even more about the tradition of Orange memorialisation of the war. Lodge number 977 is the '36th Division

282

Men of LOL 862, a military lodge of the Orange Order within the Ulster Division
SOMME MUSEUM

Memorial Lodge', based in north Belfast and founded in 1919 as a successor to Loyal Orange Lodge (LOL) 862, the temporary military lodge that was created when the Ulster Division was based in Seaford, Sussex. For many years, Orangemen had either to be veterans or belong to a veteran's family in order to join. Numbers understandably shrank as the Somme receded into history. However, the remaining members retain a proud sense of their heritage. When LOL 977 meets, a vacant chair, draped with an Orange collarette, is left standing during the proceedings as a token of remembrance, and if anyone walks in front of it, they are asked to pay a fine for dishonouring the memory of those who perished in the trenches. The lodge maintains close links with the Martyrs Memorial Lodge at Lewes, not far from Seaford – a body with its own strong sense of the distinctive English Reformed Protestant tradition.

However, in the course of the last two decades, the First World War – and the Somme in particular – has developed an even greater significance for many Orangemen, rather than fading away with the passing years. For many Orangemen, this military legacy became deeply intermingled with the controversial events at Drumcree, County Armagh, in the 1990s. The church service at Drumcree and the parade that accompanies it commemorated those who fell at the Somme, and it seemed to many Orangemen that their right to remember the Great War dead in a traditional manner was being denied by nationalist protestors who wanted the parade route changed. This undoubtedly magnified the significance of the Somme battle as a marker of Ulster Protestant identity.[7]

But it was in the wake of the unfavourable worldwide publicity surrounding the events at Drumcree that a number of key Orange figures such as Jackie Hewitt and Mervyn Gibson decided to pay more thoughtful, historical attention to the Somme, not just as a routine feature of the parading calendar but as a distinctive piece of Ulster heritage, when local communities once formed part of a momentous global story, and when local men had shown a remarkable, if tragic, courage. As a result, a new lodge was founded – LOL 1916 – which any Orangeman could join in addition to his local lodge. Among the tasks that the new institution set itself was the initiation and maintenance of a memorial at Thiepval to recognise the military sacrifices of the Loyal Orders worldwide. This structure, carved by Ballyclare stonemason, Archy Davidson, from distinctive black granite, now resides within the grounds of the Ulster Tower. With over five hundred members, LOL 1916 is now the largest Orange lodge in existence.[8]

Among other attempts by the Order to create a rich, non-controversial remembrance process has been the annual East Belfast Somme Festival, held in late June and early July, and which presents a series of relevant talks, religious services, social evenings and concerts, as well as the traditional Somme parade. The festival focuses on the memory of the battle, but also on other aspects of the unionist heritage.[9]

The Apprentice Boys and the Black Preceptory have also striven to commemorate the Somme. The musical culture that accompanies Orange parades has also been impacted by the growing interest in the First World War. A number of loyalist bands have been named after the Ulster Division and the Somme, and seek to maintain a high standard of musical performance and military bearing.[10] There are also keen archivists who gather evidence of the role of 'military lodges' in the First World War and other conflicts.[11] In various other cultural bodies concerned with the Ulster Protestant inheritance, the memory of the war is also regularly invoked. The Ulster Scots Folk Orchestra has created a CD simply entitled *Somme*.[12] Drama and poetry about the war are also being written and performed in

Orange and loyalist circles, including Brian Ervine's play, *Somme Day Mourning*,[13] and verse by the east Belfast man, Gorman McMullan.

FOUNDING MYTH OR HISTORICAL REALITY

It may seem to some observers that an horrendous battle in which there were hundreds of thousands of casualties is not a fit centrepiece for a culture that is trying to reaffirm itself. However, it must be recognised that there is a long tradition of horrendous battles forming cornerstones of cultural identity. Indeed, the First World War supplied several of these. Troops from the British Empire served and died in their own national units, and this played a role in generating autonomous national identities. Canadian losses at Vimy Ridge have given this battle profound North American political significance.[14] Gallipoli has offered Australians a vision of themselves as self-reliant, no-nonsense heroes, dying in a tragically daft imperial cause on the beaches and cliffs of the Dardanelles.[15] The same battle became a crucial founding myth for the new republic of Turkey that was being formed out of the ashes of the Ottoman Empire.[16]

Perhaps Orange culture needed to bring its historical subject matter forward from the fading pageantry of the Williamite wars in the seventeenth century to the citizen armies of twentieth-century conflict with which a younger generation may find it easier to identify. Interestingly, the Orange monument at Thiepval is in the shape of an obelisk, a form chosen because of its continuity with the eighteenth-century obelisk that stood overlooking the site of King William's victory at the River Boyne until it was destroyed by a bomb nearly two hundred years later.[17] It is also clear that in the bi-cultural Northern Irish context, where republicanism looks successfully for inspiration to the 'blood-sacrifice' of the Easter Rising in 1916 and to the more recent deaths of the IRA and INLA hunger-strikers in their prison cells, the Battle of the Somme offers evidence that Ulster Protestants can also die for their cause.

Amidst this expanding Somme culture, no young bandsman or Orange brother should imagine that it was only Ulster Protestants who went from this island to die on the barbed wire and in the shell holes of no-man's-land. Influential Orangemen such as Jackie Hewitt, of LOL 1916, are aware of the nationalist contribution made to the British army in the war. Hewitt encourages Orangemen who come to Thiepval to attend the ceremony organised by the Somme Association at the 16th Divisional Memorial, sited where many of John Redmond's men fought at Guillemont and Ginchy. Hewitt also stresses that thousands of Ulstermen probably went to fight for very prosaic and personal reasons – such as poverty, an unhappy home life, a dead-end job, the bond of comradeship or desire for adventure – rather than a mystical loyalty to Britain. The attempt by the Loyal Orders to travel to the Western Front for commemorative purposes is seen by leaders such as Hewitt as an attempt to ground the Somme legend in historical realities.[18]

A PEOPLE'S HISTORY

As the Somme story has become even more powerful in loyalist working-class communities, numerous murals on gable ends in Protestant vicinities have been devoted to the topic. The 36th Division memorial wall in the Willowfield area of east Belfast is a meticulous tribute to the various Ulster battalions, each one represented by its distinctive military insignia. Another display near Templemore Avenue depicts a Young Citizen Volunteer climbing out of the trenches into no-man's-land. Some of the murals present a link between Sir Edward Carson's Ulster Volunteer Force, the 36th Ulster Division and loyalist paramilitary organisations of the recent Troubles.

The academics Brian Graham and Peter Shirlow noted such murals on a visit to the Monkstown estate in Newtownabbey, where there is a vivid Somme mural containing the matched insignia of the 36th Division and the modern-day UVF. They also visited a memorial in the Ballysillan area of north Belfast that commemorates both a murdered modern-day UVF leader and the 36th Division, and shows an explicit paramilitary montage of four masked gunmen. The writers also observed flag posts, stone monuments, small gardens and other features of memorialisation that can often accompany these murals.[19]

There can be no doubt that when the modern-day UVF was founded by Gusty Spence in the 1960s, a continuity between 'Carson's Army' and contemporary paramilitarism was intended, even though the tactics, social composition and size of the two UVFs were very different. For some of the volunteers who joined Spence's organisation, such as Portadown man Tom Roberts, there was an explicit sense of following in the footsteps of

A loyalist mural in east Belfast: 'A' Company, 1st Battalion of the
modern-day UVF commemorates dead volunteers, who
are seen as part of a tradition that goes back to the
trenches of the First World War

forefathers who had been involved in resisting Home Rule a few decades
previously.[20] Identification with the Ulster Division was particularly
emphasised when Ulster Volunteer Force members were incarcerated in
the 1970s in Long Kesh prison, where compounds were named after First
World War battles and a striking mural of a battlefield decorated the wall
in one particular hut, before 'criminalisation' led to the imposition of the
much stricter 'H-block' regime.[21]

As Graham and Shirlow have explained, since the ceasefires and the
emptying of the jails, the Somme legend has been given fresh energy, related
to the attempts being made by several loyalist ex-prisoners to create a new
political analysis – 'For the UVF, the Somme has been reborn as an unofficial
"peoples' history", a part of the Ulster past that owes little to bourgeois
official unionism. In symbolising the suffering and exploitation but also the
pride of the Ulster working-class people, the Somme bears no shame nor is
it tainted by … sectarianism …'[22]

But Graham and Shirlow have also noted in some modern-day UVF circles
dark parallels being drawn between the Protestant working-class experiences
of the First World War and the more recent civil conflict, as disillusionment

with life in post-Troubles Northern Ireland has gradually grown. As one of their interviewees expressed it, 'The Somme and the Troubles are the same in a way. Both are about working-class Prods giving their lives for Britain, the Empire and all that … We always used to give. We fought for Britain in two wars; we worked for nothing to support unionism and the rich Prods. We fought republicans to a cease-fire and what did we get? Nothing, we got nothing. It's like after the First World War the saying "Homes fit for heroes". What did the men get after the war, crap housing, bad schools, poor wages? What did we get after the Troubles? Not a thing you could hang your hat on!'[23]

But it would be a mistake to assume that loyalist Somme culture is only about murals and band parades, or that it is just about militarism and a sense of communal gloom. In a venue on the Shankill Road in April 2008 I met with John, Stephen, Neil, Gorman and Joe, who have been involved in the promotion of loyalist culture in and around Belfast. All of them are First World War enthusiasts. Some are involved with an organisation known as the 36th Division Memorial Association. Although membership is open to all, the group primarily exists for loyalists to express their sense of the Great War heritage.

John became involved in the Great War story in the 1980s, when the Farset project took a number of young people to France to start renovating the Ulster Tower at Thiepval. His enthusiasm has turned him into a collector, and he owns an array of 'trench art.' His involvement in commemoration has taken him to Donegal, where the Farset project has links with a group in the Inishowen peninsula who are striving to pay tribute to local men who fought in the trenches.

Stephen had no particular interest in the First World War until one night he spontaneously accepted an offer to join a party that was about to travel to the Western Front. When he got to the battlefields, he was 'blown away' by the experience. He now works to promote local history, arts and culture in east Belfast. One of his responsibilities is the erection of murals in the area.

Neil has recently taken a great interest in recovering the story of his great-grandfather's experiences as a Great War soldier. What intrigues him is that neither his father nor his grandfather had much to say about this topic, and he is now trying to bridge that gap, helped by the research facilities that are available. He now works for the West Belfast Cultural and Athletic Society.

Joe is heavily involved with the 36th Division Memorial Association, and has been delighted to find new branches springing up everywhere, including Merseyside, Tyneside and Scotland. In 2006 he watched as one thousand members marched to the Thiepval Tower, including numerous former UVF volunteers. For Joe, the Somme story is something with which working-class Protestants can feel comfortable as it involves ordinary men from the streets where they live. He feels that the story of the Ulster Division enables working-class loyalists to feel proud and confident when travelling in Europe. He has also been enthused by a personal quest to find out more about this subject, a journey that has taken him to libraries and archives in Belfast city centre.

However, Joe was perturbed on his trip to France in 2006 to hear some visitors to the official Ulster Tower commemoration expressing negative comments about the loyalists whom they could see preparing to march to the site to lay their wreaths in a later ceremony. It seemed to him that there was still a hierarchy in place, as there had been in 1916, with working-class expressions of Britishness still being looked down upon, despite the fact that it is the working-man who is always expected to go out into no-man's-land and do the fighting.

For Gorman, the experience of being imprisoned as a loyalist combatant was highly formative, as he studied and gained qualifications when behind bars. Now he is deeply involved with the 36th Division Memorial Association, collects First World War memorabilia, and writes and performs ballads about the conflict, several of which have been put to music. He has travelled to cross-border locations, such as Drogheda, to see their recently restored war memorials.

When he first read Cyril Falls' book on the Ulster Division, Gorman was so taken by the story that he pasted pages from this volume on the walls of his band hall so that fellow band members could read about their heritage. Then holidaying on a beach in Spain, he read *The Road to the Somme* and found tears running down his cheeks as he absorbed the extent of the suffering of the Ulster soldiers. Now he goes three times a year to the Western Front, and is involved in planning a memorial, in cooperation with the Royal Dublin Fusiliers' Association, to the men from the 36th and 16th Divisions who fought in the Messines campaign.

It is clear that the First World War quest has offered men like these great satisfaction and focus, broadened their historical and geographical horizons, and enabled them to offer their community a story of class pride and cultural origin. It also renews the local sense of belonging that suffused each regionally raised battalion of the 36th Division. Arguably, the First World War project has also offered opportunities to acknowledge nationalism and Irish Catholics, albeit in the proxy form of military units such as the 16th Division and individual soldiers such as Willie Redmond and the boy-soldier, John Condon.[24]

SOUTH OF THE BORDER

The process of Great War remembrance in Northern Ireland must be put into context by looking at what is happening in the Republic. Two hundred thousand Irishmen are thought to have been in the armed forces during the war, from north and south, and a majority of them were from the twenty-six counties that would constitute the Irish Free State after partition.[25] The attempt to forge a post-colonial identity in the new state meant that a long tradition of soldiering for Britain was eclipsed in official ceremonies and monuments of remembrance from the mid-1920s onwards. Instead, the heroism of the armed volunteers of Easter 1916 and the Irish War of Independence was given prominence.

As a result, back in the mid-1980s I found that few in the South seemed able or willing to talk about the men who had gone from Dublin, Galway or Kerry to die for the Empire in the trenches; crusading writers such as *Irish Times* journalist, Kevin Myers, were the exception. However, the Irish Republic was standing on the verge of change. Secularism, European Community membership, huge economic growth, governmental participation in the Northern peace process and a new self-confidence in relation to Britain would all play their part. As the new millennium approached, Irish society was becoming ready to investigate the complexity of its traditions – and that meant rehabilitating its entire military history, and especially the period of the First World War, when so many Irishmen served and died.

An important start in the late 1980s and early 1990s was the government-led refurbishment and re-dedication of the Irish National War Memorial Gardens in Dublin's Islandbridge, a structure whose erection had been permitted by the Free State government in 1929, but which did not open

The Irish National War Memorial Gardens at Islandbridge in 2008
DEPARTMENT OF THE ENVIRONMENT, HERITAGE AND LOCAL GOVERNMENT

until the 1940s, and then fell into terrible neglect.[26] In the years that followed, other damaged and disused regional war memorials – mostly built not long after the First World War – were restored or rebuilt, often due to interest shown by local people who could now voice disquiet that men from their home town or village had died in the conflict and been publicly forgotten, or else had returned to a society that soon disowned their war service.[27]

Then a friendship between the Donegal politician Paddy Harte and the Derry community activist Glenn Barr led to the conception of an ambitious cross-border project for a new war memorial at Messines in Belgium, in the iconic shape of an Irish round tower. It would be sited not far from where 36th and 16th Divisional soldiers fought in proximity to one another in 1917.

The British and Irish governments became interested in the political symbolism it offered, and on the eightieth anniversary of the Armistice, in November 1998, a ceremony was held to unveil and dedicate the Island of Ireland Round Tower and Peace Park, involving the Irish president Mary McAleese and the British sovereign, Queen Elizabeth.[28] It may be argued that the event was subtly presented as a complement to the Northern Ireland peace process, which in that same year had culminated in the Good Friday Agreement. The Peace Park project was 'good evidence' that British and

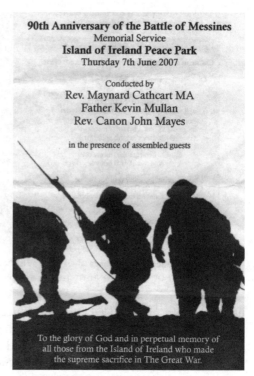

90th Anniversary of the Battle of Messines
Memorial Service
Island of Ireland Peace Park
Thursday 7th June 2007

Conducted by
Rev. Maynard Cathcart MA
Father Kevin Mullan
Rev. Canon John Mayes

in the presence of assembled guests

To the glory of God and in perpetual memory of
all those from the Island of Ireland who made
the supreme sacrifice in The Great War.

A programme for a
commemorative service held
at the Peace Park
in Messines in 2007
SOMME MUSEUM

Irish identities could be seen at last as interlinked rather than antagonistic, and
that a return to the Troubles was hopefully as unthinkable as a return to the
titanic wars that had shattered western Europe in the first half of the twentieth
century. A 'Peace Pledge' inscribed on a bronze tablet at the Peace Park
expresses aspirations for the permanent settlement of Irish domestic conflict:

> As Protestants and Catholics, we apologise for the terrible deeds we have
> done to each other and ask forgiveness … from this sacred shrine of
> remembrance, where soldiers of all nationalities, creeds and political
> allegiances were united in death, we appeal to all people in Ireland to help
> build a peaceful and tolerant society. Let us remember the solidarity and
> trust that developed between Protestant and Catholic soldiers when they
> served together in these trenches …

Despite some subsequent difficulties with maintenance, the park and tower

A detail from the programme of the 2006 Somme Memorial Service that took place in Dublin. Note the strongly Celtic design motifs.
SOMME MUSEUM

were renovated and reopened in 2004, their upkeep now securely in the hands of both Northern and Southern Irish governments.[29]

Another development has been the foundation of a Military Heritage of Ireland Trust. Since its inception, it lobbied for an exhibition dedicated to the long history of Irish soldiering. The permanent display that resulted from its vision is now housed in the National Museum at the now decommissioned Collins Barracks in Dublin, and it gives space for the Irish Great War story to be told in a manner that does justice to the allegiances of all who served.[30] The trust also promotes the Irish National War Memorial Gardens as the primary place of remembrance for all who went from Ireland to die in the conflict, north and south, as was once intended by its creators.[31]

The National Day of Remembrance has become an annual feature of the Irish memorial process. A ceremony is held at the Royal Hospital in Kilmainham to commemorate the dead of the First World War and those

Irish personnel who lost their lives in other international conflicts.[32] In 2006, on the ninetieth anniversary of the Somme, the Irish president, Taoiseach and Irish army representatives were present at another memorial service, this time held at Islandbridge, which for the first time officially saluted all Irish soldiers who had died, been injured or traumatised in the battle. The Somme had become a part of the Irish twentieth-century national narrative – a story that at one stage had been so dominated by the heroes who had stormed the GPO in Easter 1916.[33]

The full implications, north of the border, of this rediscovery of a First World War heritage in the rest of Ireland remain to be seen. For the most part, Northern unionists and loyalists seem to welcome the thought that Irish citizens might be rediscovering their lost history. On the other hand, there is honest frustration and passion in the comment reputedly made by one Ulster Protestant to a spokesman from the Republic who was emphasising the strides being made in Great War remembrance in the South: 'You'se have got the Irish Famine, can you not leave us the Somme?'

Those in the Irish Republic who are – from the sincerest and most valid of motives – establishing the First World War's commemorative programme may recognise that the Somme story has been one of the markers of 'difference' for Ulster unionist and loyalist culture within Ireland. and that what looks like 'sharing' and 'rediscovery' from the Southern viewpoint might look like cultural intrusion from the Northern perspective. As Graham and Shirlow have emphasised, this battle is not just a topic in the history of Ulster but rather an 'identity narrative'.[34] People in the Irish Republic may also recognise that many Northern Protestants are still suspicious of the moral parameters of the recent peace process, and find the project of reading the Great War as a lesson in the need for 'reconciliation' and 'conflict resolution' to be an inappropriate re-interpretation of their Great War inheritance – and a bridge too far.

THE RECOVERY OF PERSONAL STORIES

But it is not just at the institutional level that Ireland has acknowledged more of its wartime past. There has been a groundswell of interest by individuals who are deeply moved by a once-banished story of sacrifice and suffering that involves their family or their neighbourhood. Deep feeling was stirred up in several descendants of the twenty-eight Irish servicemen in the British army who were executed for desertion or other misdemeanours. An Irish 'Shot at Dawn' campaign lobbied for a British governmental pardon for these soldiers. In 2006 a pardon for all victims of military execution in the war was finally secured.[35]

I also gained a sense of how an individual Irishman's interest in the war could suddenly emerge – and have political ramifications – when conversing with the Dublin-based journalist, Patsy McGarry, in December 2007. Having returned from 'covering' Drumcree, with its connection to the Somme, he had tried to discover what remained of the story of men who had gone to the trenches from his own 'home turf', in County Roscommon, deep in the countryside of the Irish Republic. He was fascinated and disturbed to find out that more men had died from his own Catholic parish than the Protestant parish of Drumcree. In fact, well over three hundred soldiers from his home county had perished in the war. Almost no memorialisation of these young soldiers had taken place. As a consequence of his journalistic work on the topic, a cross-party group of Roscommon councillors has since been to the Western Front and laid wreaths to acknowledge their once-forgotten dead.[36]

Many individuals are involved in the retrieval of the story of the Irish regiments that recruited in the south of the island and which were thus disbanded after partition. Tom Burke of the Royal Dublin Fusiliers' Association is one such well-known enthusiast. His organisation now consists of close to five hundred members, many of whom are not motivated by any big political agenda but by the simple fact that they now want to speak and learn about their grandfathers, and cherish the memory of their service in the British army rather than feel ashamed of it.[37] Paddy Harte's idea for 'books of honour' – in which each county could list its own First World War dead – has been based on a similar recognition that each man who went to the battlefield was first and foremost a family member, friend and neighbour, and that it is among his descendants and in the place he called home that the act of remembrance should be most deeply situated.[38]

It is thus important to restate in a chapter such as this – which looks closely at the politics of public memory – that the drive to find out more about the First World War is often driven by very personal motives, on both sides of the border. Within my own circle of acquaintances are many people who, in recent times, have sought to discover all they could about the conflict because a family member was once a participant, helped by the fact that in the electronic age, genealogical research is a much easier thing for the uninitiated to undertake.

One friend – a retired surgeon – still wants to find out more about his own father's experiences as a young medical officer with the 36th Division. Another friend, since retiring, has dedicated time to recovering the story of an uncle who left a university career to join an English regiment and die in Mesopotamia. The fate that befell an earlier generation that went of its own accord to fight an unknown foe seems all the more intriguing because its challenges and sorrows are so unfamiliar in the comfort zone that many Irish people now inhabit.

Yet for some people, an interest in this subject has involved careful negotiation of the complexities of family history and cultural difference. The broadcaster, Paul Clarke, has made several programmes about Ireland's military history, but as a young boy attending a Catholic school during the fiftieth anniversary of the Easter Rising in the mid-Sixties, he heard a great deal about Patrick Pearse and the 'blood sacrifice' of 1916, but nothing at all about the deaths of thousands of Irishmen in the Battle of the Somme. Growing up in a 'very Protestant' area as the child of a 'mixed marriage', he helped his Protestant friends build bonfires until the Troubles put an end to that kind of camaraderie. The sense of having had 'a foot in both camps' was further amplified by finding out that his paternal grandfather had signed the Covenant in 1912, and that his great-uncle had been a Young Citizen Volunteer who fought with the 14th Battalion of the Royal Irish Rifles in the First World War – a history of soldiering made real by the presence of a Lee Enfield rifle in his house in Bangor.

Later in his schooling, Paul's interest in modern history grew through the influence of a good teacher. In due course, he was able to make connections between the documentary series on the Great War that he had, as a small boy, watched with wide-open eyes, the complex story of his own family, and the local history of 'both communities' here in Northern Ireland. He feels considerable respect for the Orange Order's attempt to preserve and honour the story of the 36th Division, but also sees great benefit in the Irish Republic's rediscovery of its wartime heritage, saying that 'we have found we have a common ground in places like the battleground of the Somme.'[39]

Despite the deep layers of personal significance, it is an unavoidable fact that the First World War still possesses a vast range of social and political meanings on this island. Those people who decry such 'politicisation' should recognise that it is not a modern trend. In fact, even before the 36th Division had fought at the Somme, another First World War battle had already become a source of political controversy at home.

In 1915 thousands of Irish troops had perished at Gallipoli in strategic and human circumstances that were, if anything, worse than those on the Western Front. Many had been shot while wading ashore at Cape Helles, presenting an easy target for enemy guns, or else they had drowned in the off-shore surf.[40] Others had died of thirst or disease when fighting further north at Suvla Bay in a campaign where clean water, proper food, sanitation and medical care had often been non-existent. Yet in the aftermath of the battle, as the Irish obituary columns began to fill, the sufferings of Gallipoli took on a contested political meaning. Nationalist leaders suggested that the sacrifice of so many young Catholic soldiers was a good reason for Britain to 'keep her word' and grant Home Rule to Ireland. The unionist news-paper, the *Northern Whig*, fiercely contested this interpretation, producing statistics to 'prove' that most of the 10th Division who fought at Suvla Bay were not of Irish Catholic extraction, and, furthermore, that recruitment in nationalist Ireland was lamentably poor. Thus did the First World War divide the 'two traditions' in this country, before any Ulsterman had fired a bullet in the Somme campaign.[41]

As has already been noted, recent times have seen an attempt to draw political lessons from the conflict that could bring the 'two traditions' together rather than separate them. Perhaps the most novel of these is centred on the Irish Peace Park. The most significant figure in this enterprise has been Derry-based Ulsterman: loyalist militant turned community activist, Glenn Barr. Under his guidance, Messines rather than the Somme has become the iconic battle for the project. It is seen as the campaign where nationalists and unionists fought side by side, advancing against a common enemy, whose young soldiers were also the victims of a cruel war that had engulfed most of Europe. This is the battle where John Redmond's brother Willie was carried from the battlefield by members of the Ulster Division in an act of exemplary fraternity and mercy that Barr finds inspiring.

Irish soldiers at Gallipoli. This, too, was a battle with political implications in Ireland, with Irish nationalist politicians claiming that the Irishmen who died there added to the case for granting Home Rule.
PHILIP ORR

An International School for Peace Studies now exists at Messines, supported by local politicians in Flanders. Courses in peace studies can be undertaken, and those who complete the most advanced course are eligible to become 'Fellows of Messines', in which they pledge themselves to 'resolving differences through peaceful dialogue' and rejecting 'all forms of violence as a means of creating change.' In establishing international credentials, the Irish Messines project has already forged links with similar work in Cyprus, the Balkans and the Caucasus, where ethnic strife has caused much suffering.[42]

Some might question the validity of the Messines symbolism, given the baleful hostility the men in the 16th and 36th Divisions sometimes displayed to one another. However, the Peace Park project is a positive venture that takes many people away from Ireland to a place where war is exposed in all its cruelty, and the craft of peace-building is given prominence.

It would be interesting to make a comparative study of the two towers on the Western Front at Messines and Thiepval. One tower, despite a genuine attempt to represent Ulster's dead in a non-partisan way, still possesses great political significance as a symbol of Ulster Protestant sacrifice.

The other tower speaks in idealistic language of a politics of mediation and conflict resolution, both in Ireland and around the world. They both stand as testaments to a rich memorialisation of the Great War, which continues to generate new meanings ninety years after the final gunfire faded away.

NORTHERN REPUBLICANISM AND THE GREAT WAR HERITAGE

It is one thing for people in the south of Ireland to embrace a heritage from the Great War, and another thing for Northern republicans to do so. Having been locked in conflict with the British army throughout much of the Troubles, participation in ceremonies of remembrance where British military uniforms are being worn and the Union Jack is being flown still constitutes a step too far for the republican movement. The feeling exists that First World War commemoration since the inception of the 'six-county state' has been an excuse for unionists to reassert the indissoluble Britishness of Northern Ireland, and to wear the poppy as a badge of that identity.

However, there have been signs of change. In November 2002 Belfast's first Sinn Féin Lord Mayor, Alex Maskey, laid a wreath at the cenotaph in the grounds of the City Hall, albeit in a brief and separate ceremony where no members of the armed services were present and no flags flew. The wreath was not made of poppies but of laurel.[43] In Alex Maskey's eyes, this gesture was part of an attempt undertaken throughout his mayoral year to engage with non-republican culture and represent all the people of the city.

Although he was predictably criticised by republicans who were suspicious of a dalliance with 'British militarism', and by unionists who felt the gesture was too 'lukewarm', Maskey received a number of plaudits, not least from those Ulster Catholics who told him that their family had now been given back a part of its past. Some people told him they now felt it was 'legitimate' to speak of a grandfather whose actions in joining the army had been 'hushed up' in a nationalist family as a matter of shame.[44] Interestingly, there have been recent attempts by the 'Good Relations' department of Belfast City Council to create public events in the City Hall that commemorate both World Wars through music, imagery and the spoken word, and possess no links with ceremonies traditionally cherished by only one community.[45]

The challenge for Northern republicanism is to grasp the complexity of

Belfast's first Sinn Féin Lord Mayor, Alex Maskey,
lays a wreath at the cenotaph in 2002
PA PHOTOS

allegiance presented by the First World War and its aftermath, which includes the story of Thomas Devlin – father of the SDLP politician Paddy Devlin – whose family possess both the medals he earned as a British soldier and the medal he gained as an IRA veteran in the 'Tan War'.[46] Also included is Seán McCartney, who lies buried in a republican plot in Milltown cemetery, honoured as Belfast's first dead IRA volunteer during the 1920s campaign. McCartney had been a soldier during the First World War, serving with the Connaught Rangers.[47]

The challenge to the pro-Union mindset is a different one. As Alex Maskey explained to me in a recent interview, a visit that he made to the Western Front has only made him all the more convinced of the need for the republican struggle. The rows of graves, both Allied and German, were profoundly moving, but they showed him clearly why the Easter Rising had to take place – so that thousands of young working-class Irishmen would no longer be obliged to lay down their lives for the Empire.[48] So it seems that if unionists wish to see Northern nationalists take a greater interest in their contribution to British military history, it may mean exposing them even more starkly to one of the most significant reasons why the British Empire began to fall apart in Ireland. Nationalist families did not want their sons to be slaughtered at battles such as the Somme. They were prepared to vote for the expulsion of Britain from Ireland so that slaughter could not happen again. If the vote were to be rejected, then they would have to use force.

A NEW KIND OF COURAGE

In concluding, I think it important to recognise two contexts within which I first wrote *The Road to the Somme*. One was the Cold War, in which a terrifying nuclear stand-off prevailed between the Soviet Union and the NATO powers. In 1982 I had made a visit to the Soviet Union, where I met a range of local people and had been horrified to think that ordinary Russians were my 'enemy'. The other context was the Troubles that raged around me and in which I had seen friends and neighbours killed for causes I could not understand. My study of the Somme was motivated by witnessing conflict at home and abroad during which ordinary people seemed to be caught up in destructive, half-understood enmity, just as they had been in 1916. The trenches for me were lamentably emblematic of the human condition.

Much has changed. Communism has vanished, and now the more elusive foe of militant Islamism is seen as the main threat to the West. Here in Northern Ireland, old foes sit down with one another and share power. The conflict-resolution methodology that produced the peace process is being exported to other troubled regions of the world. However, the Messines project is surely right in its ethos: the slaughter of the Western Front must still stand as a stark warning of the way that war can so easily overwhelm and destroy a generation – a warning that is especially powerful when the voices of the survivors themselves are heard.

Among the benefits of peace in Ulster for me has been the chance to know some of those men and women, both loyalist and republican, whose motivations I found so indecipherable two decades ago. As a result, I am re-evaluating my own response back then to the Somme legend, when I saw myself 'deconstructing' the mythology that had grown up around this Great War battle, and insisting on a more truthful and less partisan narrative.

Of course, as I stressed in 1987, every culture should prize historically accurate accounts of its famous battles, and every culture needs to be wary of such concepts as heroism, patriotism and national glory, which can so easily stir up the kind of enmity referred to above. However, I now know that all cultures also need pride and courage in order to survive and to adapt. The pro-Union culture of Northern Ireland has had precious few reasons to exult in recent times, especially in its working-class manifestations.

Insomuch as the tragic audacity shown on a July morning in 1916 has brought a sense of genuine pride and courage to thousands of Ulster Protestants through the past twenty-one years, it has served an important function. If, however, this story of soldiering has encouraged some young loyalists in recent decades to admire militarism and aggression, or if its dark outcome has appealed to a part of the unionist psyche that seems laden with cultural doom, then perhaps the Somme legacy has not always been completely benign.

In 2007 the funeral of the loyalist politician David Ervine took place in east Belfast. His brother Brian spoke at the service, commending David for the journey of transformation he had made from a prison cell housing members of the modern-day UVF to the parliament buildings at Stormont, where he had represented the Progressive Unionist Party and gained the respect of many, both loyalist and republican. Using imagery borrowed from the famous Christmas truce of 1914, Brian Ervine suggested that his brother had had 'the guts and the courage to climb out of the traditional trenches, meet the enemy in no-man's land and play ball with him.'[49]

The final chapter of this new edition of *The Road to the Somme* concludes with the hope that both unionists and nationalists on this island have now recognised the kind of courage required in the twenty-first century. It is not the bravery needed to climb out of trenches and race towards German machine guns with a rifle in hand, as so many of their forefathers once did, but rather the courage required to keep on tackling the causes of mutual hostility and social disadvantage here at home, while building a future that can be shared alike by former enemies and friends.

Philip Orr
Carrickfergus
May 2008

REFERENCES

PREFACE TO THE 2008 EDITION

1   The book known as *Ireland's Memorial Records* lists the men who perished in Irish regiments. It may be responsible for the inflated figure. The lower figure for Irish war-dead is accepted by such authorities as Professor Keith Jeffery in 'Ireland and the First World War: the Historical Context', an unpublished draft of a talk on the war, p. 2.

2   A book that takes account of the phenomenon of Irish-born soldiers in other units is Jeff Kildea, *Anzacs and Ireland* (Cork University Press, 2007).

3   A book that looks at the Great War soldiering of one significant part of the Irish diaspora is John Sheen, *Tyneside Irish – A History of the Tyneside Irish Brigade Raised in the Northeast (Pals)* (Pen and Sword Books, 1998).

4   Jeffery, pp. 1–2. A fuller version of this script, including a discussion of commemoration and politicisation of the Great War story, may be found at www.groupedhistoiresocia.free.fr/question_d_agreg/jeffery.html

5   Nicholas Perry (ed.), *Major General Oliver Nugent and the Ulster Division 1915–1918* (Sutton Publishing Limited, 2007), pp. 96–7.

6   Timothy Bowman, *Irish Regiments in the Great War – Discipline and Morale* (Manchester University Press, 2003), pp. 5, 65–6.

7   Interview with Amanda Moreno, April 2008.

8   Bowman, *Irish Regiments*, p. 65.

9   Timothy Bowman, *Carson's Army –*

The Ulster Volunteer Force, 1910–1912 (Manchester University Press, 2007), pp. 205–10.

10 The letter in the *Portadown News* on 19 July 1919 is quoted in a PhD thesis by Colin Cousins, completed at Queens University, Belfast.

11 Catherine Switzer, *Unionists and Great War Commemoration in the North of Ireland 1914–1939* (Irish Academic Press, 2007), pp. 117–18. The author draws on accounts by Sam McAughtry, Jack Sayers and John Simms.

12 J. Bourke, 'Shell-shock, psychiatry and the Irish soldier during the First World War' in Adrian Gregory and Senia Paseta (eds), *Ireland and the Great War – 'A War to Unite Us All'?* (Manchester University Press, 2002), pp. 155–70.

13 A useful study of memorialisation throughout Ireland is to be found in Jane Leonard, *The Culture of War Commemoration* (Cultures of Ireland, 1996).

14 Switzer, pp. 58, 119.

15 The Waringstown clock tower is noted in Leslie Elliott and David Stevenson, 'The Story of a Banner – Waringstown during World War One' (LOL 83, 2007).

16 Details on the Knockagh monument may be found in Keith Jeffery, *Ireland and the Great War* (Cambridge University Press, 2000), pp. 128–9 and at www.geocities.com/rurmuseum/knockagh.html

17 Travers' work on the Ulster Division's artillery is mentioned in Bowman, *Irish Regiments*, p. 124.

18 Information on the divisional tactics at Messines is found in Gary Sheffield, *Forgotten Victory* (Headline, 2002), p. 202.

19 Bowman, *Irish Regiments*, pp. 68–85, 109–14.

20 Perry, pp. 17–95.

21 Information on the execution of Privates Crozier, McCracken and Templeton is found in chapters 2 and 4 of Stephen Walker, *Forgotten Soldiers – The Irishmen Shot at Dawn* (Gill and Macmillan, 2007). The quotation from Leslie Bell is located on p. 64.

CHAPTER 1

1 Ronald McNeill, *Ulster's Stand for Union* (Murray, 1922), pp. 49–51.

2 Patrick Buckland, *Irish Unionism II* (Gill and Macmillan, 1973), p. 58.

3 Quoted in A.T.Q. Stewart, *The Ulster Crisis* (Faber & Faber, 1967), p. 55.

4 A.T.Q. Stewart, *The Ulster Crisis*, p. 62.

5 F.S.L. Lyons, *Ireland Since the Famine* (Weidenfeld & Nicolson, 1971), p. 317, and F.X. Martin, 'Easter 1916: an inside report on Ulster' in *Clogher Record* (1986), p. 194.

6 Cyril Falls, *The History of the 36th (Ulster) Division* (McGaw, Stevenson & Orr, 1922), p. 101.

7 D.J.H., *The Reminiscences of Capt. D.J. Bell of Ballynahinch* (Mourne Observer Press, 1962), p. 18.

8 Mina Lenox-Conyngham, *An Old Ulster House* (Dundalgan Press, 1946), pp. 200–2.

9 Mary Rogers, *Prospect of Erne* (Fermanagh Field Club, 1967), p. 156.

10 Information on use of estates by UVF supplied by various interviewees.

11 Information supplied by R.H. Stewart from interviews conducted in the Waringstown area.

12 Desmond Murphy, *Derry, Donegal and Modern Ulster 1790–1921* (Aileach Press, 1981), p. 210.

13 T. Desmond Williams, 'Eoin MacNeill and the Irish Volunteers' in F.X. Martin (ed.), *Leaders and Men of the Easter Rising: Dublin 1916* (Methuen, 1967), p. 144.

14 J. Hutchinson, 'The Recollections of a Royal Irish Rifleman 1917–19'. (unpublished), held in Royal Ulster Rifles Regimental Museum (RURRM), pp. 1–10.

15 Tommy Ervine, taped recollections in author's possession.

16 Hutchinson, pp. 1–10.

17 Ervine.

18 Buckland, p. 54.

19 Henry Patterson, *Class Conflict and Sectarianism* (Blackstaff Press, 1980), p. 89.

20 Information supplied by W. Martin, Crossgar.

21 Hugh Stewart, taped recollections in author's possession.

22 Murphy, p. 196.

23 Public Record Office of Northern Ireland (PRONI) D1327/4/3.

24 PRONI D1540/35.

25 PRONI D1327/9/17.

26 PRONI D123 8/9/17.

27 *Ulster Gazette*, 24 May 1984.

28 Quoted in McNeill, p. 163.

29 *Irish News*, 25 September 1911.

30 *Irish News*, 30 September 1912.

31 *Irish News*, 27 September 1913.

32 *Irish News*, 23 September 1913.

33 *Irish News*, 16 September 1913.

34 *Irish News*, 13–18 August 1913.

35 Philip Cruikshank, *The Tyrone Regiment UVF Record of Camp of Instruction, Baronscourt 1913* (Tyrone Constitution, 1913).

36 Rex Herdman, *They All Made Me* (S.D. Montgomery, 1970), p. 259.

37 Herdman, p. 259.

38 Cruikshank.

39 D.J.H., p. 19.

40 Corelli Barnett, *Britain and her Army* (Allen Lane, 1970), p. 391.

41 McNeill, p. 218.

42 PRONI D1540/3 6A–B.

43 PRONI D1540/23 A.

44 Ibid.

45 PRONI D1327/4/3.

46 PRONI D1540/60A–B.

47 Lenox-Conyngham, pp. 200–2.

48 A.T.Q. Stewart, *The Ulster Crisis*, p. 128.

49 F.P. Crozier, *Impressions and Recollections* (Werner Laurie, 1930), chaps. 1–7.

50 A.T.Q. Stewart, *The Ulster Crisis*, p. 124.

51 Crozier, *Impressions*, p. 149.

52 R.J. Adgey, *Arming the Ulster Volunteers*, 1914 (privately printed, undated), p. 45.

53 John Leslie Stewart-Moore, taped recollections in author's possession.

54 Herdman, pp. 24, 115, 211.

55 Quoted in James Carry (ed.), *Ireland: From the Great Famine to the Treaty of 1921* (C.J. Fallon, 1951), p. 140.

56 Herdman, pp. 24, 342.

57 Rogers, pp. 199–200.

58 P. Livingstone, *The Monaghan Story* (Clogher Historical Society, 1980), pp. 367–9.

59 Ibid. p. 272.

60 D.W. Miller, *Church, State and Nation in Ireland 1898–1921* (Gill and Macmillan, 1981), pp. 298–9.

61 Murphy, pp. 197–8, 207.

62 Stephen Gwynn, *John Redmond's Last Years* (Edward Arnold, 1919), pp. 102–3, and Michael Laffan, *The Partition of Ireland 1911–1925* (Dundalgan Press, 1983), pp. 37–8.

63 A.C. Hepburn, *The Conflict of Nationality in Modern Ireland* (Edward Arnold, 1980), pp. 77–8, and T. J. Campbell, *Fifty Years of Ulster 1890–1940* (*Irish News*, 1941), p. 57.

64 *The Times*, 16 March 1914.

65 Ibid.

66 Ibid.

67 A.T.Q. Stewart, *The Ulster Crisis*, chaps. 11–13.

68 R.H. Stewart.

69 McNeill, pp. 216–18, and A.T.Q. Stewart, *The Ulster Crisis*, chap. 16.

70 Stewart-Moore, tape.

71 Information supplied by Hugh James Adams, Crossgar.

72 Hugh Stewart.

73 A.T.Q Stewart, *Edward Carson* (Gill and Macmillan, 1981), pp. 83, 92.

74 Lenox-Conyngham, p. 221.

75 PRONI D1295/2.

76 McNeill, p. 220.

77 Lt. Colonel F.H. Crawford, *Guns for Ulster* (Graham & Heslip, 1947), p. 33.

78 *Northern Whig*, 24 March 1914.

79 YCV documents held in Ulster Museum.

80 *Belfast News Letter*, 11 September 1912.

81 PRONI D1568/5 A.

82 PRONI D1568/6/10/14.

83 *Belfast News Letter*, 8 June 1914.

84 *Belfast Evening Telegraph*, 8 June 1914.

85 *Irish News*, 8 June 1914.

86 Lyons, p. 327.

87 Murphy, p. 209.

88 A.T.Q. Stewart, *The Ulster Crisis*, chap. 18.

89 *Belfast News Letter*, 3 August 1914.
90 PRONI D1295/2.
91 Stewart-Moore, tape.

CHAPTER 2

1 Rupert Brooke, *1914 and Other Poems* (Faber & Faber, 1941), p. 11.
2 A.T.Q. Stewart, *The Ulster Crisis*, pp. 229–33.
3 *Belfast News Letter*, 8 August 1914.
4 A.T.Q. Stewart, *The Ulster Crisis*, pp. 232–3.
5 Ian Colvin, *The Life of Lord Carson* (Gollancz, 1934), vol. 3, pp. 17–26.
6 *Belfast News Letter*, 31 August 1914.
7 *Belfast News Letter*, 3 September 1914.
8 PRONI D1295/2.
9 Falls, p. 3.
10 Colvin, p. 27.
11 Falls, pp. 4–5.
12 Alice Stopford Green, *Ourselves Alone in Ulster* (pamphlet, 1918), p. 19.
13 PRONI D1.295/2.
14 Falls, pp. 9–11.
15 A.T.Q. Stewart, *The Ulster Crisis*, pp. 224–9.
16 Ibid. p. 226.
17 Quoted in A.T.Q. Stewart, *The Ulster Crisis*, p. 226.
18 Quoted in Green, pp. 8–9.
19 Quoted in Green, p. 20.
20 Ervine.
21 Hutchinson, p. 11.
22 P.P. Crozier, *A Brass Hat in No Man's Land* (Cape, 1930), p. 21.
23 Crozier, *Impressions*, pp. 159–60.
24 Crozier, *A Brass Hat*, pp. 30–6.
25 Jim Maultsaid, 'One Man's War' (4 parts), in *Cityweek*, 9, 16, 23 and 30 June 1966.

26 G.H.M., 'Service with the 14th Battalion R.I.R. in the 1914–18 War' (unpublished), held in RURRM, pp. 20–8.
27 Information supplied by Bill McFadzean, Lisburn.
28 *Newtownards Chronicle*, 12 September 1914.
29 Ibid.
30 Reprinted in *Ulster Gazette,* 31 May 1984.
31 R.H. Stewart, 'File on Formation and Training of the Ulster Division' (unpublished), in author's possession.
32 Stewart-Moore, tape.
33 D.J.H., pp. 8–9, 20–1.
34 Martin.
35 Adams.
36 Albert Bruce, taped recollections in author's possession.
37 Hugh Stewart.
38 R.H. Stewart, 'Records of interviews with First World War veterans' (unpublished), M18 RURRM. p. 4.
39 R.H. Stewart, M18 RURRM, pp. 5–6. See also R.H. Stewart, 'File on Formation and Training'.
40 Ibid.
41 Quoted in Colvin, p. 44.
42 McNeill, p. 238.
43 Green, p. 27.
44 Campbell, p. 82.
45 Poem by F.S. Boas, *Newtownards Chronicle,* 31 October 1914.
46 Falls, pp. 11–14.
47 PRONI D1295/2.
48 Ibid.
49 Hugh Stewart.
50 PRONI D1295/2.
51 R.H. Stewart, M18 RURRM pp. 7–14.
52 John Leslie Stewart-Moore, 'Random Recollections' (unpublished), in author's possession.

53 D.J.H., pp. 21–3, 39–41.
54 Hutchinson, pp. 10–20.
55 Falls, p. 15.
56 *Newtownards Chronicle*, 19 December 1914.
57 J.K. Hope, volume of reminiscences, M30 RURRM, chap.1.
58 PRONI D1568715.
59 Hope, chap. 1.
60 G.H.M., pp. 19–25.
61 PRONI D1568/16, unidentified newspaper cutting.
62 G.H.M., pp. 25–56.
63 Hope, chap. 2.
64 G.H.M., pp. 57–74.
65 Crozier, *Impressions*, p. 163.
66 Information supplied by G. McClintock, Ballykinler.
67 Crozier, *A Brass Hat*, pp. 35–45.
68 Hutchinson, pp. 47–8.
69 Elise Sandes and Theodora Schofield, *21 Years of Unrecorded Service for the British Army 1913–34* (Marshall, Morgan & Scott, undated).
70 R.H. Stewart, 'File on Formation and Training'.
71 Hutchinson, p. 49.
72 Stewart-Moore, 'Random Recollections'.
73 Ervine.
74 M26 RURRM.
75 M9 RURRM.
76 PRONI D1295/2.
77 Tommy Jordan, taped recollections in author's possession.
78 Jordan.
79 The remains of some of these trenches were shown to the author by David McCarter, Hillsborough.
80 R.H. Stewart, 'File on Formation and Training'.
81 Falls, p. 14.
82 *Newtownards Chronicle*, 3 July 1915.
83 R.H. Stewart, M18 RURRM, p. 8.
84 Jordan.
85 George Lindsay, taped recollections in author's possession.
86 *Newtownards Chronicle*, 8 January 1915.
87 *Newtownards Chronicle*, 5 June 1915.
88 M32 RURRM.
89 D.J.H., pp. 40–1.
90 Stewart-Moore, 'Random Recollections'.
91 G.H.M., pp. 79–82.
92 *Newtownards Chronicle*, 15 May 1915.
93 *Northern Whig*, 10 May 1915.
94 Hutchinson, p. 13.
95 R.H. Stewart, M18 RURRM, p. 16.
96 G.H.M.,p. 84.
97 R.H. Stewart, 'File on Formation and Training'.
98 D.J.H., p. 41.
99 Stewart-Moore, 'Random Recollections'.
100 Hugh Stewart.
101 Adams.
102 Stewart-Moore, 'Random Recollections'.
103 Hope, chap. 3.
104 *Newtownards Chronicle,* 31 July 1915.
105 Falls, p. 17.
106 PRONI D1295/2.
107 Ibid.
108 Falls, pp. 17–18.
109 Stewart-Moore, 'Random Recollections'.
110 *Newtownards Chronicle*, 24 July 1915.
111 M35 RURRM.
112 Falls, p. 18.
113 R.H. Stewart, M18 RURRM, p. 20.
114 PRONI D1295/2.
115 Ibid.
116 Stewart-Moore, 'Random Recollections'.
117 Hope, chap. 3.
118 Crozier, *A Brass Hat*, pp. 49–50.

119 Falls, p. 20.
120 Stewart-Moore, 'Random Recollections'.
121 Falls, p. 20.
122 R.H. Stewart, 'File on Formation and Training'.
123 Ibid.
124 Ibid.
125 Ibid.
126 Falls, p. 20.
127 Ibid. p. 21.
128 D.J.H., p. 42.
129 Stewart-Moore, 'Random Recollections'.
130 Crozier, *A Brass Hat*, pp. 51–2.
131 A.P.I.S. and D.G.S., *With the Ulster Division in France* (William Mullan & Son, undated), pp. 8–9.
132 *Cityweek*, 9 June 1966.
133 Quoted in Martin Middlebrook, *The First Day on the Somme* (Allen Lane, 1971), p. 28.
134 G.H.M., pp. 90–100.

CHAPTER 3

1 Patrick MacGill, *Soldier Songs* (Herbert Jenkins, 1917), p. 37.
2 Crozier, *Impressions*, p. 164, and *A Brass Hat*, pp. 53–4.
3 Hugh Stewart.
4 A.P.I.S. and D.G.S., pp. 9–10.
5 G.H.M., pp. 101–2.
6 *Cityweek*, 9 June 1966.
7 G.H.M., pp. 101–2.
8 Stewart-Moore, 'Random Recollections'.
9 A.P.I.S. and D.G.S., p. 11.
10 Hugh Stewart.
11 D.J.H., pp. 42–3.
12 Official War Diary of 9th Battalion Royal Irish Fusiliers, kept in Royal Irish Fusiliers Regimental Museum (RIFRM), 6 October 1915.
13 Stewart-Moore, 'Random Recollections'.
14 A.P.I.S. and D.G.S., pp. 12–15.
15 Hugh Stewart.
16 9th RIF War Diary, 2, 5 November 1915.
17 A.P.I.S. and D.G.S., pp. 12–15.
18 Crozier, *Impressions*, p. 164.
19 G.H.M., pp. 104–5.
20 Hope, p. 9.
21 Jim Maultsaid, 'One Man's War', part 2, in *Cityweek*, 16 June 1966.
22 Stewart-Moore, 'Random Recollections'.
23 Ibid.
24 R.H. Stewart, 'File on Formation and Training'.
25 Falls, pp. 22–6.
26 Crozier, *A Brass Hat*, pp. 60–2.
27 Hugh Stewart.
28 Stewart-Moore, 'Random Recollections'.
29 Ibid.
30 R.H. Stewart, 'File on Formation and Training'.
31 Hugh Stewart.
32 R.H. Stewart, 'File on Formation and Training'.
33 Ibid.
34 Ervine.
35 Falls, p. 28.
36 Ibid. p. 24.
37 R.H. Stewart, 'File on Formation and Training'.
38 Adams.
39 Stewart-Moore, 'Random Recollections'.
40 A.P.I.S. and D.G.S., pp. 30–2.
41 Hugh Stewart.
42 Hope, p. 9.
43 R.H. Stewart, 'File on Formation and Training'.
44 A.P.I.S. and D.G.S., p. 13.

45 PRONI D1295/2.
46 Ervine.
47 Hugh Stewart.
48 R.H. Stewart, 'File on Formation and Training'.
49 Adams.
50 Tommy Russell, taped recollections in author's possession.
51 Stewart-Moore, 'Random Recollections'.
52 Falls, pp. 29–30.
53 R.H. Stewart, 'File on Formation and Training'.
54 G.H.M., pp. 116–19.
55 Stewart-Moore, 'Random Recollections'.
56 9th RIF War Diary, 9 February 1916.
57 Crozier, *A Brass Hat,* pp. 79–80.
58 R.H. Stewart, 'File on Formation and Training'.
59 Crozier, *A Brass Hat*, pp. 65–7.
60 Hugh Stewart.
61 R.H. Stewart, 'File on Formation and Training'.
62 Hope, p. 13.
63 R.H. Stewart, 'File on Formation and Training'.
64 Hope, p. 13.
65 9th RIF War Diary, 14 November 1915.
66 Jordan.
67 Middlebrooke, p. 38.
68 Hope, p. 12.
69 Shown to the author by Hugh Stewart, Lisburn, in 1984.
70 9th RIF War Diary, 13 January 1916.
71 All information on medical matters in R.H. Stewart, 'File on Formation and Training' (section on Royal Auxiliary Medical Corps).
72 R.H. Stewart, 'File on Formation and Training'.
73 Ervine.
74 G.H.M., pp. 120–1.
75 Stewart-Moore, 'Random Recollections'.
76 G.H.M., pp. 120–1.
77 Hugh Stewart.
78 R.H. Stewart, 'File on Formation and Training'.
79 Stewart–Moore, 'Random Recollections'.
80 A.P.I.S. and D.G.S., p. 34.
81 Hugh Stewart.
82 R.H. Stewart, 'File on Formation and Training'.
83 Stewart-Moore, 'Random Recollections'.
84 A.P.I.S. and D.G.S., pp. 34–5.
85 Official War Diary of 14th Battalion Royal Irish Rifles, kept in RURRM, December 1915.
86 Falls, pp. 32–3.
87 Lindsay.
88 Stewart-Moore, 'Random Recollections'.
89 R.H. Stewart, 'File on Formation and Training'.
90 Ervine.
91 *Cityweek*, 16 June 1966.
92 G.H.M., pp. 108, 113, 130.
93 Stewart-Moore, 'Random Recollections'.
94 A.P.I.S. and D.G.S., p. 49.
95 A.P.I.S. and D.G.S., pp. 37–8, and Hugh Stewart.
96 Crozier, *A Brass Hat*, pp. 59–85.
97 Adams.
98 All information on the execution in F.P. Crozier, *The Men I Killed* (Michael Joseph, 1937), chap. 2, and Crozier, *A Brass Hat*, p. 84.
99 Adams.
100 M30 RURRM.
101 C.S.M. Adams, correspondence kept in RIFRM.
102 William Hill's letter in possession of Emily Butler, Belfast.

103 R.H. Stewart, 'File on Formation and Training'.
104 Hymnbook and pocket Gospel in possession of R.H. Stewart.
105 R.H. Stewart, 'File on Formation and Training'.
106 Bruce, and Ervine.
107 Crozier, *A Brass Hat*, p. 56.
108 Stewart-Moore, 'Random Recollections'.
109 PRONI D1631/3/2, and M32, RURRM.
110 Stewart-Moore, 'Random Recollections'.
111 All information on Orange and Masonic aspects in R.H. Stewart, 'File on the Ulster Division at the Somme' (unpublished), in author's possession.
112 Sir Frank Fox, *The Royal Inniskillmg Fusiliers in the World War* (Constable, 1928), p. 57.
113 14th RIR War Diary, 7 May 1916.
114 Hope, p. 16.
115 R.H. Stewart, 'File on Somme'.
116 Crozier, *The Men I Killed*, p. 59.
117 Jordan.
118 Jim Maultsaid, 'One Man's War', part 3, in *Cityweek*, 23 June 1966.
119 Hugh Stewart.
120 Falls, pp. 35–6.
121 R.H. Stewart, 'File on Formation and Training'.
122 A.P.I.S. and D.G.S., p. 43.
123 9th RIF War Diary, 17 March 1916.
124 Stewart-Moore, 'Random Recollections'.
125 Crozier, *A Brass Hat*, p. 86.
126 Falls, p. 36.
127 Russell.
128 G.H.M., p. 133.
129 Stewart-Moore, 'Random Recollections'.
130 A.P.I.S. and D.G.S., pp. 43–5.
131 Falls, p. 36.
132 R.H. Stewart, 'File on Formation and Training'.
133 Ibid.
134 Ibid.
135 A.P.I.S. and D.G.S., pp. 47–9.
136 R.H. Stewart, 'File on Formation and Training'.
137 A.P.I.S. and D.G.S., pp. 47–9.
138 R.H. Stewart, 'File on Formation and Training'.

CHAPTER 4

1 R.H. Stewart, 'File on Somme', and Middlebrook, chaps. 2–4, appendix 2.
2 Falls, pp. 41–8, and R.H. Stewart, 'File on Somme'.
3 Philip Gibbs, *Realities of War* (Heinemann, 1920), p. 292.
4 R.H. Stewart, 'File on Somme'.
5 Falls, pp. 41–2, and R.H. Stewart, 'File on Somme'.
6 G.H.M., p. 145.
7 14th RIR War Diary, 13 June 1916.
8 R.H. Stewart, 'File on Somme'.
9 14th RIR War Diary, 13 June 1916.
10 G.H.M., p. 145.
11 R.H. Stewart, 'File on Somme'.
12 Stewart-Moore, 'Random Recollections'.
13 Crozier, *A Brass Hat*, pp. 92–5.
14 Stewart-Moore, 'Random Recollections'.
15 A.P.I.S. and D.G.S., p. 51.
16 14th RIR War Diary, 16 June 1916.
17 14th RIR War Diary, 19 June 1916.
18 Crozier, *A Brass Hat*, p. 96.
19 Stewart-Moore, 'Random Recollections'.
20 14th RIR War Diary, 20, 21 June 1916.
21 A.P.I.S. and D.G.S., p. 51.
22 14th RIR War Diary, 23 June 1916.

23 A.P.I.S. and D.G.S., p. 51.
24 Falls, pp. 48–9.
25 Jordan.
26 Falls, p. 47.
27 Quoted in Sir Francis Evans, 'That Day of Tragic Glory', *Belfast Telegraph*, 30 June 1966.
28 Lindsay.
29 Jordan.
30 R.H. Stewart, 'File on Somme'.
31 George Birmingham, *A Padre in France* (Hodder & Stoughton, 1918), p. 111.
32 A copy of the operational instructions was shown to me by David McCarter, Hillsborough.
33 G.H.M., p. 148.
34 R.H. Stewart, 'File on Somme'.
35 A.P.I.S. and D.G.S., p. 57.
36 R.H. Stewart, 'File on Somme'.
37 Falls, p. 49.
38 A.P.I.S. and D.G.S., pp. 48–9, and Russell.
39 R.H. Stewart, 'File on Formation and Training'.
40 14th RIR War Diary, 29 June 1916.
41 A copy of the letter in the possession of R.H. Stewart.
42 R.H. Stewart, 'File on Somme'.
43 Ibid.
44 14th RIR War Diary, 30 June 1916.
45 R.H. Stewart, 'File on Somme'.
46 Ibid.
47 Stewart-Moore, 'Random Recollections'.
48 R.H. Stewart, 'File on Somme'.
49 14th RIR War Diary, 1 July 1916.
50 Jim Maultsaid, 'One Man's War', part 4, in *Cityweek*, 30 June 1966.
51 G.H.M., p. 150.
52 R.H. Stewart, 'File on Somme'.
53 D.J.H., p. 8.
54 14th RIR War Diary, 1 July 1916.
55 9th RIF War Diary, 'Report on action: Somme'.
56 14th RIR War Diary, 1 July 1916.
57 Ervine.
58 Crozier, *A Brass Hat*, pp. 97–9.
59 R.H. Stewart, 'File on Somme'.
60 Montgomery correspondence in M84 RURRM.
61 R.H. Stewart, 'File on Somme'.
62 9th RIF War Diary, 'Report on action: Somme'.
63 Hugh Stewart.
64 Alan Whitsitt, 'The War Diary of Private Berry', *Belfast Telegraph*, 12 January 1984.
65 14th RIR War Diary.
66 Stewart-Moore, 'Random Recollections'.
67 R.H. Stewart, 'File on Formation and Training'.
68 Middlebrook, p. 117.
69 Hugh Stewart.
70 *Belfast Weekly Telegraph*, 16 September 1916.
71 Hugh Stewart.
72 R.H. Stewart, 'File on Somme'.
73 Michael MacDonagh, *The Irish on the Somme* (Hodder & Stoughton, 1917), p. 37.
74 R.H. Stewart, 'File on Somme'.
75 A.P.I.S. and D.G.S., pp. 54, 60.
76 9th RIF War Diary, 'Report on action: Somme'.
77 R.H. Stewart, 'File on Formation and Training', and 14th RIR War Diary.
78 Quoted in A.P.I.S. and D.G.S., p. 62.
79 Quoted in A.P.I.S. and D.G.S., p. 60.
80 R.H. Stewart, 'File on Somme'.
81 A.P.I.S. and D.G.S., pp. 54–63.
82 Hugh Stewart.
83 Bruce.
84 *Belfast Telegraph*, 30 June 1966.

85 R.H. Stewart, 'File on Formation and Training'.
86 Ervine, and Hugh Stewart.
87 14th RIR War Diary, 1 July 1916.
88 *Cityweek,* 30 June 1966.
89 Hope, p. 18.
90 G.H.M., pp. 150–1.
91 R.H. Stewart, 'File on Somme'.
92 M9 RURRM.
93 R.H. Stewart, 'File on Somme'.
94 MacDonagh, pp. 38–9.
95 Ibid. pp. 43–4.
96 Hugh Stewart.
97 M9 RURRM.
98 *Belfast Telegraph*, 30 June 1966.
99 Hugh Stewart.
100 Falls, p. 56.
101 Crozier, *Impressions*, p. 174, and *A Brass Hat*, pp. 100–6.
102 Malcolm McKee, 'In Chains for Execution', *Belfast Telegraph*, 30 June 1966.
103 Crozier, *A Brass Hat*, p. 106, and *The Men I Killed*, pp. 82–3.
104 *Belfast Telegraph*, 30 June 1966.
105 Ervine.
106 14th RIR War Diary.
107 Crozier, *A Brass Hat*, p. 108.
108 R.H. Stewart, 'File on Somme'.
109 Falls, p. 56.
110 Adams.
111 R.H. Stewart, 'File on Somme'.
112 R.H. Stewart, 'File on Somme', and M84 RURRM.
113 M84 RURRM, and Fox, p. 69.
114 Falls, p. 56.
115 Hugh Stewart.
116 R.H. Stewart, 'File on Somme'.
117 MacDonagh, p. 35.
118 R.H. Stewart, 'File on Somme'.
119 Quoted in Jonathan Bardon, 'The Somme Nightmare', *Sunday News*, 7–24 April 1966.
120 R.H. Stewart, 'File on Somme'.
121 Falls, p. 53.
122 R.H. Stewart, 'File on Somme'.
123 9th RIF War Diary.
124 Middlebrook, appendix 5.
125 R.H. Stewart, 'File on Somme'.
126 M84 RURRM.
127 Russell.
128 M84 RURRM.
129 Falls, pp. 56–7.
130 R.H. Stewart, 'File on Somme'.
131 Ibid.
132 Middlebrook, p. 209.
133 R.H. Stewart, 'File on Somme'.
134 Crozier, *A Brass Hat*, p. 110, and M84 RURRM.
135 R.H. Stewart, 'File on Somme'.
136 Crozier, *The Men I Killed*, p. 86, and M84 RURRM.
137 Crozier, *A Brass Hat*, p. 110.
138 Crozier, *The Men I Killed*, p. 83.
139 Hope, pp. 18–19.
140 14th RIR War Diary, 1 July 1916.
141 R.H. Stewart, 'File on Somme'.
142 Russell.
143 Bruce.
144 R.H. Stewart, 'File on Somme'.
145 Stewart-Moore, 'Random Recollections'.
146 Falls, pp. 57–8.
147 Ibid. pp. 58–9.
148 Brigadier-General Sir James Edmonds, *Military Operations in France and Belgium 1916* (Macmillan, 1932), p. 142.
149 R.H. Stewart, 'File on Somme'.
150 Falls, pp. 58–9.
151 R.H. Stewart, 'File on Somme'.
152 Hope, pp. 19–20.
153 14th RIR War Diary, 2 July 1916.
154 R.H. Stewart, 'File on Somme'.
155 M84 RURRM.
156 Ervine.

157 Falls, p. 59.
158 Stewart-Moore, 'Random Recollections'.
159 Crozier, *A Brass Hat*, pp. 111–15.
160 Hope, p. 20.
161 G.H.M., pp. 150–5.
162 M84 RURRM.
163 D.J.H., p. 42.
164 R.H. Stewart, 'File on Somme'.
165 14th RIR War Diary, 5 July 1916.
166 R.H. Stewart, 'File on Somme'.
167 M84 RURRM.
168 Falls, pp. 60–3.
169 14th RIR War Diary, 11 July 1916.
170 Falls, pp. 60–3.
171 Information supplied by Mabin family, Belfast.
172 R.H. Stewart, 'File on Somme'.
173 *Belfast Evening Telegraph,* 10 July 1916.
174 Ibid.
175 *Belfast Evening Telegraph,* 18 July 1916.
176 *Belfast Evening Telegraph,* 19 July 1916.
177 *Belfast Evening Telegraph,* 11 July 1916.
178 *Belfast News Letter,* 11 July 1916.
179 *Banbridge Chronicle,* 8 July 1916.
180 Blacker's letter kept in RIFRM.
181 Quoted in R.H. Stewart, 'File on Somme'.
182 *Belfast News Letter,* 13 July 1916.
183 R.H. Stewart, 'File on Somme'.
184 Both messages quoted in A.P.I.S. and D.G.S., pp. 67–8.
185 R.H. Stewart, 'File on Somme'.
186 Middlebrook, pp. 224, 243, 266.
187 Quoted in Edmonds, p. 407.
188 Middlebrook, p. 280.
189 Falls, pp. 313–16.
190 Jordan.

CHAPTER 5

1 Colvin, p. 181.
2 Falls, pp. 298–9.
3 Ibid. chaps. 4–16.
4 Ervine.
5 Bruce.
6 Russell.
7 Jordan.
8 Adams.
9 Hugh Stewart.
10 Lindsay.
11 Stewart-Moore, 'Random Recollections'.
12 G.H.M., p. 293.
13 Crozier, *A Brass Hat*, pp. 118–19, 127–9, 229–30.
14 A.P.I.S. and D.G.S., p. 76.
15 Poem in possession of Nigel Hamill, Hillsborough.
16 Information on John Martin supplied by William Martin, Crossgar; Will Martin, Belfast; and Molly McMaster, Cookstown.
17 Information supplied by Bill McFadzean, Lisburn.
18 Official programme for unveiling of cenotaph, in possession of Bill McFadzean.
19 Reported in *Belfast News Letter,* 2 July 1923, 2 July 1925, 12 November 1929.
20 *Belfast News Letter,* 4 July 1966.
21 Information supplied by Don Cully, RURRM.
22 *Ulster's Tribute to Her Fallen Sons* (Ulster Division Battlefield Memorial Committee, undated) pp. 12–13.
23 Information supplied by Bill McFadzean.
24 Information supplied by the Mabin family.

25 Information supplied by management and staff of Ulster Volunteer Force Hospital, Belfast.

26 Recollections of George McBride, interviewed by author, August 1986.

27 Stewart-Moore, 'Random Recollections'.

28 Jordan.

29 Hugh Stewart.

30 Bruce.

31 Ervine.

32 Adams.

33 R.H. Stewart, 'File on Formation and Training'.

34 G.H.M., p. 294.

35 Falls, p. 38.

36 Herdman, pp. 342–3, and information supplied by Herdman family, Sion Mills.

37 Information supplied by Don Cully.

38 Crozier, *Impressions*, chaps. 10–12 and conclusion.

39 Lindsay.

CHAPTER 6

1 Gary Sheffield, *Forgotten Victory* (Headline Book Publishing, 2002), pp. 186–7.

2 Terence Denman, *Ireland's Unknown Soldiers – The 16th (Irish) Division in the Great War 1914–1918* (Irish Academic Press, 1992), p. 101.

3 Interview with David Wilsden, March 2008.

4 Interview with Carol Walker, March 2008, and information obtained at www.irishsoldier.org, 1 March 2008.

5 I have relied on interviews with David Wilsden, February 2008, and Carol Walker, April 2008, for information about the 2006 ceremonies and visitor numbers at the tower.

6 Information on Orange banners and lodges that have commemorated the Somme and several of Ulster's Great War soldiers may be obtained from the Orange Order's offices at Schomberg House, Belfast.

7 For one account of the Drumcree protests, see Chris Ryder and Vincent Kearney, *Drumcree – The Orange Order's Last Stand* (Methuen, 2001).

8 Interview with Jackie Hewitt, March 2008.

9 Information on the Somme Festival was found at www.ballymacarrettdlol6.com/page16.html, 23 March 2008.

10 Interview with David Wilsden, March 2008.

11 Interview with Bobby Rainey, March 2008.

12 The Ulster Scots Orchestra was found at www.naegoatstoe.com on 6 April 2008.

13 Interview with Brian Ervine, May 2008.

14 Information on the Canadian significance of Vimy Ridge may be obtained at www.vimyfoundation.ca/e-index.html. A visit to the Vimy sector of the Western Front is also recommended.

15 Information on the importance of public remembrance by Australians of the Battle of Gallipoli and the 'Anzacs' who fought there may be found at www.dva.gov.au/commemorations. A visit to Gallipoli is also essential.

16 By far the best way to become acquainted with the Turkish Gallipoli legend and the mythic status of the Turkish commander and national hero, Kemal Attaturk, is to visit the Gallipoli peninsula in European Turkey in the company of a Turkish guide.

17 Hewitt.

18 Ibid.

19 B. Graham and P. Shirlow, 'The Battle of the Somme in Ulster Memory and Identity', in *Political Geography*, 21 (2002), pp. 894–5.

20 For a sense of the belief in this connection between the 'old' and the 'new' UVF, I am reliant on an interview with Tom Roberts, March 2008.

21 Interview with Gorman McMullan, April 2008.

22 Ibid.

23 Graham and Shirlow, pp. 891–2.

24 Interview with John, Stephen, Neil, Joe and Gorman, April 2008.

25 Although several modern historians now offer this figure for Ireland's contribution to the British armed services, I am relying on the unpublished draft of a lecture by Professor Keith Jeffery of Queen's University, Belfast, entitled 'Ireland and the First World War – the Historical Context', pp. 1–2.

26 Information on Islandbridge was found at www.taoiseach.gov.ie/index.asp?docID=2746, 2 March 2008.

27 Information on the re-memorialisation process is found in Philip Orr, *Field of Bones – An Irish Division at Gallipoli* (Lilliput Press, 2006), pp. 226–7.

28 Information on the opening ceremony at Messines was found at news.bbc.co.uk/1/hi/world/Europe/212208.stm, 3 April 2008.

29 Information on the genesis and ethos of the Peace Park was found at www.ww1battlefields.co.uk/flanders/messines.html, 1 April 2008.

30 The exhibition, entitled 'Soldiers and Chiefs', is on permanent display and is located in a building that was one of the great military barracks of the British Empire.

31 Interview with Harvey Bicker, February 2008.

32 The commemorative ceremony, with Irish president and Taoiseach in attendance, is held at the Royal Hospital on a Sunday in the first two weeks in July.

33 Information on the Somme ceremony was found at www.taoiseach.gov.ie/index.asp?loc.ID, 20 February 2008.

34 Graham and Shirlow, p. 883.

35 Detailed information about the Irish soldiers who were executed – including three men in the Ulster Division – and the campaign for their names to be cleared may be found in Stephen Walker, *Forgotten Soldiers – The Irishmen Shot at Dawn* (Gill and Macmillan, 2007).

36 Interviews with Patsy McGarry, December 2007 and April 2008.

37 The Royal Dublin Fusiliers' Association website is found at www.greatwar.ie

38 The 'Books of Honour' project has had an uneven career, varying from county to county. One area where the book has been successfully produced is Donegal, and access to a copy may be had through contact with the county librarian at www.donegal.ie/library

39 Interview with Paul Clarke, April 2008.

40 Information on the Irish troops who fought at Cape Helles is found in

most of the comprehensive histories of the Gallipoli campaign. Material particularly focused on the Royal Dublin Fusiliers, Royal Inniskilling Fusiliers and Royal Munster Fusiliers at Cape Helles can be obtained from the appropriate regimental associations or regimental museum.

41 For information on the Irish role in the Suvla campaign, see Orr, *Field of Bones*.

42 Interview with Glenn Barr, March 2008. See also www.schoolforpeace.com

43 Information about the wreath-laying ceremony was found at www.4ni.co.uk/northern_ireland_ne ws.asp/id=8262, 9 April 2008.

44 Interview with Alex Maskey, March 2008.

45 Information on the Good Relations projects undertaken by Belfast City Council may be found at www.belfastcity.gov.uk/goodrelations

46 Interview with Bobby Devlin, April 2008.

47 Information on Seán McCartney may be found in Orr, *Field of Bones*, p. 229.

48 Interview with Alex Maskey, March 2008.

49 Interview with Brian Ervine, May 2008.

FURTHER READING

The following is my choice of a hundred books to be read by anyone who wants to gain a truly exhaustive knowledge of Ireland's experience of the First World War, supplemented by an insight into the Ulster Home Rule Crisis that preceded it. There are some books that did not make it onto my list. Websites, theses, scholarly articles and journalism also receive no mention. I have made no attempt to 'sort' the items on this list by topic, genre or category, and will leave readers to use the Internet and the public-library system for further investigation into those publications mentioned here that stir up their interest. It should be noted that some books on this list have been published in several editions with different publishers, only one of which will be mentioned in this bibliography.

Adgey, A.J., *Arming the Ulster Volunteers*, 1914, (privately printed and undated)

Barry, Sebastian, *A Long, Long Way* (Faber & Faber, 2005)

Beckett, Ian, *The Army and the Curragh Incident* (Random House UK, 1987)

Bew, Paul, *John Redmond* (Dundalgan Press, 1996)

Birmingham, George, *A Padre in France* (Hodder and Stoughton, 1918)

Bowman, Timothy, *Carson's Army – The Ulster Volunteer Force, 1910–1922* (Manchester University Press, 2007)

Bowman, Timothy, *The Irish Regiments in the Great War – Discipline and Morale* (Manchester University Press, 2003)

Brearton, Fran, *The Great War in Irish Poetry* (Oxford University Press, 2000)

Brett MC, Charles, *An Irish Soldier with the Connaught Rangers in World War One* (Somme Association, 2007)

Burke, Tom, *The 16th Irish and 36th Ulster Divisions at the Battle of Wytschaete-Messines Ridge, 7 June 1917 – A Battlefield Tour Guide* (Royal Dublin Fusilier Association, June, 2007)

Canning, W.J., *A Wheen of Medals* (W.J. Canning, 2006)

Canning, W.J., *Ballyshannon, Belcoo, Bertincourt – The History of the 11th Battalion, The Royal Inniskilling Fusiliers (Donegal and Fermanagh Volunteers) in the First World War* (W.J. Canning, 1996)

Clarke, P.J., *Mayo Comrades of the Great War, 1914–1919* (Pádraig Corcoran Publishing, 2006)

Cooper, Bryan, *The 10th (Irish) Division in Gallipoli* (Irish Academic Press, 1993)

Crawford, Lt. Col. F.H., *Guns for Ulster* (Graham and Hislop, 1947)

Crozier, F.P., *The Men I Killed* (Michael Joseph, 1937)

Curtayne, Alice, *Francis Ledwidge* (New Island Books, 1998)

D.J.H., *The Reminiscences of Capt. D.J. Bell of Ballynahinch* (Mourne Observer Press,1962)

Denman, Terence, *Ireland's Unknown Soldiers – The 16th (Irish) Division in the Great War, 1914–1918* (Irish Academic Press, 1992)

Doherty, Richard and Truesdale, David, *Irish Winners of the Victoria Cross* (Four Courts Press, 1999)

Donegal Book of Honour (County Book of Honour Committee, 2002)

Dooley, T.P., *Irishmen or English Soldiers?* (Liverpool University Press, 1995)

Dublin City and County Book of Honour – The Great War 1914–1918 (National Book of Honour Committee, 2003)

Dungan, Myles, *Irish Voices from the Great War* (Irish Academic Press, 1995)

Dungan, Myles, *They Shall Grow Not Old – Irish Soldiers and the Great War* (Four Courts Press, 1997)

Durney, James, *Far from the Short Grass – The Story of Kildare Men in Two World Wars* (Gaul House, 1999)

Falls, Cyril, *History of the First Seven Battalions of the Royal Irish Rifles in the Great War* (Naval and Military Press, 2002)

Falls, Cyril, *The History of the 36th (Ulster) Division* (McCaw, Stevenson and Orr, 1922)

Fitzpatrick, David, *Politics and Irish Life, 1913–1921* (Gill and Macmillan, 1977)

Fox, Sir Frank, *The Royal Inniskilling Fusiliers in the World War* (Constable, 1928)

Geoghegan, S., *The Campaigns and History of the Royal Irish Regiment, II, 1900–1922* (Blackwood, 1927)

Hall, Donal, *The Unreturned Army – County Louth Dead in the Great War, 1914–1918* (Dundalgan Press, 2005)

Hargrave, John, *At Suvla Bay* (Constable, 1916)

Harris, Henry, *The Irish Regiments in the First World War* (Mercier Press, 1968)

Harris, Henry, *The Royal Irish Fusiliers* (Leo Cooper, 1972)

Henry, William, *Forgotten Heroes – Galway Soldiers of the Great War, 1914–1918* (Mercier Press, 2008)

Henry, William, *Galway and the Great War, 1914–1918* (Mercier Press, 2006)

Hitchcock, F.C., *Stand To – A Diary of the Trenches, 1915–1918* (Naval and Military Press, 2001)

Hogarty, Pat, *Remembrance – A Brief History of the Blue Caps, the 1st Battalion, Royal Dublin Fusiliers, 1914–1922* (no publisher or date given)

Hogarty, Pat, *The Old Toughs: From Milton to Mons and the Western Front, 1911–1918 – A Brief History of the Royal Dublin Fusiliers, 2nd Battalion* (Royal Dublin Fusiliers' Association, 2001)

Jackson, Alvin, *Sir Edward Carson* (Dundalgan Press, 1993)

Jeffery, Keith, *Ireland and the Great War* (Cambridge University Press, 2000)

Jervis, H.S., *The 2nd Munsters in France* (Schull Books, 1998)

Johnson, N.C., *Ireland, the Great War and the Geography of Remembrance* (Cambridge University Press, 2003)

Johnston, Jennifer, *How Many Miles to Babylon?* (Hamish Hamilton, 1974)

Johnstone, Tom, *Orange, Green and Khaki* (Gill and Macmillan, 1992)

Juvenis, *Suvla Bay and After* (Hodder and Stoughton, 1916)

Kerr, S. Parnell, *What the Irish Regiments Have Done* (Unwin, 1916)

Kettle, Tom, *The Ways of War* (Kessinger Publishing, 2008)

Kildea, Jeff, *Anzacs and Ireland* (University of New South Wales Press, 2007)

Kilfeather, T.P., *The Connaught Rangers* (Anvil Books, 1969)

Kipling, Rudyard, *The Irish Guards in the Great War – The 1st Battalion* (Spellmount, 1997)

Kipling, Rudyard, *The Irish Guards in the Great War – the 2nd Battalion* (Spellmount, 1997)

Laird, Frank, *Personal Experiences of the Great War* (Eason and Son, 1925)

Lecane, Philip, *Torpedoed ! – The RMS Leinster Disaster* (Periscope Publishing, 2005)

Ledwidge, Francis, *The Complete Poems of Francis Ledwidge* (Poolbeg, 1998)

Leonard, Jane, *The Culture of Great War Commemoration* (Cultures of Ireland, 1996)

MacGill, Patrick, *The Navvy Poet: The Collected Works of Patrick MacGill* (Caliban Books, 1984)

Maguire, Paul, *Follow Them Up from Carlow* (P. Maguire, 2002)

Martin, F.X., *Irish Volunteers, 1913–1915* (James Duffy and Co., 1963)

Martin, Thomas F., *A Portrait of Kerry During World War One* (Nonsuch Publishing, 2006)

McCance, S., *History of the Royal Munster Fusiliers, 1861–1922,* vol. 2 (Gale and Polden, 1927)

McCullough, Elizabeth, Jack and Dorothy, *Letters from the Front, 1915–1917* (Serendipity, 2005)

McDonagh, Michael, *The Irish on the Somme* (Hodder and Stoughton, 1917)

McGinley, Niall, *Donegal, Ireland and the Great War* (An Crann, 1987)

McGuinn, James, *Sligo Men in the Great War* (Naughan Press, 1994)

McGuinness, Frank, *Observe the Sons of Ulster Marching Towards the Somme* (Faber & Faber, 1986)

McNamara, Patrick J., *The Widow's Penny – The Record of Limerick Men and Women Who Gave Their Lives in the Great War* (Hamsoft Communications, 2004)

Mitchell, Gardiner, *'Three Cheers for the Derrys!' – A Brief History of the 10th Royal Inniskilling Fusiliers in the 1914–1918 War* (YES! Publications, 1991)

Moore, Steven, *The Irish on the Somme – A Battlefield Guide* (Local Press, 2005)

Moreno, Amanda and Truesdale,
David, *Angels and Heroes – The
Story of a Machine-gunner with the
Royal Irish Fusiliers, August 1914–
April 1915* (Silverlink Publications,
2004)
O'Casey, Seán, *Silver Tassie – A Tragi-
comedy in 4 Acts* (Macmillan, 1928)
Olson, Elizabeth Cassidy, *Francis
Ledwidge: Song of the Blackbird*
(AuthorHouse, 2000)
Orr, Philip, *Field of Bones – An Irish
Division at Gallipoli* (Lilliput Press,
2006)
Orr, Philip, *Tom's Story – Sentry Hill
and the Great War* (Newtownabbey
Borough Council, 2007)
Paseta, Senia and Gregory, Adrian
(eds.), *Ireland and the Great War: 'A
War to Unite us All?'* (Manchester
University Press, 2002)
Perry, Nicholas (ed.), *Major-General
Oliver Nugent and the Ulster
Division, 1915–1918* (Sutton
Publishing, 2007)
Phelan, Tom, *The Canal Bridge*
(Lilliput Press, 2005)
Quinn, Anthony P., *Wigs and Guns –
Irish Barristers in the Great War*
(Four Courts Press, 2006)
Redmond MP, Major Willie *Trench
Pictures from France* (Somme
Association, 2007)
Samuels, A.P.I. and D.G.S. Belfast,
*With the Ulster Division in France –
A Story of the 11th Battalion Royal
Irish Rifles (South Antrim Volunteers)
from Bordon to Thiepval* (Naval and
Military Press, 2003)

Sheldon, Jack, *The Germans at Thiepval*
(Pen and Sword Books, 2006)
Sheppard, Gilbert Alan, *The Connaught
Rangers* (Osprey, 1972)
Sheen, John, *Tyneside Irish* (Pen and
Sword Books, 1998)
Stanley, Jeremy, *Ireland's Forgotten
Tenth – A Brief History of the
10th (Irish) Division, 1914–1918,
Turkey, Macedonia and Palestine*
(Impact Printing Limited,
2003)
Stewart, A.T.Q., *The Ulster Crisis –
Resistance to Home Rule, 1912–1914*
(Faber & Faber, 1969)
Switzer, Catherine, *Unionists and Great
War Commemoration in the North of
Ireland, 1914–1939* (Irish Academic
Press, 2007)
Taylor, James W., *The 1st Royal Irish
Rifles in the Great War* (Four Courts
Press, 2002)
Taylor, James W., *The 2nd Royal Irish
Rifles in the Great War* (Four Courts
Press, 2005)
Thompson, Robert, *Ballymoney Heroes*
(R. Thompson, 1999)
Thompson, Robert, *Bushmills Heroes,
1914–1918* (R. Thompson, 1995)
Thompson, Robert, *Coleraine Heroes*
(R. Thompson, 2004)
Thompson, Robert, *Innishowen Heroes*
(R. Thompson, 2007)
Thompson, Robert, *Kilrea Heroes*
(R. Thompson, 2003)
Thompson, Robert, *Portrush Heroes*
(R. Thompson, 2001)
Thompson, Robert, *Portstewart Heroes*
(R. Thompson, 2006)

Walker, G.A.C., *The Book of the 7th Service Battalion of the Royal Inniskilling Fusiliers from Tipperary to Ypres* (Brindley and Son, *c.* 1920)

Walker, Stephen, *Forgotten Soldiers: The Irishmen Shot at Dawn* (Gill and Macmillan, 2007)

White, Stuart N., *The Terrors – The 16th (Pioneer) Battalion Royal Irish Rifles* (Somme Association, 1996)

Whitton, F.E., *The History of the Prince of Wales's Leinster Regiment (Royal Canadians) in the Great War* (Naval and Military Press, 2004)

ACKNOWLEDGEMENTS, 1987

I must begin by acknowledging the role played by those veterans whom I interviewed: Hugh James Adams, David Brown, Albert Bruce, Tommy Ervine, Tommy Jordan, George Lindsay, Dan McAlinden, George McBride, John McClements, Bert Murphy, W. Quinn, Tommy Russell and Hugh Stewart. They showed clarity of mind about events that happened long ago and a willingness to undergo the painful process of confronting, once again, a number of grim, buried memories from those war years. The families of many veterans also gave help, especially with photographs.

To Robert Stewart go special thanks for making available the files of information he had built up on the Ulster Division and the Ulster Volunteer Force. These are based mainly on the excellent interviews he conducted with veterans at a time when many more of them were alive.

Two regimental museums also deserve thanks for the way in which they made their written and visual records available – the Royal Irish Fusiliers Regimental Museum in Armagh and the Royal Ulster Rifles Regimental Museum in Belfast. Staff at each of these places went out of their way to assist but Don Cully of the Rifles Museum merits a special mention for his frequent and knowledgeable contributions to my researches.

The Public Record Office of Northern Ireland provided a rich body of material and thanks are due to Dr Brian Trainor, the Deputy Keeper of Records, for permission to publish photographs and extracts from documents which are lodged there. I also appreciate the helping hand given by numerous other members of staff at the Record Office during my periods of research there.

I also received help from staff at Belfast Central Library and at Belfast's Linen Hall Library where John Killen and Robert Bell deserve particular thanks. The Linen Hall also gave permission for me to use a number of postcards and photographs. The Ulster Museum gave permission for me to use some of their photographic archives, and Tom Wylie, on the staff of the museum, provided valuable advice with interpretation of photographs.

Many other people made their contribution. Iona McFerran and Commander Claude Herdman were warm and charming assistants with the story of Ambrose Ricardo; my colleague, Pat Geary, also gave help in piecing together this aspect of the book. Ethel Taylor, William Martin senior, Will Martin and Molly McMaster were the members of my family circle who helped trace the story of my great-uncle, John Martin. Bill McFadzean was able to provide some interesting information about his famous uncle, Billy McFadzean VC. The Perceval Maxwell family also helped with details concerning Robert Perceval Maxwell, and the relatives of John Leslie Stewart-Moore, both here and in Australia, were very helpful in the attempt to piece together his intriguing war record with the Ulster Division.

Staff of the UVF Hospital, Craigavon, provided information on the history of that institution and Mrs Herbert, of the Soldiers', Sailors' and Airmen's Families' Association, gave some valuable tips in the attempt to contact veterans. Emily Butler and Nigel Hamill furnished interesting documents, and the Mabin and Leyburn families provided useful details, as did John Chambers. At various stages, staff and students of the history department at Friends' School, Lisburn, gave valued assistance with aspects of the broad historical background, and Rhoda Noble turned up some informative books about the Ulster Volunteer Force period. Howard Kinkead shared in formulating the concept of a book based on the oral record, and among other people whose enthusiasm and interest were a great spur, David McCarter and my father deserve particular mention. Bill Nelson gave advice on postcards of the period, and to Gail Pollock of PRONI and to Dermott Dunbar I am indebted for help given with photography. I am also grateful to Michael Maultsaid for granting permission for me to publish copies of his father's excellent drawings and cartoons from his illustrated war diaries.

Jonathan Bardon was of enormous assistance with the project. He diagnosed areas of weakness and suggested improvements throughout the book, but I was particularly indebted to him for the time and effort he devoted to helping me improve the chapter on the Ulster Volunteers in pre-war Ireland.

To Nigel Hamill goes a special word of thanks – his calm and good-humoured approach to the task of typing my well-nigh illegible script enabled me to proceed to the publishers in good time. My mother also gave some assistance with typing.

As someone who is not a historian by university training or occupation, I have looked back to try to discover what factors first led me into attempting to write a book about a topic in Irish history. Here I must acknowledge the role of Noel Orr, who taught me Irish history some years ago at Down High School, Downpatrick, and whose keen interest in a hitherto unglamorous subject obviously communicated itself to me and helped lay the seed-bed for a book such as this. Finally, there are all the friends and relations who, at various stages over the past three years, showed interest in my project and, at times, positively badgered me into pushing ahead, when I had lost some of the drive needed to complete it. I know they will recognise themselves in this brief acknowledgement and feel no need of an explicit mention to assure them of the lasting warmth of my regard.

ACKNOWLEDGEMENTS, 2008

I am grateful to the following for assistance with the work undertaken in 2008:

Amanda Moreno, for help with understanding and illustrating the Royal Irish Fusilier contribution to the 36th Division; Bobby Devlin, for providing information about his father, and John Moore, for helping with the story of his uncle; Bobby Foster, for use of photographs from his archives; Brian Ervine, for permission to reproduce some of what he said at his brother's funeral; Colin Cousins, for assistance with understanding the issues of recruitment and post-war reception of veterans; Davy Wilsden, for insights into his own commitment to the Somme heritage; Dermott Dunbar, for further use of his 1987 images; Glenn Barr, for insights into the Irish Messines project; Hannah Moffat, for help with the portraiture of her father; Harvey Bicker, for his thoughts on the Irish commemorative process; Jack Dunlop, for help with the Inniskilling contribution to the 36th Division; Joe Stewart and the team of Gorman, Stephen, Neil and John, who assisted with the theme of contemporary Loyalist Great War culture; Keith Jeffery, for his knowledge of the academic framework needed for a 'rewrite' such as this; Ken Dawson for his thoughtful reading of my script; Mervyn Gibson, Jackie Hewitt, Bobby Rainey, Derek Parkhill and David Hume for help given with the story of the Somme and the Loyal Orders; the McFadzean family for continued use of the photograph of their ancestor;

Michael Maultsaid, for continued use of his father's drawings; Patsy McGarry, for his insights into the impact of the First World War in County Roscommon; Paul Clarke, for continual support of this project; politician Alex Maskey, for help in understanding the Nationalist perspective on Great War commemoration; The Somme Centre, where Carol and Noel shared their knowledge of the Somme Association's work and their archive of photographs; Stephen Walker, who took a constant interest in my writing; Terence and Jackie at the Royal Ulster Rifles Museum, who were helpful with renewing the photographic record; Tom Burke, who explained the process of regenerating the Irish Republic's Great War heritage; Tom Roberts, who assisted with photographs; Will Martin, who gave fresh help with his great-uncle's story; William Thompson, who brought his own expertise to bear on looking at the new set of illustrations; and, finally, everyone at Blackstaff Press who assisted with the republication project, especially Helen Wright, whose efficiency and good judgment were invaluable.

INDEX